CROSSCURRENTS *Modern Critiques*

CROSSCURRENTS *Modern Critiques*
Harry T. Moore, *General Editor*

Angelo Philip Bertocci

From Symbolism
to Baudelaire

WITH A PREFACE BY

Harry T. Moore

Carbondale

SOUTHERN ILLINOIS UNIVERSITY PRESS

To Aili,

my wife and most patient critic,
and to my brother Peter,
philosophically present

PREFACE

KNOWLEDGE OF THE MOVEMENT known as symbolisme—
note how, in the book that follows, Angelo Bertocci carefully uses that distinguishing final e—broke upon the
English-speaking world in 1899 with publication of the
first edition of Arthur Symons' The Symbolist Movement
in Literature (not actually published until March 1900).
This had its influence, particularly in the early work of
T. S. Eliot, and the movement exerted an important effect
upon writers all over the western world—just how important Edmund Wilson showed in Axel's Castle (1931),
which linked the work of specific members of the Mallarmé group, such as Paul Valéry, with the writings of
various other modern authors of stature. These included
not only Eliot, but William Butler Yeats, to whom the
first edition of Symons' book had been dedicated, as well
as Marcel Proust, James Joyce, and Gertrude Stein. There
have been many other books on symbolism since.

In the present volume, Angelo Bertocci examines the
work of Baudelaire and its ancestry of the symboliste
movement. Professor Bertocci, who is Chairman of the
Department of Comparative Literature at Boston University, has long been an expert on French and other modern
literatures. He attended Boston University as an under-
graduate, taking his master's degree from Harvard and his
doctor's from Columbia. While at Boston University he
won a fellowship which sent him for a year to Grenoble
(and a Hautes Études Françaises diploma). As an Italian-

born boy whose family wasn't affluent, Angelo Bertocci, living in the Boston suburbs, had selected Boston University just because of that fellowship, and he single-mindedly aimed at it—as noted, with success. Before returning to Boston University as a professor in 1948, Angelo Bertocci was Chairman of the French Department at Bates College.

A frequent contributor to Yale French Studies, Professor Bertocci translated several of the essays in Justin O'Brien's edition of André Gide's Pretexts (Meridian Books, 1959). Professor Bertocci is the author of Charles du Bos and English Literature (Columbia University Press, 1949). He made an important contribution to A D. H. Lawrence Miscellany (Southern Illinois University Press, 1959; William Heinemann, Ltd., 1960). This contribution was a study of the symbolism in Lawrence's finest novel, Women in Love. The essay was reprinted in the anthology of critiques, Modern British Fiction (Oxford University Press, 1961), edited by Mark Schorer, himself the author of a notable essay on Women in Love.

And now, in From Symbolism to Baudelaire, Professor Bertocci gives a fresh and important consideration of a highly significant literary movement. His perceptive historical-background chapters range from Plotinus to Dante and on to Goethe and Coleridge. Then, after his searching discussion of Baudelaire, the heart of the book, he seeks a theory relating symbols to meaning, and so moves on to the somewhat later French writers who used symbols and to the symboliste movement itself, whose practitioners, like Baudelaire, developed an entirely new and different way of using symbols. Angelo Bertocci's approach to these matters combines a rich and varied learning with the intuitional qualities needed for penetration of the subject. He can be vigorously theoretical (his comments on other critics of the subject are discerning and valuable), but he remains intrinsically concrete. His explications of the poems of Baudelaire and others are extremely helpful—more than that, they are brilliant. And fortunately he provides the original texts as well as translations, as commentators should always do on occasions of this kind.

Professor Bertocci's arguments don't need to be discussed in detail in this preface by one of his former students: they should be followed in full, and although they are complex, as the nature of the subject demands, they also have an admirable clarity. Professor Bertocci has transmitted onto the page the excitement of his classes in symbolisme, romanticism, and literary criticism, as I knew he would do when I invited him to write this book. And certainly students and readers at all levels will feel indebted to him for sharing his insights with them.

HARRY T. MOORE

Southern Illinois University
July 31, 1964

CONTENTS

From Symbolism to Baudelaire

1 SYMBOLISM:
FROM PLOTINUS TO DANTE

A STRIKING FEATURE of English and American criticism and literary history in the last two decades has been an increasing agreement to accept as the source of what is "modern" in our poetry that aspect of the Romantic movement which in France developed its implications through the Symbolistes. It has been a difficult consensus to reach, for poets and critics who had distinguished themselves in a veritable onslaught on Romanticism have had to be persuaded that, whatever their justification, they had struck at the matrix through a power lodged in Romanticism itself, but isolated and disciplined by Symbolisme.

A consensus having been reached, our problem is again to make distinctions. What do our critics, aestheticians and poets mean by "symbolism" and by the "symbol"? What do these terms have to do with the "symbole" of that movement so distinguished by diversity and individualism, le Symbolisme of 1885? The movement imposed leadership on Mallarmé and on Verlaine; it basked in a *charisma* descending from its most distant ancestor, Baudelaire; and it was these poets, by the authority of their artistic achievements even more than by their theories, who give le Symbolisme status especially in our day. For us the study of *Symbolisme* begins with and dwells upon those whom, with unintentional humor, most manuals of literature still call the "precursors."

The key to that complex, Romanticism-Symbolism, to

which modern poetry is said to owe such a debt is Baudelaire. The reasons are more than chronological: in him we can discern not only the relation of Symbolisme to the main tradition from the Neo-Platonists to the Romantics, but also the seeds that will grow into misunderstanding and deviation. In Baudelaire's critical theory and in his poetic practice we shall find the cues, if not the sufficient causes, for an ultimate secularization of the symbol with which, we believe, the poet would have had no sympathy. In this aspect, at least, the author of *Les Fleurs du mal* is no precursor of a significant body of modern theory and practice of the "symbol." But Baudelaire, we think, can also be exemplary, and especially in a conviction of the higher meaning of poetry that he fused with what is really indispensable in poetic autonomy. One may properly speak of the "mysticism" of Baudelaire, as well as of Mallarmé and Rimbaud; but, in his case, the vision he sought to present led him neither to the attenuations of Mallarmé nor the dislocations of Rimbaud. In Baudelaire we can study an important mode of the fusion of Symbolisme and the central tradition of Western poetry, of which Yeats is our most recent instance.

To the increasing consensus in our day linking Romanticism with Symbolisme and modern poetry, one of the major contributors has been Professor René Wellek, chiefly because of his support of the view of Romanticism as a self-conscious movement characterized by its "doctrine of nature," or organicism, the theory of the Imagination, and the use of the Symbol.[1] We have it on the same authority that, when in the middle of the nineteenth century, Romanticism became in many countries "only a justification of emotionalism and nationalism," and lost its literary eminence to realism and naturalism, nevertheless its "central force, the symbolic concept of poetry," worked underground against Taine and naturalism. The force was rebaptized Symbolisme in 1886.

In the 20th century there is everywhere a return to the ideas of the years we have surveyed. In Italy De Sanctis became the intermediary for Croce, who himself went directly to Hegel and Schleiermacher. In France the symbolist movement recaptured the essence of romantic criticism and transmitted it to the 20th century. In England and the United States the French symbolists, Croce, and certainly those responsible for the revival of Coleridge have profoundly stimulated the rebirth of criticism which we have witnessed in the last thirty years.[2]

To turn to a historian of literature, Professor J. Isaacs [3] describes the Symbolist movement as a second wave of a flow of "pure poetry" following that of the Romantics and reaching its climax in Mallarmé and Valéry and its decadence in Rilke, Stefan George, T. S. Eliot, Yeats. It is this decadence which is the modernity of today. But if all modern poets are "indebted directly or indirectly" to that fusion of suggestive indefiniteness and conscious craftsmanship achieved by Mallarmé, it is in Edgar Allan Poe that Professor Isaacs finds the "confluence of the great rivers of criticism flowing from Coleridge and from German Romanticism."

As a matter of fact, even before Poe the new vehicle that was to be modern poetry had already gone from conception to blueprint to factory; it had had successful runs by the English, German and French Romantics. It needed only production in full awareness by a master-builder; and for Baudelaire Poe seems to have provided a foreign shock of recognition.

For Poe and for the Symbolistes the theoretical groundwork had been laid in Germany. The dialectical and symbolic view of poetry, according to Professor Wellek,

> grows out of the organic analogy, developed by Herder and Goethe, but proceeds beyond it to a view of poetry as a union of opposites, a system of symbols. In Germany this view was in constant danger of becoming mystical and thus of losing its grip on the aesthetic fact itself, but in the Schlegels and a few critics around them a satisfying theory of poetry was developed which guarded its fences against emotionalism, naturalism, and mysticism and successfully combined symbolism with a profound grasp of literary his-

tory. *This view seems to me valuable and substantially true even today.*[4]

The term "Symbolisme," then, came to the fore in France in 1886 to mark the consciousness of a dimension in which poetry had been implicated at least since Baudelaire with his sense of analogies and correspondences not merely between orders of nature but between the natural and supranatural. But the tradition was of remote origin; it had attained to philosophy in the Neo-Platonists. According to Plotinus, since the divine Oneness created the world through the Intellect, all things inevitably will reveal traces of the One, of the Intellect and its Ideas, of Love, and of the living Forces which drive the Ideas toward their realization in individual substances. The beauty of things depends upon the degree to which, as direct symbols, they manifest, though in an imperfect and ephemeral manner, the perfection of the One, of Intellect, and of Love. All beauty, then, is a manifestation of the divine. It is the symbol of the great prototypes or archetypes which govern existence: of the Good, of Life, of Reason, of Intelligence, of Wisdom, of Virtue, of Truth, of the Eternal. "Beauty is *perfection* and *unity*, it is the projection of Justice which assigns to everything its proper place and a revelation of Power."[5]

If natural things and processes, appreciated for their beauty, can be symbols for Plotinus, so can objects created by artists who go back for their models to the Ideas from which nature derives. Such opinions make of Plotinus, according to Professors Wimsatt and Brooks, "The earliest systematic philosopher of the creative imagination, if we are willing to give this passage the benefit of some 1,400 years of anachronism, to place it momentarily in a context shining back from, let us say, the Germany of the Schlegels and the England of Coleridge and Shelley."[6]

The Neo-Platonic tendency to interpret the whole created universe and also artistic creations as pointing to God coincided with a similar attitude in St. Paul and in early Christian thought, dominated as it was by the East and by the Hebraic concept of history in the Old Testament. An Ambrose could be influenced by the Neo-Platonist Philo of Alexandria. St. Augustine bears also a noteworthy witness to the power of the image, even as he raises the attendant problem. He is puzzled by the appearance of symbols in Scripture. Do they not substitute the outer show to the inner and pure meaning? Yet he takes a special pleasure in contemplating holy men as "the teeth of the Church, tearing men away from their errors" or "under the figure of sheep that have been shorn." He cannot deny the fact that "it is pleasanter in some cases to have knowledge communicated through figures, and that what is attended with difficulty in the seeking gives greater pleasure in the finding."

The idea of a "veiled" and difficult poetry was Augustine's and Dante's before it became Mallarmé's. St. Augustine had raised a perennial problem in the theory of the symbol. Is the pleasure we take in the symbol akin to that experienced in solving a baffling puzzle? If so, is not the interpretation of the symbol an intellectual game, and Symbolisme, as Croce will say, extraneous to art? Or is the peculiar obscurity of symbolic apprehension due to the fact that, as Coleridge says of Imagination, "the whole soul is brought into activity" and strains toward a full and living knowledge? There is no more crucial question than this in theory of literature.

To this question the Aristotelian St. Thomas gave at least a forthright answer:

> Poetic knowledge concerns matters which through a deficiency in their truth cannot be laid hold of by the reason; hence the reason has to be beguiled by means of certain similitudes. Theology deals with matters which are above reason. So the symbolic mode is common to both types of discourse; neither type is suited to reasoning.

Yet even St. Thomas seems not to have struggled free of the dreamlike web of Neo-Platonism. Between the fifth century of St. Augustine and the thirteenth of St. Thomas, according to Wimsatt and Brooks, the "concretely historical, bloody and suffering claim of Christianity" had developed its effect in aesthetics as well as in metaphysics and theology. Plotinus' doctrine of emanation from the Godhead, a shading away of things in truth and value from the nevertheless everpresent One, had once seemed sufficient to account for moral and metaphysical evil. A different approach to the problem of evil now led St. Thomas to an emphatic distinction between God and his works. The Creator, the source of the beautiful, can be known only by reasoning from the separate works of His hands. Yet there is a "subjective accent" even in St. Thomas' definition of beautiful things as those which are apprehended with pleasure—*quae visa placent*.

> As with Augustine and Plotinus, we are once more in the presence of a basic assumption of radical harmony between man the knower and the external universe which he knows —and in some parts of which he takes a special delight. The beauty of a beautiful object consists not merely in a self-enclosed character but in a corresponding external rela- tion of fitness to the knowing subject, a relation of know- ability. All knowledge, and especially the knowledge of the beautiful, and pleasure in the beautiful, arise by a kind of union between subject and object.

Professors Wimsatt and Brooks refer to the creed in the latter pages of Joyce's *Portrait of the Artist as a Young Man* as a "retrospective and romanticized piece of scho- lasticism," an "idealistic modification" which rings very naturally against the background of the nineteenth cen- tury.[7] Evidently no more than Ambrose, Augustine, or Thomas in the case of Neo-Platonism, could James Joyce sever the bond, with Mallarmé as one of the intermediate links, between himself and Schelling and the Schlegels, who were in some respects the heirs of Plotinus. It is the influence of Plotinus, we think, working through Schelling and especially Bergson, which is at war in T. E. Hulme as theorist of the symbol with his radical ethical dualism.

ii

We must remember, however, that the symbolism of the Middle Ages, whether Aristotelian or Plotinian, is in its emphasis theological and recognizes God's ontological participation in His creation. Not only is such participation vertical, but it is diffusive. Every beautiful visible thing is the image of the invisible beauty of God. Thus a woman may be considered the symbol of such impersonal ideas as the Good, Reason, Life, or the expression of the eternal Feminine in the human species; but she may also be, through her beauty, the symbolic revelation of God as well as the synthesis of the beauty of the World. Beauty not only is indefinable, it is as De Bruyne insists, *the symbol of the inexpressible*.[8] Likewise, Baudelaire's poet in the presence of beauty will feel a love "éternel et muet ainsi que la matière" and Mallarmé's Saint Cecilia will be "musicienne du silence."

Yet symbolist doctrines in the Middle Ages have special, though not exclusive, reference to what God makes. And what God makes in nature or accomplishes in history not only manifests Him in His presence of immensity but it may bear a specific message. He will speak in allegory. For the Middle Ages also had an incorrigible tendency toward allegory, nourished by the belief in the authoritative revelation of the Scriptures. Thus the believer reads in the Bible that Noah's ark was made of beams well-squared, as one would expect of a water-tight, floating structure. But in the Bible itself and in the writings of wise commentators there are hints of other meanings. In Holy Writ God uses words to present things, and things not merely to mean themselves, but the higher meanings of His plan for man's salvation. What can the ark be also but the spiritual Church, outside of which there is no salvation? The "beams well-squared" recall the four-square man of ancient and profane tradition, the perfect man. Thus the text means allegorically and mysteriously that the Church is made up of perfect saints.

When objects are *symbolic* they point toward God in the universal aspect of His presence. Everything, in this sense, *means* God. But when you inquire about the mysterious *relations* felt between physical realities and realities of *another order* that cannot be perceived by the senses, you have *allegory*. It is thanks to the mysterious immanence of the invisible God in the visible world that the four rivers of Eden are also the four rivers of Paradise and the four Gospels.

We have been describing, to be sure, the "allegory of the theologians," buttressed by the Bible's undoubted authenticity as the word of God. But what of visible *things* outside of Scriptures? They, too, according to Richard of St. Victor, convey as it were a painted image of the invisible world. All natural realities have some resemblance with supernatural realities: "Habent omnia corpora ad invisiblia bona similitudinum.[9]

The crucial question with relation to *belles lettres* follows logically. If God in the Scriptures can use words so that the things or events or persons signified stand for themselves and for meanings of *another order*, can a poet ever use words to name things and events which stand in a literal sense for themselves and, *at the same time*, stand for authentic meanings of another order, such as the allegorical, the moral, and the anagogical? Especially if such a poet should be named Dante and the work should be the *Divine Comedy*?

Dante acknowledged his use of another mode in an earlier work, the *Convivio*. There was an "allegorical sense after the use of the poets" which was different from that of the theologians. The allegorical sense

> is a truth hidden under beauteous fiction. As when Ovid says that Orpheus with his lyre made wild beasts tame and made trees and rocks approach him; which would say that the wise man with the instrument of his voice makes cruel hearts tender and humble; and moveth to his will such as have [not] the life of science and art; for they that have not the rational life are as good as stones.[10]

Ever since the middle of the second century before Christ allegory had been systematized as one of the ornaments of artistic prose. Yet it seems probable that it was the sacred writers who imposed on the Middle Ages its allegorical interpretation of the Bible and nature and expounded the theory of allegory. Bringing together the Bible and the Greeks, the Middle Ages saw in allegory a transcendental property of beauty. They praised the triple aesthetic pleasure derived from allegory: the sharpening of the wit, the giving of freshness to expression, the ornamentation of style. But even reality itself, they felt, takes on a mysterious charm as its unity diversifies itself in such a rich and unthought-of multiplicity of semblances! [11]

Some writers will go further and will aspire to nothing less than a poetry based upon "the objective structure of a world created by God, in its reality at once physical and supernatural." De Bruyne suggestively points to the *Divine Comedy* as evidence that there was sometimes a passage from a profane parabolism, where a bridge is thrown between words only and things, to theological allegory in a writer who came all the closer to the Bible and Nature as he sought to make his allegory an imitation of reality. In our day and in America, Professor Charles S. Singleton affirms the position in the fullest and most emphatic form. "The fiction of the *Divine Comedy* is that it is not fiction." [12]

Professor Singleton accepts, with many modern scholars, the authenticity of the Letter to Can Grande della Scala ascribed to Dante. In this letter Dante describes the *Divine Comedy* as

> polysemous, that is, having several meanings; for the first meaning is that which is conveyed by the letter, and the next that which is conveyed by what the letter signifies; the former of which is called literal, while the latter is called allegorical, or mystical. And for the better illustration of this method of exposition we may apply it to the following verses: "When Israel went out of Egypt, the house of Jacob from a people of strange language; Judah was his sanctuary, and Israel his dominion." For if we consider the letter alone, the thing signified to us is the going out of the children of Israel from Egypt in the time of Moses; if the allegory, our redemption through Christ is signified; if the moral sense, the conversion of the soul from the sorrow and misery of sin to a state of grace is signified; and if the analogical, the passing of the sanctified soul from the bondage of the corruption of this world to the liberty of everlasting glory is signified . . .

This being understood, it is clear that the subject, with

regard to which the alternative meanings are brought into play, must be twofold. And therefore the subject of this work must be considered in the first place from the point of view of the literal meaning, and next from that of allegorical interpretation. The subject, then, of the whole work, taken in the literal sense only, is the state of souls after death, pure and simple. For on or about that the whole work turns. If, however, the work be regarded from the allegorical point of view, the subject is man according as by his merits or demerits in the exercise of his free will he is deserving of reward or punishment by justice.[13]

Of special interest for our study of the symbol are the terms which Professor Singleton uses to express his conviction that the *Divine Comedy* has in common with the "allegory of the theologians" a grounding in the nature of things. "To anyone who knows this poem well it amounts to a steady feeling that somehow beyond his words there is a reality which would remain even if the words were taken away." "His song is a song to the will of man directing it to the Good." Professor Singleton takes issue with C. S. Lewis and many Dante scholars even concerning the *Vita Nuova*. "The *Vita Nuova* is no allegory. It is full of symbolism and mystical analogy, but symbol and analogy are not allegory. The *Roman de la Rose* is an allegory. The rose has another meaning and there is a key to it." Allegory offers "this for that," Dante's poetry presents "this and that" within the "focus of a single vision."

In the *Divine Comedy*, according to Professor Singleton, the pilgrim's journey in the other world is presented literally in a certain fashion so that it becomes our journey in this world. "It is because this is so that we have never before known an allegory like Dante's allegory."[14] Francis Fergusson in his study of Dante's *Purgatory* is equally explicit. Dante "wanted to make a poem which would be true as he believed Scripture was true. He wanted it to reflect the drama of man's life in the real world, in actual history, and in hidden but perpetual relation to God, as the Christian faith sees that drama."[15]

The kind of literary effect that Professor Singleton seeks

to describe could be identified by a modern theorist of the literary symbol as that of *symbolism in its post-Goethean sense*. "At the bottom of Dante's poetry . . . there is an imagination at work which is more mythical than poetic." Dante's poem is "myth" in the sense of Genesis and Plato. "This is a vision, not of things as we would wish them to be, but of things as they are." [16] But is this not to say of Dante's achievement what Goethe will say of the symbol: "In a true symbol the particular represents the universal, not as a dream or shadow, but as the living and instantaneous revelation of the unfathomable"? [17]

The answer is "yes," but with qualifications. "Yes" since the so-called "allegory" of Dante is symbol, as Singleton insists, in the sense that it conveys a higher and ultimate reality. Yet there is *one* sense in which Dante's practice is more like Baudelaire's than like Goethe's. For, as we shall see, a poem which Goethe calls "symbolic" need not possess what, with Baudelaire and the post-Baudelaireans, we call a symbol. A Goethean symbol can be a presentation with a minimum of indirection, no more, for instance, than in Tolstoy's *War and Peace*. The Baudelairean *symbole* is presented more indirectly. In Dante such indirection is demonstrated in the narrative of a journey in another world even if that journey is meant to suggest the real conditions and the real meaning of man's journey in this world. Despite Dante's pilgrim's meetings "over there" with so many characters who were historical or thought to be historical "down here," we approach the narrative on the oblique and with greater indirection than is the case with a novel like Tolstoy's which aims to present the meaning of human life and of history through a fiction embodying some historical and some nonhistorical characters.

Among modern Dante students there seems to be a considerable confusion of terminology influenced perhaps by the systematic inversion of terms to be found in C. S. Lewis' *The Medieval Allegory of Love*.[18] Symbolism, he tells us, came from Platonism, Neo-Platonism, Augustine and others; it is a sacramentalism, the attempt to represent a something else through its sensible imitations, to see the archetype of the copy. The "poetry of symbolism" belongs principally to the Romantics. Symbolism is a "mode of thought, but allegory is a mode of expression." Then Professor Lewis proceeds to make of every metaphor "an allegory in little," and rejects "purely conceptual equivalences" in allegory as "vulgar." The allegorical characters of the *Roman de la Rose* are "true incarnations of human experience," [19] a formulation hard to distinguish from Etienne Gilson's statement that Dante's Virgil, "far from being the expression of a symbolical meaning . . . is the origin of it." But Gilson's point of view seems post-Goethean as, again in his statement: "it is not the meaning that creates the symbolical being, but the symbolical being that creates its own symbol." [20]

It seems likely, then, that Dante scholars are involved in the perplexities which we hope to begin to disentangle as we proceed from Symbolism to Baudelaire.

THE DISTINCTION between symbol and allegory is known to the English speaking world through Coleridge's contrast in the *Statesman's Manual* between "a translation of abstract notions into a picture language," and "the translucence of the special in the individual, or of the general in the special . . . above all, by the translucence of the eternal through the temporal." Yet, according to Professor Wellek,[1] it was first clearly drawn by Goethe who declared that

> it makes a great difference whether a poet starts with a universal idea and then looks for suitable particulars, or beholds the universal *in* the particular. The former method produces allegory, where the particular has status merely as an instance, an example, of the universal. The latter, by contrast, is what reveals poetry in its true nature. It speaks forth a particular without independently thinking of or referring to a universal, but in grasping the particular in its living characters it implicitly apprehends the universal along with it.[2]

The passage reveals the all-important shift of the focus of definition that characterized the late eighteenth century and the nineteenth century. Allegory and symbol will not be defined by their external characteristics, nor in their relation to objective truth, but in terms of the process in the mind of the poet. Furthermore Goethe's distinction between allegory and symbol cuts deeper than a mere discrimination between genres. It approaches the normative, and has been in our time used as a norm. The way of recognizing true literature is by its recalcitrance to the treatment one can give allegory. If the writer does no more than "blow up" a concept even by the latest and trickiest techniques of photography and illustration, then it also can be satisfactorily reduced to its epitome, a paraphrasable meaning. But this proves that the piece of writing is "allegory" or "prose" in the absolute sense, a statement that can be exhaustively represented by an equivalent.

Goethe holds to symbol as a means of implicit knowledge of the universal even though the poet had his mind, to start with, on a particular. We have already quoted his statement: "In a true symbol the particular represents the universal, not as a dream or shadow, but as the living and instantaneous revelation of the unfathomable." Yet the heart of the difficulty for theory of knowledge is exposed in this brief statement. It is the "universal" that is known in the particular, nevertheless it is "unfathomable." How does one know, then, that it is universal? Moreover the knowledge given by the "particular" is a "revelation" (and not an outcome of an investigation using concepts), and it is obtained through the "particular" as its own evidence instantaneously, where the "instantaneous" and the "living" are one. But to become "knowledge," must not "revelation," especially of the "universal," be interpreted through concepts? On the other hand, does Goethe mean by "universal" here a sense of totality, of the cosmic?

Goethe's view of the symbol, and hence of the essence and the task of art, arises as Professor Karl Viëtor points out, from the assumption that God and existence are one. There can be no direct recognition of primal concepts like the true and the divine, just as we cannot perceive light itself, but only the things illuminated by it. Everything that is, then, is a representative-in-particular—a symbol—of the ultimate reality. To be sure there are single cases of an "eminent" nature, that is, they can become representative of many others. The highest symbol of the organization of nature is the primal phenomenon which comprehends all cases. It is an archetype. But the symbol has no meaning that could be abstracted from it. It is a "picture assembled in the mirror of the mind, and yet identical with its object." [3] Furthermore, though reality must provide the stimulus and the substance, yet "the elements of the visible world lie in the poet," this hidden aptitude to harbor them being strengthened gradually through repeated encounters with reality. "Had I not already carried the world within me by way of anticipation," Goethe said to Eckermann, "I should have remained blind with seeing eyes." The Absolute must remain inaccessible, though the divine essence is recognizable in modes or single phenomena. Professor Viëtor sums up appositely:

> The basic note in his ideas is the conviction that everything real is akin to us, but that at the same time the special uniqueness of every individuality constitutes a mystery which we are not in position to unveil . . . He does not attempt to explain nature by the laws of pure thinking, or to understand the universe as a rational system. Out of idea, feeling, and thinking our creative genius forms for itself a picture of the universe which preserves the fullness and the animation of the actual because it is not converted into concept and system. Goethe's "world piety" (*Weltfrommigkeit*) is something other than Spinoza's *amor dei intellectualis*.[4]

Thus for Goethe, as for Plotinus and the Neo-Platonists of the Middle Ages, symbolism is part and parcel of a metaphysical view, and in Goethe it develops a consonant literary doctrine. For him, too, as for Plotinus, art is the mediator of the inexpressible. But he rejected in Plotinus what left him cold in Plato, that eventual separation of the world of the Idea from the world of sense. For man there cannot be any knowledge, even on the highest level, severed from sense. Contemplative thinking is "anschauliche Denken" and with more than the purely mental or the spiritual eye focused on the object. Thus though Goethe may have received more than he realized of Plato through Shaftesbury, the "amiable Plato of Europe," as Herder called him, who gave a modern stamp to Neo-

Platonic ideas and from whom Goethe took over the idea of inner form so important to his aesthetics, there was another mysticism with some of whose doctrines and attitudes he found himself in greater sympathy.

We refer to the Alexandrian mysticism transmitted by German pansophists and theosophists with its doctrine of the universe as an organic whole, man as microcosm being an analogue of the macrocosm. Goethe read Paracelsus and the hermetic philosophies of the Renaissance; its alchemists and its occultists influenced him, and always in the direction of the affirmation of life, of nature, of the feeling that the soul is one with God and God one with nature. The ancient occultist view of the world seems to crop up wherever there is symbolism, be it in Goethe, Baudelaire, Mallarmé or Yeats, and we shall pause later to see it at work in the Romantic philosophers of nature and the dream.

ii

Nevertheless it was to the views of the philosopher Schelling that Goethe owed the largest debt. "In Schelling," Professor Viëtor writes, "Goethe found his own *Weltanschauung* presented, but in a systematic relation and in the language of modern speculation." Schelling in his famous essay on "The Relation of the Plastic Arts to Nature" (1807) had distinguished between the imitation of nature, *natura naturata* and that of *natura naturans*, that of "the world's holy, eternally creating primal energy, which engenders and actively brings forth all things out of itself." According to the German philosopher, the artist can create something true only through a living imitation of the spirit of nature in whose speech form and shape are merely symbols. Schelling's insistence that a thing's perfection is not a static form but "nothing else than the creative life within, its power to exist," and his stress on the "inner essence" which is this energy, effected a shift in the conception of the Idea, and the artist's relation to it. Whether for the Plato of the *Republic* who denied the artist's ability to imitate the Idea, or in Plotinus' doctrine of emanations making art possible as mediation between man and the Idea, the Idea remains in itself a static, time-less Form. According to the new doctrine, what gives form to anything is not the limits by which we "define" it but "the energy that inhabits it, by means of which it asserts itself as a whole on its own in relation to the whole." Thus "if the artist recognizes the vision and essence of the idea creating within him and stresses these, he fashions the individual into a world of its own, a genus, an eternal prototype." Yet the artist's timing must be perfect. He must seize the phenomenon at its one moment of complete existence. Only then it is what it is for all eternity. Art, by depicting the creature at this moment, raises it up out of time and presents it in pure being, in the eternity of its life. Thus for Schelling success in art will depend upon the same capacity that for Pater will make for "success in life"—to train oneself for recognition of those moments when what is in process and gestation flashes in full manifestation of itself.

Such ideas bear witness to a radical shift in the meaning of the symbol. For Plotinus and the Middle Ages the symbol brought a glimpse of something more excellent in its nature and therefore ineffable. For Schelling and Goethe the symbol no longer "brings together" (*symballein*) time and eternity in its dimension of perfection or holiness but time and eternity in the relation of meaning as process. The model for thought becomes biological and organic, the great commendatory word is "living." By means of this analogy Goethe, who can quarrel with Newtonian abstraction and for whom law is a "living" kind of universal and knowledge a function of the whole man congruent with nature, brings together the delights of the mind and of the senses. What is Beauty itself but the perfect revelation of the law-like reason which governs the processes of life, an objective norm in which we behold "the law-governed phase of life in its greatest activity and perfection"? [5]

One could object, and quite rightly, that what is here being described is an intention rather than an achievement. As Plato saw long ago it would require no less than a god to bring the One and the Many together. Schelling will not free himself from the Platonic, especially after 1801,[6] just as Whitehead in our day could not seem to do without "eternalism" in some form. Nevertheless the very significant effort was made to bring together "activity" and "perfection" and it was not easy either for Romantic poet or philosopher, any more than for Yeats, to let a Plato or Plotinus go, though with a "blessing" on his head. For earlier generations of thinkers, where "perfection" is, activity must have ceased. What really happened was that the new generation, with its eye on "nature," insisted that the vital must be one of perfection's attributes. Essence must be shown coming into existence in order to be commended, both in art and metaphysics.

The artist, Coleridge writes, in that essay "On Poesy or Art" where he has Schelling most in view,

> must imitate that which is within the thing, that which is active through form and figure, and discourses to us by symbols—the *Natur-geist*, or spirit of nature . . . The idea which puts the form together cannot itself be the form. It is above form, and is its essence, the universal in the individual, or the individuality itself,—the glance and the exponent of the indwelling power.

Thus it is the "idea," Schelling's *Idee*, the spirit of nature, the essence or energizing power, the inmost principle of the possibility of anything as that particular thing, that is made known to us by its bodily form or symbol in natural objects. The artist must succeed in mastering "the essence, the *natura naturans*, which presupposes a bond between nature in the higher sense and the soul of man." It is the Imagination as "essentially vital" that is the source of the symbol by which the artist in turn can come to a knowledge of nature. For the Imagination is, according to the *Statesman's Manual*, "that reconciling and mediatory power, which incorporating the reason in images of the sense, and organizing (as it were) the flux of the senses by the permanent and self-circling energies of the reason,

gives birth to a system of symbols, harmonious in themselves, and consubstantial with the truths of which they
are the conductors."

Though Baudelaire, so far as we can determine, derives
something both from Coleridge and the Germans upon
whom the English critic so largely draws, we shall be
satisfied with a long passage from the *History of Modern
Criticism* to characterize the thought of the latter and
limit further description to the German thinkers:

But beyond verbal reproductions and close paraphrases, we
must also realize that many or even most of Coleridge's key
terms and distinctions are derived from Germany. The
general aesthetic position—the view of the relation between art and nature, the reconciliation of opposites, the
whole dialectical scheme—comes from Schelling. The distinction between symbol and allegory can be found in
Schelling and Goethe, the distinction between genius and
talent in Kant, the distinctions between organic and mechanical, classical and modern, statuesque and picturesque
in A. W. Schlegel. Coleridge's particular use of the term
"Idea" comes from the Germans, and the way in which he
links imagination with the process of cognition is also
clearly derived from Fichte and Schelling. It is true, of
course, that some of these ideas have their ultimate source
in antiquity and can be found occasionally in the English
neo-Platonists. Coleridge was acquainted with Plato, Plotinus, Cudworth, Henry More, and others, but still he draws
on the Germans, for only they use the same dialectical
method as he, the same epistemology and the same critical
vocabulary. The neo-Platonists remained essentially scholastic mystics. Coleridge could not have been known to
Schopenhauer, Hegel, De Sanctis, or Belinsky, and still
most of the concepts, theories, and ideas which in the
English-speaking world are today ascribed to Coleridge can
be found in them. In Germany there was a large body of
aesthetic thought which slowly radiated to France, Italy,
Spain, and Russia. In England Coleridge stood quite alone,
sharply distinct even from his close associates, Wordsworth,
Lamb, and Hazlitt, who had only very slight German con-
tacts. The vocabulary, the dialectical scheme, the whole
intellectual atmosphere sets Coleridge apart. The differ-

ence is explainable only by Coleridge's adaptation and im-portation of the Germans. This in itself constituted an important historical merit which should not be minimized. Coleridge was the main source, in this respect, not only for a long line of English critics but also for the American transcendentalists and for Poe, and thus indirectly for the French symbolists.[7]

At important points, moreover, where Coleridge draws his inspiration from German thought, he is, in Professor Wellek's opinion, eclectic to excess, seeking to reconcile incompatibles of beauty and truth, the universal and the particular, imitation and symbol, now emphasizing Platonic mystical terminology, now exalting the metaphysical role of art. Symbol he confuses with synecdoche, metaphor he will consider a fragment of allegory, even *Don Quixote* becoming "a substantial living allegory." And he is relatively indifferent to myth.

iii

It was in A. W. Schlegel especially, then, as well as in Schelling, that Goethe's concept of the symbol found its true development. His theory of poetry centers on metaphor, symbol and myth. Metaphor is for A. W. Schlegel the basic procedure of poetry, and no comparison can be too bold if only apt and meaningful. It restores original vision and immediacy of perception, and for the system of nature metaphor signifies the inter-relationship of all things so that each part of the universe mirrors the whole. Imagination breaks through what we have made a commonplace reality; it both plunges us into the universe and makes it move within us "like a magic realm of eternal metamorphoses, where everything rises out of everything by a marvelous creation." As Professor Wellek remarks, Schlegel here propounds a theory of correspondences, "which is practically identical with that of the much later symbolist movement."

The German critic sees that metaphor and symbolism may be used in a purely decorative and intellectual way; nevertheless, properly speaking, allegory is "the personification of a concept, a fiction contrived only for this purpose; but (symbolism) is what the imagination has created for other reasons, or what possesses a reality independent of concept, what is at the same time spontaneously susceptible of a symbolic interpretation; indeed it even lends itself to it." [8]

All art must then be symbolic or, as Schlegel later preferred to say, "sinnbildlich," and must present meaningful images, just as nature reveals the inner by the outer. By the way in which the artist shapes the physiognomy of things, he enables the reader to penetrate to the inner core of things. Art is a thinking in images and poetry a "bildlich, anschauender Gedankenausdruck." But what does the language of poetry, at once so close to sensation and image and thought, present? At times Schlegel answers "Ideen," i.e. necessary and eternally true thoughts and feelings which soar above earthly existence. He thus occasionally comes close to Hegel's "sinnliches Scheinen der Idee" and the intellectualism that makes poetry the embodiment of ideas. For the "symbolist view of poetry," Professor Wellek observes "an analogy of the totality of the universe and its relationships, is a precarious position, which has to be guarded carefully against two dangers: intellectualism and mysticism." But, as we shall observe in our study of Baudelaire, there is the opposite danger that in seeking to "guard" the symbol well, we may abstract the symbol from its philosophical and religious contexts and reduce it to an empty rhetorical term.

For the Germans, however, as had been true in the past, the idea of symbol involved the self-evidence of a "higher" or "deeper" reality. Thus if, according to Professor Wellek, Schlegel's critical practice usually holds him firmly to his original idea (derived from Herder) that poetry must be concrete, he does add the necessity of a symbolic relationship to the whole universe: a microcosmic-macrocosmic parallelism which has its ultimate roots in Neo-Platonism. A work of art has the "inexhaustibility of creative nature whose counterpart it is in miniature." [9] But it is to mysticism that Schleger is more often attracted than to intellectualism. He modifies a phrase from Schelling, "beauty is the infinite represented finitely" to read "beauty is the symbolic representation of the infinite." The "infinite" here, Professor Wellek explains, is the mystery behind appearances and the mystery in us, a mystery which, though cosmic, is not completely beyond this world. It is intimated through "the oracular verdict of the heart, these deep intuitions in which the dark riddle of our existence seems to solve itself."

Nevertheless it is the concept of myth, the idea of the poet as neither philosopher nor mystic but myth-maker that, according to Wellek, organizes A. W. Schlegel's views of poetic activity and gives him a strong claim to modern interest. The state of myth is for the German critic natural to man; it is a stage of his past; it remains with him as a boundless shudder in the midst of physical security despite every effort of the Enlightenment to reduce it to mere fear or the machinations of priests. For myth is not merely the raw material of poetry, it is poetry itself as operative, a complete view of the world. If myth is indeed a living force in mankind, if it arose and still persists as an unconscious fiction of mankind by which nature can be humanized, then it may be possible for an individual poet like Dante to let the most essential forces of nature become for the poet symbols of spiritual existence, so that a "scientific mythology" rises from the union of his physics with his theology.[10]

The emphasis on poetry as metaphor, symbol, and myth accords with the image of art as organism. Art "should create living works like nature created independently, organized and organizing." Schlegel tends to press the organism metaphor far, Professor Wellek thinks, not content to use it merely as a biological analogy, tenable if moderately interpreted, that will help the critic to grasp the unity of form and content. He distinguishes between "mechanical" form, which is impressed upon the object from the outside, like a shape given to a soft mass, and "organic form," which "unfolds itself from within and acquires its definiteness simultaneously with the total development of the germ." For the German critic, "from the first conception of a poem, content and form are, like soul and body, indivisible."

Such a view of artistic creation would seem to demand a definition of genius as unconscious power. But Schlegel rejects the Kantian view and holds that genius brings together in intimate union the unconscious and self-conscious activity, instinct and intention, freedom and necessity. Certainly the idea of the fusion of the conscious and the unconscious both in creation and interpretation lies behind those modern theories of poetic suggestiveness, warning us against understanding poetry too well, and of creative obscurity, which we may consider our heritage from Symbolisme. A Baudelaire or a Mallarmé are illuminated by August Schlegel's remark that in modern poetry, in contrast to the ancient, "a higher reflection must in its works submerge itself again in the Unconscious." Today's poet must be "clearer in his knowledge of the nature of art than great poets of former ages could be." [11]

Furthermore, it is only insofar as such emergence of an advanced intellectual consciousness from the unconscious, but without abstraction, is indeed thought possible, and felt by the critic to be achieved in actual works of art, that one can turn back Croce's attacks on Symbolisme in Mallarmé, Rimbaud, Claudel, and even Baudelaire.[12] The critic reproaches Symbolisme for its emotionalism (on the side of "suggestiveness") and for its intellectualistic hermeticism (on the side of its "obscurity"), his own ideal seeming to be a poetry simple, sensuous and passionate, stemming from experience directly confronted, the resulting state of soul being cognized in a universal form. But the Symbolisme of Baudelaire and of Mallarmé has its source in le rêve, which is presumed to be a special organization of consciousness where volupté and connaissance are fused, but at a remove from ordinary experience. Such a state, if credible, would be the basis for the reconciliation, which Schlegel takes for granted, of the conscious and the unconscious, freedom and necessity.

iv

We are ready, then, to pose the question: When Schelling and the Schlegels proposed the theory of poetry as symbol, did they envison poems like those of the later Mallarmé or even like the more novel specimens among the poems of Baudelaire? Speaking for Goethe, Fritz Strich, the eminent student of Romanticism, replies in emphatic negative. He objects especially to the conscious symbolism of the French poets, denying them even the name of symbolists. "Ich kann den französischen Symbolismus, der mit bewusstester Absicht symbolisiert, in meinem Sinne überhaupt nicht symbolisch nennen." [13] Only a Verlaine, in spite of a deliberate symbolism, attains to the symbolical, though his art may be only a "Suggestion-kunst"!

As an example of the Goethean symbol Professor Strich quotes the well-known lyric "Wanderer's Nachtlied" (translation by Longfellow):

> *Über allen Gipfeln*
> *Ist Ruh,*
> *In allen Wipfeln*
> *Spürest du*
> *Kaum einen Hauch;*
> *Die Vögelein schweigen im Walde.*
> *Warte nur, balde*
> *Ruhest du auch.*

> *O'er all the hill-tops*
> *Is quiet now,*
> *In all the tree-tops*
> *Hearest thou*
> *Hardly a breath;*
> *The birds are asleep in the trees.*
> *Wait; soon like these*
> *Thou too shalt rest.*

In this lyric the scholar sees an example of Dilthey's *Erlebnis*, an experience in which life as lived reaches its highest meaning. The poet here is expressing a moment of experience, a particular and, at the same time, without thinking of it, a universal, a law. The symbol does not mean, it is. Yet the reader is in the presence of an *Urphänomenon*, which deepens in meaning the more it is contemplated, and is literally endless. The poem needs no explanation, yet it is true symbol because of its power to transport the reader into the universally human directly and freely, *and not as it were in spite of himself by suggestion*. It appeals to the *Geist*, or the Spirit that is in man, *Geist* as an urge toward universality. Whatever the truth of Professor Strich's interpretation, one fact would seem to stand out: the modern reader would not, at first blush, call this poem "symbolic" at all. Where is the "symbol"? At most there is in this poem a metaphor that might easily pass unperceived! But what distinguishes Baudelaire, Mallarmé and the Symbolistes is metaphoric vision, a more energetic "projection" of vision than Goethe's.

Certainly the attitude toward metaphor marks a major difference in the theory and practice of Goethe and Baudelaire. Unlike an A. W. Schlegel, for instance, Goethe distrusted metaphor. Speech with its signs and metaphors, like the hated eyeglasses, seemed to him to give only a clouded view of reality. He was the man, as Charles Du Bos said, of the *"erfüllte Augenblick,"* the direct, serene and completely satisfying view of "objective" reality. He maintained a certain solid balance even in the pursuit of mystery.[14] Sometimes Goethe seems to illustrate unintentionally his own definition of allegory, as when he praises the Greek sculptor Myron's group of the cow giving suck to a calf as an object of the highest art, for it is the principle of nourishment represented in its most beautiful form. "This statue and others like it I call symbols of the omnipresence of God." Again, Goethe's tendency to identify symbol and "Laconismus," encouraged by his interest in the plastic arts, is of doubtful augury. For an epitome is not a symbol.

No wonder, then, that Philip Wheelwright, quoting Goethe's definition of the symbol as involving "the fullest coalescence of the particular instance and the general idea," comments that it "suggests a perhaps too great readiness to move in the direction of allegorical poetry." [15] Yet the case of Goethe is far from clear. One may stress with Professor Wellek the importance of great motifs, legends, myth and mythology for Goethe's thought and creation. Once Goethe will even say of some sketches by Tischbein that "the most beautiful symbols are those which allow a multiple interpretation," and he will acknowledge that there is something "totally incommensurable" in the *Faust*.[16] Even Professor Strich testifies to a period in Goethe's symbolism when the poet plunges not only into the "archetypal" but also the mystical. Once past his middle years, he thinks, Goethe the sage and seer stepped back into the realm of the *Urphänomenon* from the world of the *Phänomenon* and of the "Classische Symbolik"; in "die Mütter," "die Sorge," "das Ewig-Weibliche" and the older Faust himself, he brought us into immediate contact with ultimate reality by stripping his figures even of the mediatory role of symbols.

Goethe's use of the word "symbolic" seems at first to have been an attempt to characterize the impression made upon him by certain objects when he revisited Frankfurt-am-Main. They are "eminent cases," he wrote to Schiller on August 16, 1797, "which are representative of many other cases, include a certain totality, require a certain order, excite something similar or strange in my mind and make claims both from outside and inside to a certain unity and totality." [17] Here we note the stress on what Baudelaire will term the "concatenation" of inner elements in a poem. But the "something similar or strange" excited in the mind by an object seems incommensurable with the Baudelairean "spectacle, however ordinary" which in "certain states of the soul almost supernatural" reveals the "depth of life in its entirety" and "becomes its symbol." [18]

Goethe seems, both in the earlier and later stages of his use of the symbol, to have distrusted the mediation of metaphor. The Symbolisme of Baudelaire and of Mallarmé is constantly metaphorical in the presentation of its world, and the metaphors are structured into symbols. If for Goethe, then, all true poems are "symbols," for Baudelaire, as we shall see, not only are poems symbols but often, and most characteristically in his practice, they *have symbols.*

It is to the credit of Professor Eliseo Vivas among recent critics and aestheticians to have emphasized a distinction that should help to clear up a source of considerable confusion. The "constitutive" symbol (as distinguished from "symbol" used for any word or for a mathematical "X"), he points out: "may refer to the elementary means we use to grasp the world perceptually, the means which Kantian philosophers call categories, and which give the world the basic order it has for us. Or it may refer to the more or less sophisticated works of art we find in all cultures, however primitive these cultures may be. Or it may refer to components of works of art." [19]

The "symbol" in Professor Vivas' second sense, which he would apply even to a so-called naturalistic or realistic novel of Jane Austen's like *Emma,* is what we mean by the "Goethean symbol." The symbol in Vivas' third sense, the "symbol as component," is a very useful term. Thus it would be very convenient to say that the novelty of the *symbolisme* of Baudelaire and Mallarmé lies—in the most general fashion—in their preponderant use of "the symbol as component." The structuring of poetry by metaphors of symbolic force, we would add, involves a "musical" conception of poetry. Yet Baudelaire's poetry, even in its most novel form, remains closer than does the most characteristic poetry of Mallarmé and Rimbaud to the central tradition of European poetry. Likewise, in Baudelaire's critical ideas, a view of poetry broadly perennial takes on a "modern" Romantic cast, just as, in his belief, beauty should.

3 BAUDELAIRE:
THE ESOTERIC CONTEXT

FROM 1820 until the death of Baudelaire in 1867, three more or less parallel forces are at work in French poetry: first, the strictly "romantic" conception of poetry as the spontaneous overflow of emotion; secondly, around 1830 the revival, from *Les Orientales* of Hugo to Gautier and the eventual Parnassian school, of interest in poetry as "art," conceived in terms of painterly and sculptural effects, with a rejection of at least the more direct claims of morality and utility; and thirdly, a slowly developing sense of poetry as a special and mysterious experience. In the new valuation set upon the poetic experience as such, according to Professor Margaret Gilman, "the penetration into literature of the illuminist and occultist traditions plays a large part." The poetic image, once an ornament, becomes a symbol. The result is a poetry "liberated from convention yet concerned with form, intensely aware of mystery yet translating that mystery in terms of the visible world."[1]

The "mystery" is characterized by such words as "le rêve," "l'analogie," "les correspondances," terms whose meanings and implications are at least the apparent context of the aesthetic theory and of the poetry of Baudelaire. The terms belong to a tradition which we shall call "occultist" or "esoteric." Certainly some of Baudelaire's most striking pronouncements on art and literature echo this tradition, and a major problem in the case of the

French poet (as later in the case of Yeats) is the relation of "occultism" to his idea of the symbol and to his poetry. Shall we say of Baudelaire what Paul Valéry alleges concerning Edgar Allan Poe: "I shall not conceal the fact that Poe's ideas are connected basically with a certain personal metaphysical system. But this metaphysic, if it directs and dominates and suggests the theories in question, nevertheless does not penetrate them. It engenders them and explains their generation; it does not constitute them." [2] For a theory to engender without penetrating or constituting what it dominates, directs, and suggests, strikes us as a brilliant evasion of an unpalatable truth. At any rate Poe's "personal metaphysical system" certainly smacks of "occultism" and was one of his attractions for the French poet.

Such speculations seem to have been perennial, occultism manifesting itself in the Babylonian ziggurat, a kind of "magic mountain," and the pyramid, in the myth of Tammuz, in Ikhnaton, and in that common core of all Indian philosophies: the recognition of the identity of the *atman,* man's essential self, and the *brahman* the essential universal force. Professor John Senior, to whose volume *The Way Down and Out* we are indebted, points out that in *yoga* we have a form of the "great descent," the journey into the hell of the self as a necessary condition to attaining heaven. One may, according to the doctrine of some Hindu schools, achieve salvation not only through asceticism, but also through "sin," and, in Senior's opinion, this was the path followed by romantic and symbolist literature. At any rate, we think of the Castorps and the Leverkühns of Thomas Mann's novels.

Senior follows his thread into the labyrinth of the Greek mystery religions and Orphism, into Hellenistic cults and, in the Alexandrian world, into the circle of Hermes Trismegistus and of the Kabbala, with its doctrine that En-Soph creates by numbers and letters, all words being capable of reduction to twenty-two Hebrew letters. The tradition comes to Europe via Spain in the twelfth century and will blossom in the Renaissance. The astrological mysteries which Senior describes will not seem so strange to readers of Yeats' *The Vision*.[3]

In his poem "Vers Dorés," Gérard de Nerval, by many considered the first authentic voice of Symbolisme, sang: "Un mystère d'amour dans le métal repose." Alchemy, Senior writes, is the astrology of the earth. All nature strives toward a return to its single source: the mystic, therefore, strives to transmute the self into the Godhead; the alchemist, baser metals into purer ones. One acts on the self as on living metal. The alchemists are allied with every occult system. They were Pythagoreans, the seven metals being the seven strings of the lyre; they became Kabbalists with Paracelsus. They seek and find correspondences of colors and sounds, stars and matches. To their lord Trismegistus they attribute the Emerald Tablets whose thirteen precepts sum up the "great work." (One thinks of Mallarmé's "Oeuvre" which was to contain the "Orphic explanation" of the earth.)

Though science in the seventeenth century repelled the occultist world view, Bacon piercing the very heart of its method in his attack upon analogy, the "circle of perfection" will be revived in the imagination of Romantic poets. The eighteenth century already had produced Swedenborg, the type of the modern occultist, at once student, scientist, and seer. His premise of the immaterial substance working everywhere in a common world of spirit and matter, his insistence that the universe has a human form, his doctrine of correspondences, which will be brought into the realm of poetry by Baudelaire—these are reformulations of very ancient ideas.

In fact, a plethora of self-consciously occult sects swarms over the intellectual centers of Europe at the time of the French Revolution. In France Claude St. Martin, "the illuminist," has for disciple the unfrocked Abbé Alphonse Constant, who, taking the name of Eliphas Lévi, becomes the leader of the Western *avant-garde* which, according to Senior, "is about to discover Eastern thought by the back door." For this "perennial philosophy" or "esoteric tradition," the symbol is defined in Yeats' terms, an attempt to entangle the divine essence—to represent the single living substance which expresses itself in time and space as an infinite number of contradictory things by means of one of the separate things.

Metaphor is an analogy based on "correspondence." Its two terms create a "third thing" which, ricocheting off the world of physical reality, generates the "fourth thing." Such metaphor unites poetry with the fourfold universe of occult tradition. The fourfold vision is, according to Senior, the vision of Dante, of Blake, and of all the most successful poetry. It follows that the "chief symbolist poets" are "to some extent occultists"; though, in their effort to evoke mystical vision, all the symbolists "more or less fail." *Les Fleurs du mal* of Baudelaire aims to induce in the reader a participation in the experience of "vision." Baudelaire's life and work Senior sees as a "real descent into Hell" to destroy the ordinary self in order to discover the true self. But nowhere, not even in "Le Voyage," which is "great—as poetry—as a poem without vision can be," does he do more than "foresee" the glittering shores of light. In Rimbaud, too, who is squarely in the occultist tradition, there is evidence of a descent into Hell but not of an ascent. At most Rimbaud achieves "two-fold" vision. Mallarmé, on the other hand, succeeds, according to Senior, in destroying the physical world by "a kind of linguistic yoga in order to project the reader into that infinite beyond occasions." The abolition of chance to which Mallarmé dedicated both life and work is "the equivalent of 'moksha'" or yogic "release"; yet "Un Coup de dés n'abolit pas le hasard," with its attempt at fourfold vision, has too much of the negative purity of a glimpse of the Absolute and not the "great embrace, the continuous awareness of the entire created universe *as* God," the "ecstatic naturalism" of love.[4]

ii

A less doctrinaire approach to the relation of Baudelaire, Rimbaud, and Mallarmé, and indeed of French poets after the first world war, to the "esoteric" and to the German "philosophers of nature and the dream"—that of Albert Béguin in *L'Ame Romantique et le Rêve*—will fill in backgrounds that appear authentic for our Symbolistes if elusive of exact depiction. The French scholar defines "le rêve" broadly to include not only nocturnal dreaming but also the varieties of waking dream and the response to sensation, be it of a natural object or of a work of art. Including in his term all images that, by the nature of the response which they evoke, suggest more than a meaning to be utilized by thought or action in an ordinary fashion, Béguin seeks to suggest an affinity of "familles d'esprit" between French Symbolistes and German Romantics. Such affinity will not be the result of a direct influence but rather of the working upon similar human needs and aspirations of common forces of nature and of culture. Thus one can find in Baudelaire the echo of a passage from E. T. A. Hoffmann's *Kreisleriana*: [5]

> It is not so much in my dreams as in that state of delirium which precedes sleep, and particularly when I have heard a good deal of music, that I perceive a kind of *accord between colors, sounds and perfumes*. It seems to me that they become manifest side by side in the same mysterious fashion in the sunlight, only to fuse soon afterward in a marvelous concert.
>
> The perfume of dark red carnations has a singular magic power over me: involuntarily I fall into a dreamy state, and I hear then, coming it seems from far away, swelling and then fading, the sound of a horn.

The hero of one of Hoffmann's stories reports:

> A special star reigns over me at important moments; it mingles with reality fabulous things which nobody believes and which often seem to me to have issued from the profoundest depths of myself. But, suddenly, they assume, outside of myself, another value and become the mystic symbols of that marvel which at every moment in life offers itself to our gaze.

It must be remembered, Béguin points out, that the sense of "correspondances" in Baudelaire, however remark-

able in itself, is the fruit of a state of revery, of an
"authentic experience of ecstasy and of the innate tendencies of his being." The link between Baudelaire and
Hoffmann, we may add, is not a curious psychological
observation, i.e., synaesthesia, but a common dream experience. The French poet, according to Béguin, distinguishes
between the natural dream which is "the man himself"
made up of the experiences of the day, and the absurd
dream, unforeseen, with no relation or connection with
the character, the life and the passions, of the sleeper. The
former which is "hieroglyphic" represents the "supernatural side" of life.

Again, in the *Paradis artificiels*, Baudelaire distinguishes
between authentic dream states and those due to the use
of drugs. Now and then a man is granted the rare boon "of
happy seasons, happy days, delightful minutes"—an exceptional state of mind that can be called "paradisiacal."
"We must recognize that often this marvel, this kind of
prodigy occurs as if it were the effect of a superior and
invisible power, external to man, after a period in which the
latter has abused his physical faculties . . . I prefer to
consider this abnormal condition of spirit as a veritable act
of grace, like a magic mirror to which man is called to see
himself in beauty . . . a kind of angelic excitation, a call
to order in the form of delicate flattery." In the knowledge
of such moments Baudelaire compares himself with "those
who know how to observe themselves and who retain the
memory of their impressions, those who, like Hoffmann,
have been able to construct their spiritual barometer." [6]
One may relate to a species of experience described by
Hoffmann, also the famous text from *Fusées* which defines
the meaning of Baudelairean ecstasy: "In certain states of
soul almost supernatural, the depth of life reveals itself
entirely in the spectacle, however ordinary it may be, that
is before one's eyes. It becomes its *Symbol*." Thus to
become a symbol may be the property of any object,
provided it is envisaged by a state of soul "almost supernatural" and the object reveals the "depth of life." But to
such moments of vision not only Hoffmann but his
contemporaries and forbears in German Romanticism

testified frequently. Upon them they based their psychologies, their philosophies and theologies, even their poetics.

iii

The philosophical and critical thought of Schelling and the Schlegels, according to Albert Béguin, developed to a degree of rational coherence materials whose modern source was the Neo-Platonism of the Renaissance. For Kepler, Paracelsus, Nicholas of Cusa (whom Yeats was to read), Agrippa of Nettesheim, Giordano Bruno, the universe is a living being with a soul. Since all particular beings are bound together as emanations of the great All, every act has its repercussions throughout the universe, and such universal sympathy makes possible magic and astrology.

The view that everything is in some mode or to some degree analogous to everything else is also an ideal premise for any thoroughgoing symbolism. Such a conception of relationships was forced to give way to Cartesianism and post-Cartesianism with their analytic and often reductive approach to reality; yet even at the height of the Enlightenment, Béguin tells us, ideas of a Neo-Platonic cast were introduced into Germany through the writings of Dante's contemporary, Meister Eckhart, as well as of such late-Renaissance figures as Paracelsus, Agrippa, Van Helmont, and Jacob Boehme. These ideas were mixed with the alluvia, oriental in origin, of a traditional occultism renewing itself in Germany and France.

In France Louis-Claude Saint-Martin (1743–1803), already preoccupied, as were to be the philosophers of nature generally, with the problem of the fall of man, declared matter to have been created in order to arrest man's course into the abyss when he turned to another light than that of which he was to be the supreme manifestation. Thus man was given a world in which he might redeem himself by seeking to reconstitute the harmony of which he finds an imprint in himself. The world, an analogy of the Logos, is the principal agent of such a reintegration. Thus only the poet can restore the lost unity through his use of the language of angels, the perfect discourse in which the visible symbol and reality are fused. The poetic act is sacred and literally creative.[7]

In Germany the thought of Saint-Martin interested, for all their mistrust of its occultist elements, such men as Lavater, Hamann, Herder and Jacobi; the next generation with Baader, Zacharias Werner and Schubert among others, was to be even more receptive. Johann Georg Hamann, whose *Mémoires Socratiques* appeared in 1759, made, according to Béguin, the first attempt at the psychological study of a human being which went beyond the simple description of the faculties and their mechanism. He was the first to insist that genius cannot be otherwise explained than by an unconscious: "Only the knowledge of self, that descent into hell, opens the way to divinization." Already in Hamann, the idea of attaining a superhuman power through the uncontrolled intuitions of poetry announces Rimbaud.

For Hamann's disciple, Johann Gottfried Herder (1744–1803), analogical knowledge is not static but rhythmical, as in the Renaissance. (We think of Wordsworth's "truth" as a "motion or a shape, Instinct with vital functions" in *The Prelude*, VIII.) What is living in the individual seeks and finds its analogy in the life of nature. There are internal sensations, converging in imagination, and they give a higher knowledge. Thus imagination produces not only images but sounds, words, signs, feelings for which language has no name. The theory for a poetry like Baudelaire's has already been outlined.

In Goethe's time, Béguin continues, the very discoveries of empirical science seemed to be meant to provide a pretext, an example, or at least an image for cosmic speculations. The discovery of oxygen showed that a similar vital element pervaded the inorganic and organic world; the work of Galvani in electricity and of Mesmer in magnetism suggested the idea that the same force governed the world of things and of nature. Zacharias Werner, among whose students were Baader, Novalis, and Schubert, speculated from a base in geology that there must be an analogy between grammar, "that minerology of language," and the internal structure of nature. (Less strange in view of such speculations, however transmitted, will appear Mallarmé's attempt to re-create in the sound of poetry and in the interrelation of its parts an identity with the ultimate structure and meaning of things.)

These philosophers of nature and of the dream, Béguin insists, were no mere vulgarizers of Schelling. They were at some points his precursors and had surprising intuitions of their own. In this succession we shall list Ignaz-Paul-Vitalis Troxler, a pupil of Schelling and, Béguin suggests, a pre-Bergsonian in his insistence that true knowledge must grasp living wholes; Johann Jakob Wagner, jurist, journalist, professor of philosophy; Johann Karl Passavant, physician, physicist, and mathematician who believed in the poet as "seer"; Dietrich-Georg Kieser, professor at Jena and the director of the Archiv für Magnetismus; the Norwegian Henrick Steffens who wrote works on natural science, anthropology, and moral philosophy; Lorenz Okenfuss who studied sex for the main clue to the enigma of the universe; Georg-Christoph Lichtenberger, who discovered a profound analogy between the functioning of dreams and the birth of myths in primitive mentality and who directly related the personal unconscious and the collective unconscious.[8] From the last named one line goes to Jung, another to Wittgenstein. Carus also, in his psychological writings on the personal and impersonal unconscious, offers more than a hint of Jung. In Karl-Philipp Moritz ideas of memory and imagination foreshadow Proust as well as Baudelaire. In an autobiographical novel, *Andreas Hartknopf*, Moritz writes: "There are certain material objects whose sight gives us a dim perception of our entire lives and perhaps of our entire existence." Baudelaire, as we have seen, describes his symbol in very similar language.

The world view of these men can be summarized in a series of theses:

Cosmic becoming aims at a return to a lost unity.

Nature is an animated organism.

Man the microcosm can decipher the macrocosm. Hence the need and value of analogy and correspondences.

The individual himself only truly lives when lifted into the absolute by a state of ecstasy.

The Unconscious is God in the heart. We ask the questions, and the heart, as in hypnotism, gives the answers. For the Unconscious is the very root of the human being, the point of insertion into nature which makes possible human participation in its rhythms. It is an awareness of cosmic flux. In sleep consciousness enters into the fulness of its hidden life. The dream unites not with the flux but with the primal creative force in nature.

Inspiration combines in ways which the reason does not understand the fulness of night and the clarity of day, the unconscious and the conscious.

Yet poetry, not abandoning itself to the unconscious, but seizing it and raising it as far as possible into consciousness, only prefigures a final reconciliation of the two.

The Imagination is the creative force of dream; it is the "inner sense" or the "universal sense"; essentially inventive and creative it really sees into the relations and the life of things. Thus a Baader in 1820, Béguin suggests, would have agreed with Rimbaud in his famous dictum "Je est un autre"; but the creative power in poetry, he would have said, is one with the power in all things.

Among these "philosophers," Gotthilf Heinrich von Schubert, a constant reader of Novalis, seems especially, in Béguin's opinion, to be feeling his way toward a conception of poetry which "was to find full expression only in the lineage of Baudelaire, of Mallarmé, and of Rimbaud." In his *Symbolik des Traumes* (1814), an original theoretical work on the dream state, he observes that the metaphors of dreams are linked by a new law of association. The mind works through a language of hieroglyphics which is innate, and whose images participate in reality. Thus for all people "darkness" is associated with melancholy; but there can be constrasting images, "burial" suggesting "marriage," and also remote associations, thanks to which "morning" is known through "yellow" or a "yellow landscape," joy through "red," deep suffering through meteors, the native land through the image of the umbilicus, the bed partner through the image of a shoulder. Thus poetry is the key to our hidden wealth; rhythm with its spell restores the harmony between us and the universe; and the irony in the poet's life and words comes from his sense of the unexpressed.

iv

What such an *Anschauung* can mean for the writing of poetry and the theory of poetry can be observed especially in Friedrich von Hardenberg (1772–1801), called "Novalis," whom Albert Béguin considers the initiator of German romanticism and of the "philosophy of nature." Poetry for Novalis terminates in experience, a mystical consummation here below, *hic et nunc*. The supreme state is a harmony of a musical nature: "Gemüt-Harmonie aller Geisterkräfte—gleiche Stimmung und harmonisches Spiel der ganzen Seele." [9] "Gemüt" is a state of musical harmony superior to consciousness and unconsciousness which another recent student of Novalis, Maurice Besset, identifies with the "moi profond" of Bergson and his "cime de l'âme."

Such perfect consciousness, not possible for all nor permanent for any, is consciousness of everything and of nothing; it is a chant, the simple modulation of states of soul. It may come upon us at the sight of certain people, faces, eyes, expressions, gestures, or at the sound of certain words or the reading of certain passages, or when we have a sense of the unity of body and soul. The state is more than a simultaneous seeing and feeling. In its calm we are filled with an immediate certainty of our truest and most intimate life. Such sovereign consciousness, with its absolute clarity, is also irony, a testimony to the spirit's sense of an absolute superiority. [10]

If Symbolisme means in part the creative consciousness functioning not only as poetic insight but as control and pressure, the new rigor is already in the Romantic Novalis. The root and the fruit of poetry for Novalis is to be possessed and self-possessed. His conception of poetry as the conveyance of a state of soul makes him, for Charles Du Bos, the precursor of modern poetry.[11]

Poetry, Novalis says repeatedly, must be treated as a rigorous art. Not a mere expression of emotion, it is the creation of a state of mind both calm and comprehensive. Its language can never be too particular, evocative, or exact, for the right word is a force evoking an awareness that may affect our whole life. Words themselves think, paint, and sing. The poet uses words like musical notes, and if Novalis thus far prepares us for Flaubert and Mallarmé, his stress on poetry as a free association of ideas, a spontaneous, arbitrary and yet ideal production based on chance announces a Valéry, but in the key of faith.[12]

Poetry is for Novalis symbol thanks to the primitive and marvelous capacity for interchange between nature and spirit. The symbol must suggest, and though the reader follows the scenario, the symbol provokes in him a spontaneous spiritual activity which rhythm only strengthens and accelerates. A symbol is not the equivalent of a reality of another order; it works indirectly through the spontaneous activity of spirit which it energizes. As "hieroglyphic," it must necessarily be obscure, play with ambiguities, arouse a multiple interest, and be known and loved in different ways. Mystery in poetry has the power both to attract and to "distance." In a number of ways, then, the poet of *Hymen an die Nacht* unites before Baudelaire *volupté* and *connaissance*.

v

Whether it be in the *Paradis artificiels*, Baudelaire's translations and adaptations of Thomas de Quincey, or in the intimate journals or the critical articles, the informed reader becomes aware of the context which we have been describing. At the end of his article, "Du Vin et du

Haschisch," Baudelaire quotes approvingly the words of a certain Barbereau, theorist of music and professor at the Conservatory, directed at users of drugs:

"I do not understand why rational and spiritual man uses artificial means to attain to poetic beautitude, since enthusiasm and will suffice to raise him to a supranatural existence. The great poets, the philosophers, the prophets are beings who through the pure and free exercise of the will reach *a state where they are at once cause and effect, subject and object, magnetizer and somnambulist.*" [italics supplied] I think exactly as he does.[13]

Baudelaire has been listening to a man who uses the language of a German "philosopher of nature and the dream" and of the voluntarism of Novalis.

It is the same context that helps to explain Baudelaire's sense of affinity for Edgar Allan Poe, who had some slight knowledge of Novalis, and later for Richard Wagner. In such cases influence does not initiate—if indeed it can ever initiate for truly creative spirits—it confirms and it consecrates. For Baudelaire to feel as if he had himself written Poe's tales or created Wagner's music, is either an empty boast or a confident testimony to what one recognizes in himself as powerful tendencies and talents.

No doubt the image of Poe was not the same for Baudelaire, Mallarmé, and Valéry, though they all were fascinated by his conception of a poem as something constructed with an almost scientific calculation. But Baudelaire, more than the others, found in Poe, as Enid Starkie says, "for the first time, someone of his own spiritual family." Perhaps Miss Starkie underrates, in her effort to measure influence precisely, the significance of her own statement. It is true that by 1856, when Baudelaire had seen the whole of Poe's writings, he had already written the bulk of his own poetry, and that even by 1843, before he had encountered Poe, he had written poems that were to seem to later critics strongly influenced by the American poet. In this sense "the influence of Poe on Baudelaire is very much less significant than has hitherto been suggested." But the confirmation of a poet's thought, especially when it is rejected by contemporaries, can be an important influence. Yet we press this point not to determine an influence but to establish an affinity, a "context" for Baudelaire's feeling and thought.

Upon Miss Starkie's own authority, Baudelaire, at least after he had reached his maturity, was "an austere moralist preoccupied chiefly with the problem of sin and temptation," whose art "even in its form" is "closely linked" with his dominant interest, the search for a spiritual ideal. For in 1852, when the poet's mind was turning increasingly toward philosophy and mysticism, "his interest in the American writer came to hasten his maturity at a critical stage in his psychological evolution." And "Poe became, as it were, the lay figure on which he draped his own aesthetic and spiritual conceptions."

In this same period, Miss Starkie adds, Baudelaire's philosophic, and later, aesthetic beliefs, were being colored by the theories of Swedenborg which affected even his interpretation of Poe. Accordingly he saw the American poet as a solitary figure wandering and lost in a world of mystery and supernatural problems which he was trying to solve. In the 1852 article on Poe, he describes him as a man whose sole aim was to interpret the life to come, and it ends with a peroration in the Swedenborgian manner picturing the purified and spiritual essence of the poet interceding among the heavenly beings for the rest of struggling humanity. Such an interpretation of Poe's writings, Miss Starkie concludes, "coupled with his view of the philosophy of Swedenborg, becomes the basis of Baudelaire's spiritual poems after 1852." [14] Whatever, then, the exact measure of the influence of the American poet upon Baudelaire, the latter connected with Poe and shared with Poe the kind of context we have described in our account of the German "philosophers of nature and the dream." Poe and the "philosophers," as well as Swedenborg and Baudelaire, are all in the familiar passage:

> It is that admirable, that immortal instinct for Beauty which causes us to consider the Earth and its spectacles as a

glimpse, as a *Correspondence* of Heaven. The insatiable thirst for what is beyond, and which life reveals, is the most living proof of our immortality. It is simultaneously by means of poetry and *across and beyond* poetry, by means of music and *across and beyond* music, that the soul glimpses the splendors situated beyond the tomb; and when an exquisite poem brings tears to the eyes, these tears are not the proof of an excess of enjoyment but they are much rather the witness of an irritated melancholy, of a postulation of the nerves, of a nature exiled in the imperfect and which would like to take immediate possession, on this earth of ours, of the paradise revealed. Thus the principle of poetry is, strictly and simply, the human aspiration towards a superior Beauty, and the manifestation of this principle is in an enthusiasm, a rapture of the soul; an enthusiasm quite independent of passion, which is the intoxication of the heart, and of truth, which is the nourishment of the reason.[15]

Thus, whatever the differences between Poe's poetry and Baudelaire's, whatever the latter may have misread in Poe's theory or read into Poe's theory, to whatever degree he spiritualized what seems mechanical in that theory, it seems a fact that Edgar Allan Poe fulfilled Baudelaire's (and Mallarmé's) need of a "myth" in the sense of a concrete organizing image which grounded in history their faith, with its ebb and flow of conviction and aspiration, that poetry was par excellence *the spiritual activity* of man, and somehow metaphysical in its relations and implications.

4 BAUDELAIRE:
THE CRITIC'S THEORIES

OUR ELABORATION of the context of the poet's work has been meant to counteract a very influential effort to draw him subtly out of that context and thereby to shift the meaning of symbolism in Baudelaire. Perhaps no single writing on Poe, Baudelaire and Symbolisme matches the influence of Paul Valéry's article of 1924, "La Situation de Baudelaire." [1]

What makes Baudelaire extraordinarily important for French poetry—and we may add the whole "modern" poetic movement—is the combination of "critical intelligence" and "poetic proficiency." He might have remained merely a rival of Gautier but for the mental curiosity which "led him to the discovery of a new intellectual world in the works of Edgar Allan Poe, through whose influence," according to Valéry, "his talent was transformed . . . his destiny magnificently changed." Poe appeared to Baudelaire as "a genius of analysis and an inventor of the newest, most seductive combinations of logic and imagination." He was the first to reduce the problem of literature to a "psychological problem" to be solved deliberately by the "logic and mechanics of effects" applied to the relation between the work and the reader. Poe, moreover, in conformity with the tendency of an age "which drew a sharper and sharper distinction between forms and provinces of activity," understood that poetry could claim "to realize its own object and produce itself, to some degree, in a pure state." Such was "the strict and fascinating doctrine in which he united a sort of mathematics with a sort of mysticism."

Now Baudelaire, with others, had already been reacting against Romanticism in a "will to perfection—the mysticism of 'art for art's sake'—the demand for observation and an impersonal recording of things." In his desire *"for a more solid substance and for a subtler, purer form,"* he had taken up arms against "impassioned facility, stylistic inconsistency, and the excesses of silliness and eccentricity." He belonged to the school of "reflective" rather than "spontaneous action." In accordance with Poe's precepts, *Les Fleurs du mal* contains no poems based upon narrative, no flights into philosophy, no political verse, and the rare descriptions are always *"pertinent."*

Valéry will characterize Baudelaire's best poems as "a combination of flesh and spirit, a mixture of solemnity, warmth and bitterness, of eternity and intimacy." The duration and ascendency of this poetry he attributes to "the plenitude and the unusual clearness of its timbre" and, in spite of an occasional "eloquence," to an admirably pure melodic line and a perfectly sustained sonority which distinguishes it from all prose. In Baudelaire, "all is charm, music, powerful, abstract sensuality."

It is as he seeks to define the "charm" and the "miracle," words which he is forced to use almost in spite of himself to characterize the poetry, that Valéry in 1924 effects what could be called "the Valéryan shift":

> It should be shown that language contains emotive resources mingled with its practical, directly significant properties. The duty, the work, the function of the poet are to bring out and render active these forces of enchantment, these stimulants of the emotional life and intellectual sensibility, which are mixed together in the customary language with the signs and means of communication of ordinary superficial life. Thus the poet consecrates himself and consumes himself in the task of defining and constructing a language within the language; and this operation which is long, difficult, and delicate, which demands a

diversity of mental qualities and is never finished, tends to constitute the speech of a being purer, more powerful and profound in his thoughts, more intense in his life, more elegant and felicitous in his speech, than any real person. This extraordinary speech manifests itself and is recognized by the rhythm and the harmony which sustain it, and which should be so intimately and even mysteriously bound to its origin that the sound and the sense can no longer be separated, responding to each other indefinitely in the memory.

This enormously influential passage, with the sentence, "what was baptized Symbolism is summed up quite simply in the intention common to several families of poets to take back from music what belonged to them," has become for many a classic definition of Symbolisme. Yet a close reading will reveal the "Valéryan shift" from a conception of poetry in which language in privileged moments "almost supernatural" in their difference from ordinary "life" uses the objects offered by experience in such a way as to reveal the profounder meaning of that life, to a notion of poetry as the "language within the language." Though tending to "constitute the speech of a being purer, more powerful and profound in his thoughts, more elegant and felicitous in his speech than any real person," such poetry *says nothing which can be taken as all the more uniquely characterizing the nature of life* because of the operation of the "forces of enchantment, these stimulants of the emotional life and intellectual sensibility." We have shifted from "miracle" to "miraculism." Now miracle in religion calls special attention to a "truth" needed in the life of men for their guidance and "salvation"; its very difference from the ordinary events of history is meant to serve history. "Miraculism" calls attention to the miracle within itself, invests landscape and spectator with its radiance, but points to nothing outside of itself and defines salvation in terms of itself. The purely reflexive operation described by Valéry may appeal to many as the most valid definition of poetry. For us the relevant question is: "Does it conform to Baudelaire's definition of poetry?" We seriously doubt it. "La grande poésie est essentiellement *bête*, elle *croit*," said Baudelaire, criticizing a friend and fellow-poet who wrote of Jupiter without believing in Jupiter.[2] This does not mean, as the same article makes plain, that even "atheism" may not result in good poetry, if the poet sees and feels, that is, if he believes. Belief for Baudelaire is not all of poetry, but it never evaporates into the rainbow hues of language alone.

ii

There is a downright literalness, even naïveté, in Baudelaire's character and in his theory of poetry which must be allowed to pierce through even the major texts in which he sought to convey his conception of poetry. What is symbol? First of all, it is an *object* seen under special conditions: "Dans certains états de l'âme presque surnaturels, la profondeur de la vie se révèle tout entière dans le spectacle, si ordinaire qu'il soit, qu'on a sous les yeux. Il en devient le symbole." A symbol, then, is an object that opens up the depth of life for the poet in moments extraordinary enough to be considered almost supernatural. What is this "depth of life"? Is it figurative language for a purely aesthetic pleasure or delight? Is it a depth of emotion and of sentient being, made conceivable by symbol, as Susanne Langer says "something much deeper than any intellectual experience, more essential, pre-rational, and vital, something of the life-rhythms we share with all growing, hungering, moving and fearing creatures"?[3] Or is this depth to be interpreted rather in terms of the traditional moral and religious meaning of life?

The latter would seem to be the case as much for Baudelaire as for a Wordsworth whose "spots of time," described especially in the twelfth book of *The Prelude* (208–335), have much in common with the almost supernatural moments when the spectacle before the poet's eyes becomes a symbol. Or the depth of life is revealed by such a conflict between heaven and hell as

Baudelaire recognizes in *Tannhäuser* and asserts in *Mon Coeur mis à nu:* "In every man, at every moment, there are two simultaneous postulations, one towards God, the other towards Satan. The appeal to God, or spirituality, is a desire to take a step up; that to Satan, or animality, is the joy of going a step down." [4] The very title of Baudelaire's poems, *Les Fleurs du mal*, supports this interpretation. In his book he seems to have explored the conditions under which simultaneous and contradictory postulations toward God and Satan can be unified in a triumph which is both a triumph of art and a self-examination of the poet, heart and soul. [5]

We need not determine for our purposes the exact quality or degree of Baudelaire's "Catholicism" or of his "satanism." But we can characterize Baudelaire's imagination "mythic" in the sense that he needed to envisage human life as a conflict of cosmic powers in which the poet participates as man. In those moments when any object may become a symbol and the depths of life are revealed, the true poet becomes an "incarnation" of humanity, transmitting in "more melodious vibrations," the human thought handed down to him, "a collective soul who asks questions, weeps, hopes, and now and then divines the truth." [6] But Baudelaire's mythic view is fragmented into the poems of *Les Fleurs du mal*, to whose ordering, nevertheless, he gave great importance in the various editions, achieving perhaps in his mental landscapes what has been recently identified as an accomplishment of Blake and the Symbolistes, "narrative seen as a simultaneous unity." [7]

iii

Baudelaire's mysticism can easily be underrated because it is channeled in the aesthetic and is subject to the analyses and the strategies of the literary craftsman. Thus he notes, "Deux qualités littéraires fondamentales: surnaturalisme et ironie." What is supernaturalism in this context? No doubt, it is connected with what Baudelaire describes a few paragraphs below as "moments of existence in which time and space are deeper, and the sense of existence immensely increased." The "supernatural" in things is to be detected also in the "individual point of view, the way in which things stand in the presence of the writer." It includes the "general color and accent, that is to say intensity, sonority, limpidity, vibratory quality, depth and capacity for reverberation in space and time." And these seem to be not only qualities intuited in objects on special occasions but effects the literary artist must achieve.

A passage from another context will serve to illumine and extend the significance of the one in hand. Writing on "L'Exposition Universelle de 1855," Baudelaire refers to Poe's description of the effect on the senses of opium: it gives to nature a "supernatural interest" pervading every object with a "meaning deeper, more willful and despotic." Then he adds:

> Without having recourse to opium, who has not known those admirable hours, veritable feasts of the brain, where the senses unusually attentive perceive sensations unusually striking in effect, where the sky of more transparent blue recedes in depth like a more infinite abyss, where sounds ring out as in music, where colors speak, where perfumes tell us of their worlds of ideas? Well, the painting of Delacroix seems to me the translation of those happy days of the spirit. It is invested with intensity and its splendor is privileged. Like nature perceived by ultra-sensitive nerves, it reveals supernaturalism.

Indeed Delacroix, like Rembrandt, combines "le sens de l'intimité et la magie profonde."

The effect of the supernatural and of the magical is dependent, then, on the privileged moment. It is characterized by synaesthesia in the vertical sense, i.e., in which colors speak and perfumes tell of thoughts, as well as in the horizontal sense, i.e., where "perfumes, colors and sounds answer each other's call" as in the sonnet "Correspondances."

Some critics make much of Baudelaire's olfactory sense; his frequent eulogies of the painter Delacroix suggest a cult of color as more expressive of Romantic *intimité*. Indeed he tends to equate color and true creativity. Hence Baudelaire's coldness to realism and even to the new school of landscape painters. What is reality, he asks, if not "the magic of verisimilitude," or a "second reality created by the sorcery of the muse."

Color, then—hence Baudelaire's relative indifference to line and to the plasticity of sculpture—seems to be the medium through which the soul can best infuse itself into a created world. "Un paysage d'âme" would be a creation not of line, nor of music, but of color. If in general the Symbolistes sought to "reprendre à la musique leur bien," as Valéry has said, one might specify that, in the case of Baudelaire, he saw even music as color.

Thus Baudelaire will define color as the "accord of two tones." And melody is "unity in color." But "melody demands a conclusion," and wherever there is a melody of color there is a conclusion. The way to tell whether a painting is "melodious" is to stand far enough away from it so as not to be able to make out its subject or its lines. "If it is melodious, it already has a meaning, and it has already taken its place in the repertoire of memory."

For Baudelaire the meaning that painting and poetry convey is qualified in color. And this meaning can be of the broadest universality. Thus the work of Delacroix will seem sometimes to Baudelaire "a kind of mnemotechny of the native passion and grandeur of universal man." To express "simply with contour, the gesture of a man, however violent, and with color, *what one might call the atmosphere of the human drama, or the state of soul of the creator* [italics supplied]—this quite original merit has always won for him the sympathies of all the poets." Delacroix is also the most "suggestive" of painters, "suggestive" works being defined as those that "provide the most food for thought and recall to memory the greatest number of feelings and poetic thoughts already known, but which one believed buried forever in the night of the past."

Sometimes Baudelaire will make color an element in a

triad, as when he writes that Delacroix has translated better than anyone, "the invisible, the impalpable, the dream, the nerves, the *soul*," and this with nothing but line and color and "the eloquence of a passionate musician," thus illustrating how the arts in his day "aspire, if not to take one another's place, at least to lend one another reciprocally new forces." Yet it would seem safe to say that the magic, the sorcery, the "supernaturalism" in a work that makes the effect of symbol would consist largely for Baudelaire in its power to suggest as color suggests. Color tones can be "gay," "sad," "frisky," "rich," "common," "original," or any combination of these qualities. And Baudelaire, quoting E. T. A. Hoffmann's testimony from *Kreisleriana* to the sound of music in which he finds "an analogy and an intimate union between sounds, colors and perfumes," wonders whether any "analogist has established solidly a complete gamut of colors and feelings." Or, as he writes elsewhere, "the art of the colorist is evidently related at some points to mathematics and to music."

Thus color, for all its suggestivity, does not, for Baudelaire, evoke the merely subjective. Nature, enveloping us like a mystery," presents itself to us in "certain simultaneous states," "form, attitude and movement, light and color, sound and harmony"; and to some one of these, each individual responds especially as senses, mind or heart command. But Hugo, sculptor, painter, and musician, expresses "le mystère de la vie" and may through the "triple impression" made upon the brain convey *la morale des choses*. And though he is a universal artist in contact with the forces of universal life, yet he knows how to express "with its *indispensible obscurity*, what is obscure and confusedly revealed." Thus he expresses, among other aspects of the world,

> the most fugitive, the most complicated, the most moral (I say expressly moral) sensations which are transmitted to us by visible being, by inanimate, or so-called inanimate nature; not only the shape of some existence external to man, vegetable or mineral, but also its physiognomy, its glance, its sadness, its gentleness, its joy bursting out, its

repulsive hate, its enchantment or its horror; in short, in other words, everything that is human in anything whatsoever, and also everything in it that is divine, sacred, or diabolical.

The passage suggests the importance of Hugo's poetic achievement for Baudelaire as critic and poet. We draw attention again to the paradoxical phrases "moral des choses" and "sensations morales," for they seek to convey the experience that made Baudelaire a "symboliste" poet. That objects of sensation can have an inner meaning for man's values, his sense of good and evil, his scarch for his nature and destiny, that they can be more than repositories of aesthetically self-sufficient associations of thought and emotion, such is the meaning and scope of the symbol for Baudelaire.

But he adds immediately: "Ceux qui ne sont pas poètes ne comprennent pas ces choses." And confident of the poets' superior understanding of such matters, Baudelaire takes Fourier to task for a rather pompous revelation of "les mystères de l'analogie." Yet there is some merit in the *phalangiste's* "minute discoveries" though his mind is "too taken with material exactness not to commit errors and to attain directly the moral certainty of intuition." Besides, Swedenborg, who possessed "a much greater soul" had already taught "that *the sky is a very large man*; that everything, form, movement, number, color, perfume, in the spiritual as well as in the *natural*, is significant, reciprocal, converse, *correspondent*."

Therefore, Baudelaire concludes, "we arrive at this truth, that everything is hieroglyphic, and we know that symbols are obscure only in a relative way, that is, according to the purity, the good will or the native clairvoyance of souls." The poet is a "translator, a decoder [déchiffreur]." "In excellent poets there is no metaphor, no comparison or epithet which is not mathematically exact in the given circumstances, for these comparisons, these metaphors, and these epithets are drawn from the inexhaustible supply of *universal analogy*, nor can they be drawn elsewhere." Faith united with mathematics as in

Pascal and, on another plane, in Swedenborg, can cut dazzling patterns of paradox, and Baudelaire belongs to this family of spirits.

Thus "supernaturalism" means for him analogy, correspondences that are objective, permanent, and yet not completely resistent to the strong poetic will. For him, as for a Friedrich Schlegel and a Novalis, to bring together *volupté* and *connaissance* was not to achieve a mere wonder in a work of art, but rather, like a good engineer, to use in an efficient way, and for purposes that are not entirely those of nature in the ordinary sense of the word—but which are not entirely opposed, as the finished work will show, to "nature" in some sense—resources and powers placed at the poet's disposal by reality. But by "reality" Baudelaire did not mean the naturalist's reality. This we must not forget unless we would repeat in the case of Baudelaire the mistake of I. A. Richards in the case of Coleridge. Baudelaire no more than Coleridge is to be understood in terms of incipient and unconscious naturalism concealed by an old-fashioned vocabulary.

Thus, the poet notes that "inspiration always comes when man *wills* it, but it does not always go away when he desires." He will also distinguish between creative *rêverie* as an idle daydreaming, and that which evokes inspiration. "Il faut vouloir rêver et savoir rêver." In the same passage he will speak not only of "magic applied to the evocation of the famous dead, to the re-establishment and perfectionment of health," but "of language and writing, taken as magical operations, an evocative sorcery." On the next page he will speak of prayer as "magical operation."

The poet for Baudelaire is dealing with forces which have a mechanism, although their result does not belong to the order of the mechanical. Once more Delacroix's painting is the stimulus of a telling observation: "There is no chance in art, no more than in mechanics. A happy discovery is the simple result of a good line of reasoning, of which one has sometimes skipped the intermediate deductions." Yet the method of Delacroix is also the product of a grace of temperament, and Baudelaire concludes with a quotation from Heine: "In matters of art I am a super-naturalist. I believe that the artist can find in nature all the types, but that the most remarkable are revealed to him in his soul and all at once like an innate system of symbols for innate ideas." [8]

iv

For Baudelaire, then, the supernatural can be manipulated and controlled without reduction to what we ordinarily mean by the "natural." And if we inquire now concerning the second quality of the two fundamental literary qualities, "ironie," we find ourselves at no great distance from "supernaturalisme." For irony, as the context reveals, means "Satanism," that is, "une tournure d' esprit satanique."

Baudelaire gives no explanation of this phrase, but in the preceding section of *Fusées* he has described "[his] beauty"—"something ardent and sad, a little vague, leaving room for conjecture." Thus the head of a beautiful woman would lead to a "revery,—in a confused fashion,—of *volupté* and sorrow; which involves an idea of melancholy, of lassitude, and of satiety,—yet also a contrary idea, that of ardor, a desire for life, associated with an access of bitterness, as if it came from privation or despair. Mystery and regret are also characteristics of the Beautiful."

A fine man's head would have some of the same qualities, with a suggestion of unused and potentially explosive powers," an *"insensibilité* vengeresse," so becoming to the ideal type of the Dandy, a certain mystery, and finally *le malheur*. Joy can be one of the more vulgar ornaments of Beauty, but melancholy, writes Baudelaire, is "so to speak the illustrious Companion, to the point that I can hardly conceive (is my brain a mirror bewitched?) a type of Beauty in which there is no *sorrow*. Leaning on,—others would say: obsessed by—these ideas, one can see why it would be difficult not to conclude that the most perfect kind of viril Beauty is *Satan*,—after the fashion of Milton."

Such Satanism, no doubt, is to be connected with

Baudelaire's remarks in "Le Poème du Haschisch" concerning the vices of man as "proof (if only on the basis of their infinite expansion!) of his taste for the infinite; only it is a taste that often loses its way." It may also involve that "delightful contemplation of remorse, in a kind of voluptuous analysis; and an analysis so rapid that man, that natural devil, to talk like the Swedenborgians, does not realize how involuntary it is, and how, from second to second, he approaches diabolic perfection. He *admires* his remorse and he glorifies himself while he is about to lose his liberty." But Satanism can undermine its own appeal. The sense of the infinite, originally a warning against complacency, can nourish a spiritual pride as the soul, misunderstood, says to itself: "Do you not possess that sovereign disdain which renders the soul so good?" [9]

v

In the spirit of Poe, then, Baudelaire has analyzed the main sources of his poetic effects —*supernaturalisme et ironie*. Poetic sincerity for him evidently lies not in the unconscious expression of *what you cannot help* but in the maximum rendering given to the spiritual force at your command. Likewise a Swedenborg, to the amazement of Valéry, can write a treatise on representations and correspondences, the *Arcana Coelestia*, with the collaboration of the inhabitants of another world, which nevertheless makes the effect of having been "meditated and composed by an author more systematic and master of himself than inspired and lost in contemplation." [10]

The name for that faculty or that state of our faculties in which there is union of *volupté* and *connaissance*, *surnaturalisme* and *ironie*, is "Imagination." Baudelaire describes this power especially in the famous "Salon de 1859." [11] Imagination, mysterious "queen" of the faculties "created, at the world's beginning, analogy and metaphor." "It is imagination which taught man the moral meaning of color, contour, sound and perfume." Imagination is not to be confused with the other faculties though it touches them all, excites them, and brings them into play. (Coleridge will not otherwise describe Imagination as bringing "the whole soul of man into activity.") For Baudelaire, as for Coleridge, Imagination is fundamentally a synthesizing power. "It decomposes all creation, and, with the materials amassed and disposed according to rules whose source can be found only in the profoundest depths of the soul, it creates a new world, it produces a sensation of the new. Since it created the world (one may say that, I think, even in a religious sense), it is just that it should govern it." After having written this last sentence and sent it off "not with a certain timidity," Baudelaire is pleased to discover in that "excellent Mrs. Crowe, whose capacity to believe I have often admired, as developed in her as in others the tendency to disbelieve," the following sentence which he quotes from *The Nocturnal Side of Nature:* "By imagination, I do not simply mean to convey the common notion implied by that much abused word, which is only *fancy*, but the *constructive* imagination, which is a much higher function, and which, in as much as man is made in the likeness of God, bears a distant relation to that sublime power by which the Creator projects, creates, and upholds his universe."

But the creative power of imagination for Baudelaire is not limited to artistic activity. Its possession distinguishes the mere soldier, however excellent, from the conqueror, the mere diplomat from the statesman with a vision of the future, the savant from the genius who will discover the new laws, for the "imagination is the queen of truth, and the *possible* is one of the provinces of truth. It has a positive kinship with the infinite." Imagination can enhance but also criticize. Its absence will nullify the keenest powers, its presence will give due strength to the weakest faculties. It can "proudly and simply divine" what weaker faculties and missing faculties might come to discover after much trial and error. It even "contains the critical spirit."

This inclusion of the critical spirit in the imagination strikes the dominant chord in Baudelaire's conception. The creativity of imagination seems to mean for him not the *creatio ab nihilo* but the ineffaceable imprint set upon the materials by the shaping spirit, which is nevertheless proudly conscious of its own nature and identity. Here Baudelaire remains a Romantic, however classical his appearance. For the Aristotelian, the poet as maker is essentially one who forms a structure which is individual only in its re-arrangement of elements taken from a world which itself determines a general pattern for its "imitation." For Baudelaire, the artist selects *out of* materials offered in a more discrete form, as one chooses words out of a dictionary, guided by an internal image. The real value of the "dictionary" metaphor for the poet consists, however, in suggesting the freeing of words and meanings from the structures of "common sense," though not of syntax, so that they can be suffused by, indeed infused with, the internal image. Even here there is something external in our own images. Perhaps a better analogy is to be found in the contrast between the classical painter whose color fills in spaces between lines already drawn and the Romantic colorist whose color constructs line as it constructs volumes. In this way the *état d'âme* becomes a *paysage d'âme*, not fluid like a moodiness blurring everything, but qualitied in variety and unified, as the inner and outer aspects are fused into a single reality. Intimacy itself becomes another name for a living unity of informed vision.

Baudelaire's cult of color is not the cult of the emotional splash, otherwise it could not have been connected with both mathematics and music, with the "sensibilité de l'imagination" rather than "la sensibilité du coeur." What steadies Baudelaire and gives objectivity to his colorist's view of things is the sense of "analogies" and "correspondences." Not every object or situation or feeling can become symbol, but only certain ones that seem to implicate the higher realm.

When Baudelaire repeats after Delacroix, "Nature is only a dictionary," when with Delacroix he insists that all aspects of a work of art are the very humble servants of a "faculty that is unique and superior," and that "everything must serve to illuminate the "generating idea and continue to wear its livery," he is stating the conditions under which, for him, form and content can be one in an act that truly deserves to be called creative.

Thus Symbolisme, in its most general sense, to revise or interpret Valéry's definition, in that emphasis by which it has exerted its greatest influence, may be seen as the aspiration common to several families of spirit *toward a thorough-going poetic unity conceived in terms of the metaphor of "color"* (which, as we have seen, has also its "music") *in a philosophical context which permits inter-fllow and interglow of meanings, both horizontally and vertically, between areas of experience formerly maintained distinct.* For "organic unity" is as old as Aristotle, but though the image was taken from biology, it was translated in terms of structures easy for logic to distinguish. Hence in the arts the emphasis on "plot" and on "line," and the distinctions between the genres. But lay stress upon the individual and the particular, upon change and mobility, upon dynamism, upon interfusion, upon an organicism intuited as "life"—and this was the tendency of thought from the Renaissance on—and that unity can be conceived more "coloristically" and more "musically." From "line" to "color"; from "plot line" as the very sinew of unity, to recurrence in patterned shapes of images, events, sounds, rhythms as the real inner "life" of this unity; from the "fable" or "story" developing in linear fashion and conveying "meaning" easily susceptible of paraphrase, to an "import" suddenly, if fleetingly, "coming together" in consciousness, so that the "whole story" or "what the story has to say" consists of a perception distorted if lifted out of context—it is of this development in Western art that Symbolisme itself is for the historian the "symbol."

We insist that Symbolisme, in its major figures, would never have accepted the allegation of "subjectivity." In a society that had become used to "seeing" objectivity, so to speak, only in structures of lines imitating, though with some difference, structures in nature, Baudelaire, living in a world of pictures even as a child came, with the aid of

Delacroix, to "see" structures of meaning conveyed by "color." Color revealed, becoming its symbol, the *living* nature of objective form. It is a wild surmise that Goethe's theories of color-vision and his quarrel with Newton should be conceived as a confusion between a symbolist's intuition and the *philosophical* or *aesthetic* point it impels him to make, and a *scientific* point inexpugnable enough in its own context. The "apology" for color becomes the modern "defence of Poetry."

Again, if Symbolisme for Baudelaire does not mean "subjectivity," neither does it mean the "mystery" of obfuscation. To put it more exactly, it combined a *maximum mystery of result* and a *minimum mystery of means*. Here, again, Baudelaire chooses an analogy from painting:

> A good painting, faithful and equal to the dream which gave it birth, must be produced like a world. Just as creation, such as we observe, is the result of several creations of which the preceding ones are always completed by the subsequent one; thus a painting brought to a final harmony consists in a series of paintings superposed, each new layer giving more reality to the dream by causing it to take one step more toward perfection.

Such a process, for Baudelaire, constitutes the surest method at least for "rich imaginations." Rhetorics and prosodies evidently can serve the dream, for they are "a collection of rules that the very organization of spiritual being demands" and they actually "help originality to blossom forth."

Of special significance in the "Salon of 1859," from which we have been quoting, is Baudelaire's belief that what he has said of rhetoric is one of the many corollaries resulting from the

> formulary of a true aesthetic, and which can be expressed thus: The whole visible world is nothing but a storehouse of images and signs to which imagination will give its relevant place and value; it is a kind of nourishment that imagination must digest and transform. All the faculties of

the human soul must be subordinated to the imagination, which brings them all into requisition at the same time.

In the end, to make clear his meaning, Baudelaire contrasts the "*réaliste,*" or better the "*positiviste,*" with the imaginative artist, the former saying, " 'I want to represent things as they are, or as they would be, supposing that I did not exist.' The universe without man"; the latter, " 'I want to illuminate things with my mind and project the reflection upon other minds.' " [12]

vi

Symbolisme, then, for Baudelaire, seems as a doctrine firmly grounded upon analogy. Images and signs of things, to be found in sensations, objects (and presumably in characters and events), if they be rightly treated (that is, if nature be used as "dictionary," indeed as a "hieroglyphic dictionary"), can be illuminated and can serve to illuminate. But just as in all systems of meaning, anything "illuminated" is revealed with reference to a larger whole of meaning, for the "supernaturalist" and Swedenborgian Baudelaire, meaning reaches out to what is "completely true only in another world." For the "immortal instinct of Beauty" always made him think of earth as a "correspondence" of Heaven even when it seemed that Satan reigned. Intimacy, supernaturalism, Satanism, objectivity are in the same continuum. "What is pure art according to the modern conception? It is the creation of a suggestive magic which contains both subject and object, the world external to the artist and the artist himself."

Such structures of meaning are those that color and music insinuate with a most delicate science. Symbolic seeing for Baudelaire is a kind of "color-vision," but we must repeat that for him "the art of the colorist is related at certain points to that of mathematics and music." What he "makes" is in a continuum with what he "makes out" and "makes up" —a reality as ineluctible as mathematical logic, as intimate as music

Because this total conception of symbolism was both

new and related to something perennial, it took time to recognize itself and to develop a specialized vocabulary. But in art, as so often in life, the moment of supreme self-consciousness may also contain the supreme danger. A movement reaching self-recognition seeks to situate itself in society, to dramatize its success, to define and rationalize its terms and procedures for the convenience of its disciples and the public. The symbol, which was a discovery and a means of discovery in a world of real magic, may become a device among the later Symbolistes for creating a magical "effect"; those unheralded if privileged moments when the heights and depths of life open up before us "l'horreur de la vie et l'ecstase de la vie," can become "aesthetic" settings like enchanted forests or pagodas by a lakeside with ritual swans. On a more intellectual level they can be transmuted into the self-reflexive marvels of "language."

With Baudelaire, however, we are still at the heart of discovery. The ancient terms in the general context are made to suffice, and they appear almost interchangeable: *symbole, allégorie, mythe*. The French critic's fundamental definition of a *symbole* we have already presented: it is any *spectacle* which in certain privileged moments of the soul reveals the depths of life entire. Allegory, the critic says, can be a very "spiritual" genre even in painting, and is "truly one of the primitive and most natural forms of poetry" and can assert its "legitimate domination in an intelligence illuminated by intoxication," and this all the more so if that intelligence is under the influence of hashish. But *allégorie* in this context occurs under conditions which Baudelaire has described as among those which give rise to symbol.

Baudelaire's review of the philosophical poem *Prométhée* by Louis Ménard can be made to yield without too much coaxing even the Goethean denigration of allegory which will become a standard definition of the term. After reminding us that "la grande poésie est essentiellement *bête*, elle *croit*," Baudelaire warns: "never confuse the phantoms of reason with the phantoms of imagination;

the former are equations and the latter are living beings and memories." In emphasizing that the "phantoms of the imagination" are more like memories than exact equivalents of thought, Baudelaire seems to be pointing, as did such German philosophers of the dream as Schubert, toward Jung, especially since he viewed the poet as a "collective soul who questions, who weeps, who hopes and sometimes guesses the answer."

Yet Baudelaire's conviction of the metaphysical outreach of poetry, which makes it possible for him to use "symbol" and "allegory" interchangeably if the latter is the product of an "illumination," is revealed in the assertion that "Poetry is essentially philosophical; but since it is above all fatal, it must be involuntarily philosophical." Here *"philosophique"* seems to imply that, like philosophy, poetry aims at conveying the broader and deeper truths about the relation of man, nature, and the divine, while the "fatale," which is also involuntary, may refer to the unconscious and perhaps "mythic" aspects of poetry.

Sometimes Baudelaire will use the term "symbolique" when he means what post-Goethean criticism defines as allegory. Thus he points out that Rabelais is very French and also, *"raisonnable,"* because amid his most fantastic creations he remains "directement symbolique" so that his comedy has almost always "the transparence of an *apologie.*" Or he will use "symbole" for what we should call at most a pseudo-symbol: thus the *poire* to stand for Louis-Philippe. Sometimes even *mythe* will be found in a context of didacticism as, when again attacking the French penchant for a philosophical art, the critic writes: "La France aime le mythe, la morale, lé rebus." Yet he will speak somewhat more properly of "myth," though confusing it with legend and fable, as "concentrations of national life, as deep reservoirs where sleep the blood and tears of people." [13]

We may therefore affirm that Baudelaire was at least working toward Goethe's, Schlegel's, and Coleridge's distinction between symbol and allegory. His belief that metaphors must be discovered where they are stored among universal analogies and that they must be selected with precision belongs with his idea of symbol. A symbol, as we have seen, is found among objects, though the finder, as well as the interpreter, must be in a state other than that of cool reason. Symbol and imagination, moreover, go together. For Baudelaire alone, according to Margaret Gilman, the "imagination, little understood and viewed with some misgivings by most of the romantics," was the "greatest of all poetic faculties." The genius of a Diderot had in the eighteenth century already almost attained to the concept which, however, still remained primarily an active, combining, creative faculty; but Baudelaire thought of the imagination as "both creative and visionary, the faculty which penetrates beyond the surface of reality, both into that spiritual world whose existence Diderot denied, and into the human correspondences of the natural world in which it finds its symbols." [14]

BAUDELAIRE:
"SYMBOLIQUE" AND "SYMBOLISME"

IN THE CHAPTERS which have followed our account of the development, along philosophical lines, of the idea of the symbol since the beginnings of the Christian era, we have been considering, in connection with the various forms of "occultism" and in relation to the German "philosophers of nature and the dream," the "mystical" context of the idea of the symbol in Baudelaire. In our study of "sur-naturalisme et ironie," of the significance of "color" for Baudelaire, of the meaning of Imagination and symbol, we have stressed the "mystical" aspects of his doctrine. We have sought to provide a counterweight for attempts by modern students, along lines sketched by Paul Valéry, to distinguish between Baudelaire's theory and his practice in his poetry, with the result that the Baudelairean symbol is reduced practically to T. S. Eliot's "objective correlative." Such theories we shall now describe but only in connection with a narrative of the symbolist tradition in France and of the transmission of German philosophical views in Baudelaire's times.

The studies of Jean Pommier and, more recently, of Lloyd Austin, acquaint us with an early French tradition in the theory of the symbol. It seems that the Jesuit Nicholas Coussin (1583–1651), the confessor of Louis XIII, in a work published in Paris in 1618, *Electorum Symbolorum et parabolarum historicarum syntagmata*, had carried the definition of the symbol toward an amalgam of the religious, metaphysical and occult from which one might later attempt to distinguish the literary use. From this volume in which "the whole *Symbolique* of Creuzer is contained in the germ," according to Professor Austin, a certain Robert Estienne was to borrow practically the whole of his two chapters on hieroglyphics and "symboles" in his own book published in 1645 and translated into English by Thomas Blount in 1646 as *The Art of Making Devices*:

> In short the characteristic of Symbols is to be hidden and enveloped in labyrinths of obscure phrases . . . There must be a rich meaning comprised in the gravity and brevity of Symbols . . . Brevity then conjoined with a certain gravity which includes many things under a single meaning, distinguishes the Symbol . . . It must furthermore be observed that there are three kinds, Moral, Natural, and Theological. And what is proposed to us in these Symbols, through the bodily senses, penetrates into our Spirits.

A definition of this kind is the source of Diderot's statement concerning the suggestive function of language: "Un tissu d'hiéroglyphes . . . Toute poésie est emblématique." [1]

Though Baudelaire's road, no doubt, connects eventually with the ancient tradition, its better known stretches pass through Kant and Schiller and Goethe. The investigations of Jean Pommier in *La Mystique de Baudelaire* seem to indicate no direct and massive influence upon Baudelaire of historical and speculative writers, not even that of Creuzer whose influential *Symbolik*, a work on the symbolism and mythology of ancient peoples published in 1810 and introduced into France by Benjamin Constant in *De la Religion* (1834–31), owed much to the ideas of Goethe and of the German Romantic circles.

It was, then, not from the specialists in the study of religious symbol and myth that Baudelaire seems to have educated his mystical sensibilities but through Gérard de Nerval and, as we have seen, the phalangist, Fourier, through the German E. T. A. Hoffmann, the Swiss Lavater, and through Swedenborg whose Illuminism had flourished in the earlier Romantic period. A link with the tradition whose importance has increased with more recent investigation is Balzac, whom Pommier calls the guide of the young poet into "the realms of the abnormal, of the nebulous and of the fantastic." [2]

But what does Baudelaire seem to know of the more important German theorists of the symbol? He appears to have had some acquaintance with Schiller's theatre, but not with his theoretical writings. Goethe he knows somewhat better, but perhaps only through his friend Gérard de Nerval, the translator of *Faust*. The influence, then, of German ideas must have been of a general nature and more easily traceable through French philosophers. Increasing attention has been directed to Victor Cousin who influenced Poe in America and who as early as 1818 began to interpret Kantian ideas in France. His "Cours de Philosophie," published in 1836, became in 1845, after radical revision, the celebrated *Du vrai, du beau, du bien.*

The ideas of Cousin were given considerable extension, but with an emphasis upon the psychological, by Théodore Jouffroy whose *Cours d'esthétique,* offered in 1827, was not published until 1843. In Jouffroy, according to Lloyd Austin, we find ideas relevant to Baudelaire's thought at a number of points: the conception of poetry as a succession of symbols conveying the invisible, a distinction between natural symbols and allegory, a polemic against philosophical art, the notion that everything is hieroglyphic. Key ideas, even key terms are common to both theorists, but unfortunately not to both alone. For instance, one of the philosopher's auditors had been Sainte-Beuve, whose *Pensées de Joseph Delorme,* published in 1829, declares that the artist "participates in the invisible play of forces, and sympathizes with them as with souls: he has received at birth the key to symbols and a knowledge of the *figura*." And Mansell Jones traces to *Le Génie du Christianisme* of Chateaubriand key terms of the sonnet "Correspondances." [3]

Baudelaire, who knew enough English to translate Poe

and to adapt in part De Quincey's "Confessions of an Opium Eater," might have found in the writings of the English Romantics examples, a stimulus, and certain affinities as Henri Peyre has shown.[4] Yet he seems to have known the English Romantics, with the exception of Byron, only through intermediaries. The theories of Coleridge on the Imagination and the symbol, themselves conservative when compared to those of A. W. Schlegel, came to Baudelaire in their echoes in Poe and in Mrs. Catherine Crowe's *Nocturnal Side of Nature* (1884). Of greater actual importance than any Coleridgean theory of the Imagination, in Austin's opinion, was the example of Delacroix who revealed to him its role in artistic creation.[5] We have ourselves pressed this point further in our suggestions concerning the deeper meaning, for Baudelaire, of color.

In the argument of our foregoing sections we have presented the grounds for our rejection of what we have termed the "Valéryan shift," the attempt to minimize the significance of the doctrine of analogies and correspondences in Baudelaire and to reduce his symbol to a kind of "objective correlative." This tendency we can observe at work in various ways in volumes which are otherwise of unusual distinction by Robert Vivier, Jean Prévost, and Lloyd Austin. The latest of these, *L'Univers poétique de Baudelaire*, exhibits the general drift, though with a particular emphasis. According to Austin, the doctrine of "correspondances" was essential to Baudelaire's conception of the Imagination; the poet did not, at first, merely "imagine that things correspond to one another," as Jean Prévost maintained; nevertheless, when Baudelaire sought to apply his mode of vision, to see, as it were, how things are in heaven by their correspondences on earth, he was led by human sin and wretchedness to Satanism. "It is on the ruin of his religious hopes that his new poetic construction was built." Following Prévost, Austin agrees that "poetic correspondences *have man always at their center*," and that the poet, proclaiming as "true in the external world" what is true only "in his soul," "creates thus a new anthropomorphism." He concludes: "In our opinion, the essential originality of Baudelaire in this connection is to have secularized what had been from time immemorial a theological and metaphysical attitude and doctrine. According to the distinction that we are establishing, the itinerary of Baudelaire goes from a transcendent 'symbolique' to a purely human 'symbolisme.'"

In Valéryan fashion, then, Austin concludes that the "victory of *symbolisme*, studied in its great authors and not in the teeming multitude of its *epigoni* is found in the demonstration that poetry, 'the perfect application of the properties of language,' can exalt human speech to the level of equality with the voices of the gods." [6] But this is to beg the question. Are the "voices of the gods" *only a metaphor*, as Valéry would say, "une sorte de pirouette de l'idée," [7] or is it to be presumed that these "gods," for all their magnificence of language, speak the truth or even make truth-claims? Is Baudelaire to be understood as aware that what he had achieved was not a transubstantiation of the real stuff of existence, valid for man as a soul to be saved, but only an act of linguistic "miraculism?" Austin himself quotes a passage from "L'Alchimie de la douleur" where the poet cries out:

> *Anges revêtus d'or, de pourpre et d'hyacinthe,*
> *O vous, soyez témoins que j'ai fait mon devoir*
> *Comme un parfait chimiste et comme une âme sainte.*
> *Car j'ai de chaque chose extrait la quintessence,*
> *Tu m'as donné ta boue et j'en ai fait de l'or.*

(Angels in cloth of gold, of purple and of hyacinth, / O be my witness that I have accomplished my duty / like a perfect chemist and like a holy soul. / For I have extracted the quintessence from everything, / You have given me mud and I have made of it gold.) Does the "voice" here, in all its magnificence, overlay the tone that rises *De profundis* with a biographical authenticity? Or shall we say of the poet that literally "il se payait de mots"?

Literary expression here coincides with autobiography, the biographical and the poetic personality are one, if not completely the same. It is Baudelaire who has taken the dregs of human experience, a rejected sediment apparently incapable of structure and value, and has known how to find and extract a quintessence in the form and glitter of gold, the highest value. An impossible task if even in the lees of things were not buried structures continuous with, corresponding to, and magically evocative of the objective value-structures of the world or, to put it into religious language, the goodness of God.

It was not, then, on the "ruin of his religious hopes" that Baudelaire built his new poetry with its "purely human symbolism." The lines suggest the very opposite: that Baudelaire, in his very extremity, had rediscovered the ancient religious and philosophical secret, that all forms can only be structured out of good. There is no stuff so valueless, no experience so degrading as to have dropped entirely out of rapport with the ideal, and therefore it is capable of reconstitution by poetry. The poet, too, can seek and save what is lost, and restore it by the intelligence of art to the world of ideal analogies which give it reality and meaning. This restoration of the fallen world by a power that can bestow a beauty even upon the perversity and the blasphemy that nevertheless turns toward art is in the very title of *Les Fleurs du mal*.

From our point of view then, short of a Manicheanism which Austin suggests but then rejects, there can be no "originality" for Baudelaire in a "symbolique renversée, non plus céleste, mais infernale." [8] Even in certain moments of exasperation carried to the pitch of bravado, *Les Fleurs du mal* offers for our contemplation not the triumph of Satan but various forms of the pathos of the absence of God: impatience that He is *incognitus* in a world where action is not "sister to the dream," indignation because of man's appetite for infinite happiness which God has instilled but unaccountably refuses to satisfy *hic et nunc*, the resultant *ennui* or *spleen* driven to seek surcease even in mere novelty or on the other side of Death, and sometimes, as in "Receuillement," a resignation where the quality of sorrow seems as sweet as bliss.

In *Les Fleurs du mal,* of course, there are moments also of bodiless exaltation and of fulfillment of sense and spirit; yet the poet knew that his way must be that of "surnaturalisme et ironie." It is the approach by indirection. We shall be made aware of God's presence by the very quality of lamentation for His absence, or of blasphemy in the announcement of His defeat. In the *ironie* of his approach Baudelaire opened a path of modern literature, much of which asserts its positive values through the very tone of its negations. From Baudelaire, to Nietzsche, to a certain Existentialism, increasingly modern man seems inhibited in the assertion of values unless God is considered absent or dead—like a child who refuses to behave in view of its parents. The values nevertheless get themselves asserted, and the indirection, from an artistic point of view, adds the surprise of a new "slant."

Yet, even for Austin, "more than to God, more than to Satan, Baudelaire relates everything to himself, and thus creates a symbolism of his own." As we shall see, this is not quite true: Baudelaire's symbolism is not "personal" in Yeats' sense, for instance, but starts with "realistic" objects, persons, and events in the public domain, though his novelty does consist in his very use of such material as analogies and correspondences with the ultimate structures of things.

For this reason, though acknowledging that every symbolism must be "humain," since the symbol is generally considered a way of making accessible to human beings what would otherwise be closed to them even more completely, it seems to us misleading to suggest that Baudelaire either aimed at, or was forced to be satisfied with, a "symbolisme purement humain." An image conveying no more than one person's attitude toward experience needs no "hieroglyphics," and no poet as "decipherer." Nor is it likely that, for a mind like Baudelaire's, had his practice of poetry ever departed so far from his theory, there would have been no explosive recognition of the fact.

We are not driven to such a position because the poet departed from the established *symbolique.* Like many an innovator Baudelaire showed that an "old" truth or an "old" structure can encompass a greater variety of manifestations than the mere traditionalist comprehends. Just as beauty has its undeniably "modern" cast without losing its eternity, so with the realm on which analogies and correspondences are based: the Word can be made the flesh of modern life and modern poetry.

One may of course seek to interpret statements of Baudelaire that we take to refer to the transcendent as purely psychological. We can isolate a statement which is amenable to this kind of interpretation: "Il y a des moments de l'existence où le temps et l'étendue sont plus profonds, et le sentiment de l'existence immensément augmenté." Yet the passage is in a context of "opérations magiques, sorcellerie évocatoire," and it is followed soon by definition of the "symbole" as revealing in ordinary objects "la profondeur de la vie toute entiére." The feeling in a state "almost supernatural" Austin interprets as no more than a heightened sense of "vitality." Baudelaire is alleged to be speaking only as a "psychologist" when he uses such terms as "intensité," "splendeur," "nerfs ultra-sensibles"—as though this would invalidate in good logic the insights acquired.[9]

Yet such a passage as the one on "Le Goût de l'infini" which we have discussed in another context seems ample proof of the literalness with which Baudelaire interprets his exceptional states which reveal the depths of life. Even the dissipation of the drug addict with its "culpable orgies of the imagination" and "sophistic abuse of the reason" contains a "kind of angelic excitation, a call to order in the form of a delicate flattery." And if we were wise, the poet adds, we would draw from these states the certitude of a better existence and hope to attain to it by a better exercise of our wills. Just as he does not separate the will to form from inspiration, Baudelaire, with his belief that even debauch may be seeking an infinite, will not separate the natural from the supernatural.

In the context of his idea of poetry, one cannot very plausibly reduce Baudelaire's *symbole* to T. S. Eliot's "objective correlative" or to "a metaphor whose first term is abstract, the second concrete." [10] And to add, as Austin does, that "we really need to go no farther," is to reach the nadir of reductionism.

There is another path open to us if we grant that Baudelaire's *symbolisme* was not merely the established *symbolique*. We can relate Baudelaire's symbolism more directly to primary forces in the Romantic movement, with its stress on the particular, the mobile and dynamic, on process, on the *natura naturans* of Coleridge and Schelling rather than the *natura naturata*, on art's function, in Coleridge's terms, to "elaborate *essence* into *existence*" (italics ours), and thus to create Beauty whereby "truth" is "humanized" for the feelings. Romanticism conceived of the symbol as the medium for reconciling time to eternity, the particular to the universal, the organic vitalism of immediate experience with the enduring structures of reason. In Neo-Platonism itself, as Lovejoy has shown, especially as it was interpreted in the Renaissance, there was a conflict between ideas of static perfection and of creative process. We catch more than a hint of the conflict in Baudelaire, as well as in the English Romantics, and, of course, in Schelling. Yet, on the whole, for the Romantics, life with its "dome of many colored glass" stained "the white radiance of eternity" with good effect both practically and aesthetically; and poets called attention here and now to the resulting beauty in variety, even if these colors were thought to fuse ultimately into whiteness.

The brilliant facets of the "symbol" were now more than ever to mediate the eternal as poets, under the influence of science and of everything in modern life that directed attention to particulars, experimented with these particulars in the creation of what they nevertheless, like a Wordsworth and a Baudelaire with their realisms, believed could be a high poetry. It remained to be seen whether modern experience in Paris, offering its objects and situations, could under certain conditions be related to the eternal. Baudelaire found the way, at least for him, by combining *surnaturalisme et ironie,* thanks to a sense of the absence of God that haunted him like a presence.

Baudelaire, then, achieved a new equilibrium, a new synthesis of time and eternity in his actual use of the symbol. But every true equilibrium, by bringing together forces that hitherto have been deemed incompatible, one of the forces usually bearing a stigma, gives status to a power that, once the equilibrium is broken, sets itself up independently. In the case of the symbol, the hitherto despised particular sets up in business for itself with the aid of all the nominalisms and atomisms from other areas of modern life. Therefore, as we have seen, the Baudelairean symbol is reduced to something "personnel," to something "purement humain," and, as we shall see, it tends to be related to theories of the "aesthetic monad," and to ideas of "symbol" that amount to little more than the realization that poetic language is to be distinguished from discursive language and is marked by a special kind of unity. To such ulterior developments we have sought to explain in what sense Baudelaire may be considered "transitional." But a historical figure is often declared "transitional" not because of what he means but because of what others have thought he meant or found it convenient to think he meant. As we have tried to make clear, Baudelaire in his own way still believed in the "miracle," though his *charisma* was to be used in the interests of a poetic "miraculism." From our point of view "la situation de Baudelaire" consisted in a peculiarly precarious equilibrium between the eternal and the temporal, his sense of evil and sin in life and in himself being redeemed by beauty, that intimation of another world where the vision of poetry found its complete truth even *hinc et nunc.*

6 BAUDELAIRE'S SYMBOLISME:
THE POETIC ELEMENTS

IN PRECEDING SECTIONS we have presented evidence to show that the inalienable context of Baudelaire's poetic activity was a sense of the transcendent. "Happy man! enviable man! he has loved nothing but the Beautiful, he has sought only the Beautiful; and when an object grotesque or hideous presented itself, he has known the secret of extracting from it a mysterious and symbolic beauty!" [1] In 1861, à propos of Gautier's work, Baudelaire seems to be describing, and finding a tradition for, his own *Fleurs du mal* of 1857.

We are keenly aware today—and partly as the result of the Romantics' emphasis on the work of the subconscious in artistic creation—that the poet's intent is most surely to be discovered in his practice. Yet to study poetic practice does not have the self-sufficing virtues some critics attribute to it; indeed such study often seems to substitute for the poet's theory of his poetry the critics' theory. Nor is there any infallible way to demonstrate that a given poem has a "mystérieuse et symbolique beauté" since, as Baudelaire himself recognized, though everything is hieroglyphic, the obscurity or clarity of symbols will depend on the purity, good will, and native clairvoyance of souls.

Nevertheless the study of theory relating to the elements of the poetry of *Les Fleurs du mal* and an examination of the poetic practice can nourish our sense of probability if they cannot guarantee discovery of the true meaning of the *symbole* for Baudelaire. As we have seen, "surnatu-

ralisme" as a fundamental literary quality comprehends
"la couleur générale et l'accent, c'est-à-dire intensité,
sonorité, limpidité, vibrativité, profondeur et retentisse-
ment dans l'espace et dans le temps." Of these qualities
"sonorité" and "vibrativité" are certainly musical, and the
"rententissement," a reverberation in time and space,
is an auditory image for a kind of import conceived
horizontally and probably affiliated with "profondeur"
conceived vertically. Elsewhere Baudelaire notes "how
poetry verges on music by a prosody whose roots plunge
more deeply into the human soul than is recognized by any
classical prosody." [2] Most of Baudelaire's thought on that
subject will not be published until he really discovers
Wagner in 1860. Since by this time the greater part of his
poetry and his general aesthetic had already taken shape,
the poet, unlike Mallarmé and Valéry later, found in the
musician less a challenge than a confirmation of his
poetics.

Baudelaire's letter to Wagner on February 17, 1860
concerning the previous concerts of January 25, February 1
and 8, and his article in the "Revue Européenne" for April
1 entitled "Richard Wagner et *Tannhäuser*" are the main
documents. [3] "It seemed to me that the music was *mine*,
and I recognized it as any man recognizes what he is
destined to love." As we have already observed, Baudelaire
identifies the "happy moments" of creative production or
appreciation through a sense of vastitude, and Wagner's
music "représente le grand, et . . . pousse au grand . . .
la solennité des grands bruits, des grands aspects de la
Nature, et des grandes passions de l'homme."

He confesses to a frequent if rather bizarre experience;
"the pride and the enjoyment of understanding, of allowing myself to be penetrated, invaded, in a truly sensual
volupté, and which resembles that of mounting in the air
or rolling on the sea." He excuses himself for sensations "which derive probably from my turn of mind and
my frequent preoccupations." "Everywhere there is something of the ravished and the ravishing, something aspiring
to mount higher, something excessive and superlative."

Taking his terms of comparison from painting, he sees "a vast stretch of dark red. If this red represents passion, I see it arrive gradually, through all the transitions of red and rose, to the incandescence of a furnace. It would seem difficult, impossible even to reach a more burning intensity; and yet a last rocket traces an even whiter furrow against the whiteness of its background. This will be, if you please, the supreme cry of the soul reaching the height of its paroxysm."

In the article on Wagner Baudelaire stresses especially the power of music to suggest ideas, feelings and visual images. He denies the subjectivity of music: for real music suggests "analogous ideas in different minds." "What would be truly surprising is that sound *should not* suggest color, that colors *should not* be able to give the idea of a melody, and that sound and color should be unfitting to translate ideas; things always having been expressed through a reciprocal analogy, since the day when God uttered forth the world as a complex and indivisible totality."

Thus in 1861, when most of Baudelaire's best poetry and criticism have been written, he can take the correspondences for granted, at least in the "horizontal" sense, and quote the first two quatrains of his sonnet, "Correspondances." It would be a strange dissociation of thought if Baudelaire, who speaks with such unquestioning confidence in 1860 of correspondences made inevitable by God himself, creator of a *"complex* [italics supplied] and indivisible totality," should be describing what he thought he had himself affirmed but not practiced as a poet.[4]

Baudelaire's description of the effect upon him of the overture of *Lohengrin* suggests affiliations with the German theorists of the dream and throws light upon some of the terms which he uses in describing "supernatural" states.

I remember, from the very first measures, I experienced one of those happy impressions that almost all imaginative men have known, by means of the dream and in sleep. I felt myself freed from the *bonds of weight,* and I found again, through memory, the extraordinary *volupté* which circulates in the *high places* . . . Then I pictured involuntarily the delightful state of a man subject to a prolonged revery in an absolute solitude, but a solitude with *an immense horizon* and a *large diffused light; immensity* without any other ornament but itself. Soon I experienced the sensation of a more vivid *brightness*, of an intensity of light growing with such rapidity, that the nuances supplied by the dictionary would not suffice to express the *overplus constantly renewed of intensity and whiteness*. Then I conceived fully the idea of a soul moving in a luminous medium, of an ecstasy made of *volupté and of knowledge*, and soaring above and far beyond the natural world.

There is enough similarity between this experience of *Lohengrin* and his poem "Elévation" which had already appeared in the 1857 edition of *Les Fleurs du mal* to suggest that what Baudelaire felt in the presence of Wagner's music was his own typical response to the highest beauty. Austin attributes the similarity of response to a possible earlier hearing of Wagner's music in 1845. In a letter in 1860 to Poulet-Malassis, Baudelaire writes that for fifteen years he has not felt such an "enlèvement," though the reference may be to the music of Weber and Beethoven. As we have seen, he wrote to Wagner: "It seemed to me that I recognized that music . . . that music was mine."

But it is quite possible, we think, that Baudelaire's response to Wagner's music was an intensification of his own characteristic response to beauty in "states almost supernatural." It will be observed below that he also attributes to Wagner his own moral dualism. Comparing his response to this music with Wagner's and Liszt's accounts of their responses, Baudelaire insists that it is the similarities that count, that is "the sensation of a *beatitude both spiritual and physical; of isolation*, of the *contemplation of something infinitely beautiful; of an intense light* which rejoices *the eyes and the soul to the fainting point*; and finally the sensation of space extended to the last conceivable limits."

Such an experience Baudelaire sometimes presents positively in his poetry; its absence interpreted sometimes as a betrayal of man's legitimate expectations by the Higher Power, is the substance of the poems of rebellion and spleen. It is especially significant that the *volupté et connaissance* in this experience elevates him far above the natural world. Yet the experience is "objective." It can be expected to have essentially similar results in competent auditors because of a common element in them responding to the same musical structure. As for the distinction between music and language, the poet makes it clear that music "must adapt itself to feeling with the same exactness as language, but evidently in another way, that is, to express the indefinite part of feeling that language, too positive, cannot render."

ii

The relation of music to such meaning as is provided by language is discussed further by Baudelaire. Observing that the composer's subject matter is in general "decidedly legendary," he adds that it "is a propensity natural to every poetic spirit which has led Wagner to this apparent specialty." Quoting the latter approvingly to the effect that "the myth is the primitive and anonymous poem of the people" and that the myth, going beyond what is intelligible only to the abstract reason, shows what "life has of the truly human, eternally comprehensible, and shows it in that concrete form, exclusive of all imitation," Baudelaire cries out, "How would Wagner not understand admirably the sacred, divine character of myth, he who is at once poet and critic?" Here Baudelaire observes what some critics miss: Wagner did not seek to combine music and language, but music and the *language of myth*.

He proceeds to a discussion of the theme of *Tannhäuser* which for the French poet "represents the struggle of two principles which have chosen the human heart as the principal field of battle, that is to say, of the flesh with the spirit, of hell with heaven, of Satan with God." Whence, he asks, did the master derive "this furious song of the flesh, this absolute knowledge of the diabolic side of man?" "Every normal mind bears in itself two infinities, heaven and hell, and in every image of one of these infinities he recognizes suddenly half of himself."

Such an analysis of the theme of the opera may seem quite Baudelairean. But the poet's very emphasis enforces two points. His own presentation of the conflict of Heaven and Hell in *Les Fleurs du mal* might well be understood by him as "mythic" in the same sense as *Tannhäuser*. For Baudelaire the ideas informed in a poem may not in themselves determine whether the work be poetry, but they determine its value and affect the intensity and whole-heartedness of response. Poetry may express for Baudelaire un *état d'âme*, but it is the relation of that state of soul to the deep truths of a man's experience that produces the highest ecstasy of *volupté et connaissance*. Thus a work that he interprets as a metaphysical vision, whose hero is not an "ordinary libertine, but general, universal man, living morganatically with the absolute ideal of *volupté*, the queen of all the devils . . . with the indestructible and irresistible Venus," is the source of one of his most complete aesthetic experiences.

The article on Wagner and *Tannhäuser* throws further light on the poet's conception of the role of meaning in music. The composer "translates" into sound the "tumults of the human soul," but in music's own way. If such translation seems imprecise, we must remember that in painting and even in the written word, "which is nevertheless the most positive of the arts, there is always a lacuna completed by the imagination of the auditor." Sensitive people will conceive of ideas in relation to those that the composer inspired, Baudelaire remarks revealingly, if there is enough eloquence: "plus la musique est éloquente, plus la suggestion est rapide et juste." Unlike Verlaine, in order to add to music, he does not think it necessary to twist the neck of eloquence.

By "ideas" Baudelaire does not mean verbal ideas or concepts, but images of agents and kinetic images of psychological response. The poet quotes Wagner's program for the overture of *Lohengrin* distributed at the Théâtre-Italien:

> From the very first measures, the soul of the pious hermit who awaits the sacred vessel *plunges into infinite space.* He sees a strange apparition take on, little by little, a body, a shape. The apparition becomes increasingly clear, and *the miraculous troop of angels,* carrying in their midst the sacred cup, passes before him. The whole procession approaches; the heart of the elect of God is exalted little by little; it swells, it is dilated; ineffable aspirations awaken in him; *he yields to a growing beatitude* as he finds himself closer and closer to *the luminous apparition,* and when finally the Holy Grail itself appears in the midst of the sacred procession, *he sinks into an abyss of ecstatic adoration, as if the entire world had suddenly disappeared.* [Italics Baudelaire's.]

Baudelaire continues to quote, underlining images which, when compared with those which the overture evoked in Liszt and in himself, have, he believes, an essential element in common. To be sure, he adds, "my revery is much less illustrated with material objects: it is vaguer and more abstract." And so it is.

Nevertheless, we should not reduce Baudelaire's response to the operatic music to a *schemata* of psychological thrusts, colors and states. He would not deny the importance of the fable, the human predicament suggested, in guiding responses of feeling. Nevertheless, at least under the conditions of Wagnerian opera, the poet attests his belief in common structures which competent auditors of music, an art seemingly more subjective than painting and literature, can apprehend. The condition for such objectivity seems to be a tight inner coherence of a work. Thus Baudelaire will write: "In fact, without poetry, the music of Wagner would still be a poetic work, being endowed with all the qualities which constitute a well-made poetry; having its explanation in itself, so well unified are all things, conjoined, reciprocally adapted, and, if a barbarism may be permitted to express the superlative degree of a quality, prudently *concatenated*."

iii

What Baudelaire does in his poems to enable structures of words to attain as far as possible to the "condition of music," to use Walter Pater's terms, has been studied effectively in the already mentioned works of Robert Vivier and Jean Prévost. We lean upon their conclusions as we describe the new musicality in *Les Fleurs du mal*. For it is not in the logical development of his poetry, in his syntax and vocabulary—elements which derive from classicism—nor is it in the detail and expression of images, where he learned from his contemporaries, that Baudelaire is most independent, but in the creation of atmosphere, in his tone and his verbal harmony.[5]

His cadences, as Jean Prévost points out, are slower than those of the other great lyric poets of the century. As we shall show later, Baudelaire's ideal movement evokes a sunlit sea where the waves' forward motion seems one with their up-and-down swell. The frequent use of refrains works toward such an effect. The poet's preference for poems whose metrical shape is known in advance goes with his love of rich rhymes and of the repetition of rhymes. In the sonnet especially he seeks that same suppleness and amplitude within the imposed concentration that Mallarmé and Valéry were to favor. Thus he is able to achieve, as Prévost remarks, "une obscurité proprement poétique," that holds the thought in order that feeling may penetrate. Antithesis, very natural to Baudelaire, is a means of amplification, and, like a musician, he amplifies by images around a theme.

Yet in his poems one will come upon no vast crescendos of stanzas as in Victor Hugo. His longest strophe consists of five alexandrines as in "La Chevelure," for instance, or "Le Balcon." Prévost, whose work on Baudelaire is especially interesting for its study of "le souffle," the relation of breathing to emotional effects, pronounces the poet's "sensibilité respiratoire . . . vive." We know that he tends to punctuate for pauses of breath rather than for sense. But the poet's breath span is rather short and, if in a poem like "Spleen" ("Quand le ciel lourd et bas pèse comme un couvercle") one sentence runs through the first four stanzas, it is not for the sake of amplitude but to suggest through difficulty in breathing a mounting exacerbation of the nerves.

The alexandrine, Prévost continues, pronounced in four seconds, seems to be the measure of a full breath, and the habit of the alexandrine affects even the lines of ten syllables, adding a kind of exalted fullness to their speed. The shorter the line, the more important the stanza, and when such strophes are linked together, we experience an "émotion légère, heureuse, la grâce." [6]

Studies of "le souffle" like Prévost's, properly interpreted, describe one aspect of the physiological mechanism of verbal expression and only to that extent do they "explain" the poetry. Certainly there seems to be in Baudelaire's poetry what Vivier has called a "continuité des effets sonores—cette musique apaisante où tous les problèmes se résolvent dans une logique supérieure à l'évidence même des faits." [7] This is the victory of art everywhere, from *Oedipus Tyrannus* on, but in Baudelaire the entire scheme of sound is a greater factor in the triumph than, for instance, in Mallarmé who, though he developed "musicality" more elaborately than his predecessor, seeking even the effect of superposed notations in a page of music, triumphed more often in the single line.

iv

"Suggestiveness," perhaps even more than "music," has been the "word" for Symbolisme. We have dealt with "music" first, however, because what distinguishes the suggestiveness of Baudelaire is its aspiration toward music. Poetry has always been suggestive in some sense for it has always taken an indirect approach: even when it seems to be saying "This is that," poetry says "This is like that." The "suggestiveness" of Symbolisme means emphasis upon a use of language which will enlist the reader's response to enact an ideal unity of thought, image, feeling and sensation—in Coleridge's words, "to bring the whole soul of man into activity." The aim is to recreate the matrix from which words and their meaning emerge, but at a higher level of order.

In our "prose" we attempt to follow a "line" of thought which we raise above its living matrix in sense and feeling and direct toward "objectivity," that is toward a valid reference beyond itself. We seek to keep the attention of the reader or auditor focused upon that "line" whose very logic insures its relevance to external fact. In our poetry, according to the classical doctrine, our thought immerses itself anew in the matrix only so far as to make possible an adhesion to its "line" of selected elements entwining themselves around it to give it life, though they are not its life. In such art the "motive" is directive and determinative; in such poetry a paraphraseable meaning is not the whole meaning but it makes a great deal of sense.

For the Romantics at their best and for Baudelaire and the Symbolistes we should have to modify our image. Here the effect, relatively speaking, is not of words emerging into meaning by issuing from the life-giving matrix to a maximum degree, but of words appearing to emerge while remaining as much as possible immersed in the matrix. This is the "paradox" of poetic language: to be and not to be, to gain by losing discursive distinctness. In Baudelaire, the meaning's *emergence out of immersion* is relatively maximum, in Mallarmé relatively minimum, while remaining an emergence. The Rimbaud of *Les Illuminations* will seek to contrive, through juxtaposed images of great sensory force, a minimum emergence from the matrix at that depth which he would persuade us by his poetry is the true matrix. The "dérèglement de tous les sens" is an attempt through self-torture to present evidence of a "primitive" matrix overlaid by a pseudo-matrix accruing from habit. In Verlaine the Symboliste meanings sometimes "emerge" to the same extent as in Baudelaire; but, more characteristically, they are so cunningly infused into elementary simplicities of feeling that we can be deceived into thinking that the poems are "romances sans paroles," attaining symbolic force through a transparent self-evidence, with words tending to become pure musical "notes."

Jean Prévost accounts in more pragmatic fashion for the novel "obscurity" of the Symbolistes by the way in which the poet produces an "impression of shadow" with a "few strokes of light" and imposes "slowness" upon thought, "thus permitting emotion to follow it or equal it." This "very modern resource" appears in Baudelaire and becomes "one of the essential instruments of Mallarmé." [8] We should add that this "resource" was itself the result of Baudelaire's effort at adequate expression in full "color" and intimacy, of a vision granted him at certain "happy moments," and which he sought to control and even to command. Such expression involved tone as well as atmosphere, synaesthesia, and a rich texture of metaphor.

Vivier has distinguished especially four "tones" in Baudelaire: the oratorical, with its air of premeditation, its nobility, its obvious balance, a certain pomp and a taste for apostrophe; the confidential, with its quiet intensity bespeaking intimacy of feeling; the prayerful; and the ironic. Even in the poet's intimate tone he has discerned a certain control, an "air of ceremony" which ennobles the pervasiveness of a given mood.

If tone can be described as a mood in its social relations and dramatic aspect, "atmosphere" means intimacy through slow envelopment. This atmosphere, especially in poems of a confidential or prayerful tone, is "heavy, static, warm or velvety," not conveyed by concept but insinuated by the poet's sensibility through images general in nature and hardly plastic. For the "sorcellerie évocatoire" of Baudelaire, according to Vivier, is based on feeling and is caused by a certain ritual evenness of tone, by concision, and by an unerring knowledge of the psychological connotations of words, of correspondences of sound and sense, of the repertoire of effects of rhythm, of the call and recall of rhymes. There is no effect of a stream of consciousness or of a spontaneous juxtaposition of impressions as in Rimbaud. [9]

We should like only to add to this description of

"sorcellerie évocatoire" that ability to impart to the whole the effect of a poetic locus not in ourselves but in what is objectively brought into being as though implicit and rediscovered. Gundolf spoke somewhere of a "monumental intimacy" in Keats' lyricism. Baudelaire shares that quality with Keats, though perhaps with a little more reserve and solemnity. That "moi" of which Baudelaire is proud in spite of his scorn for a poetry of confession, succeeds in effecting the sorcerer's magic, bringing on to the stage a noble voice speaking, as if without the poet's complicity, for humanity. His distinction between "la sensibilité de l'imagination" and "la sensibilité du coeur" is another way of saying the same thing. *Les Fleurs du mal*, it has been said, could be given as subtitle "Mon coeur mis à nu"; but what distinguishes Baudelaire is the projection of "le coeur" through "l'imagination," an effect that the earlier T. S. Eliot sought to describe as poetic "impersonality."

Synaesthesia, as Austin points out, is far less important in Baudelaire than has been said and more complex in meaning.[10] We see its significance especially with reference to "music" and "suggestiveness." For to have a perfume evoked by a color or a sound means to enjoy two sensations as well as their merging. It is to subordinate, but not to subject, one sense to the profound unity of all the senses, to make for that interflow that, as in good piano-playing, asserts the distinctness of the individual note and multiplies suggestion. The correspondence between sensations and ideas — "rouge idéal," "rouge amour" — may lessen individual color intensity, for instance, but it diffuses color through other areas of experience. And perhaps what Vivier has observed as an abundance of abstract nouns, the use of concrete terms in an abstract sense, as in expressions like "végétal irrégulier," a certain liking for archaic terms, and yet, in contrast, the importance given to the adjective and especially to the verb as active forces, suggest what we have already stressed — Baudelaire's sense of the world as made up not of assertive, atomistic intensities and obstructive solids but of structures and relations eminently fusible in harmony, the world of a certain kind of musician.

Analogy and correspondence imply a reality not of su-perposed tiers, the one "below" evoking the one "above" part for part, but a reality in which the very possibility of a perfect inner organization of what is "below" brings conviction of the reality of a structure "above." In similar fashion, for some hearers, the perfection of Bach's music in its known structure bears an intimation, somehow, of its existence in eternity.

The poet will make a note in *Fusées* on the color violet—"amour contenu, mystérieux, voilé, couleur de chanoinesse." He sees the arabesque as the most "spir-itualiste" of designs, a taste shared by Mallarmé. The "infinite and mysterious charm" of a ship he explains as due not merely to its symmetry, which the mind demands as much as complication and harmony, but also to

> successive multiplication and generation of all the imagi-nary figures and curves operated in space by the real elements of the object. The poetic idea which one abstracts from this operation of movement in lines is the hypothesis of a vast being, immense, complicated, but eurythmical, of an animal full of genius, suffering and breathing all the sighs and ambitions of humanity.

Even the line of poetry, Baudelaire writes, can "touch on musical art and on mathematical science" by imitating "the horizontal line, the ascending straight line, the descending straight line" and can follow the "spiral, describe the parabola, or the zigzag." [11]

Baudelaire's ability to envisage a suffering animal "full of genius" in the operation of a movement in lines testifies to a strong sense of the living and the dynamic. We must not underrate his sensory powers—to judge from the studies of visual and auditory, olfactory, tactile and gusta-tory qualities in his verse by Vivier, Prévost, and Austin. We need fasten only on certain general conclusions. Among these are the recognition that the poet's gamut of sense is broad, not restricted, that in spite of the im-portance of the olfactory sense, the so-called "higher" senses of sight and hearing predominate in his poetry, though "sensibilisés," just as the lower senses are intellectualized. Most important is the conclusion that the aim of Baudelaire's sensory images is not to represent things but to make them the means of a "sorcellerie évocatoire." [12]

v

To stress as we have the "straining" from one order of experience to another and the striving for interfusion which we have found to be at the root both of "music" and "suggestiveness" in Baudelaire is to imply a richly metaphorical way of grasping and expressing meanings. For metaphor implies motion (*phora*) that is also change (*meta*)—that is, semantic motion. It is "metaphor" rather than "image" that we shall use as a comprehensive term. Vivier, Prévost, and Austin use the term "image" which the last-named defines as "any rhetorical figure which relates two areas in order to render exactly a sensation, a feeling or any idea by bringing out a point of comparison." "Image" thus includes metaphor, symbol, and allegory. American critics have offered at least two effective definitions of "image," which is for Ezra Pound "an emotional and intellectual complex in an instant of time," and for Allen Tate the source of a response that is a "single act compounded of spiritual insight and physical perception." But as a basic category of poetry we agree with Philip Wheelwright that "image" may lead too easily to misunderstanding to be acceptable as an inclusive term.[13]

What is metaphor, and shall we distinguish it from simile? Baudelaire's practice supports Wheelwright's suggestion that we largely ignore the grammarian's distinction between metaphor and simile. "Comme" meaning "as" or "like," occurs 349 times in *Les Fleurs du mal*, quite freqently as an introduction to a figure of speech.[14] But, as we shall see, figures introduced by "like" or "as" often match in force those where comparison is implied. The "quality of semantic transformation," the "psychic depth" of transmutation, as Wheelwright suggests, are what matters. It may be that the frequent use of "comme" in Baudelaire (and for that matter in Mallarmé) is the expression of his sense of analogy, that is, that metaphor does not merely perform a virtuoso dance of linguistic forces enjoying their own marvelous superfluities, but parallels an objective character of the world.

To understand the Baudelairean metaphor it will be helpful to follow Wheelwright in another of his distinctions. Metaphor reaches out and combines, and these two functions appear most effectively in combination and are perhaps always at least implicit. But one can distinguish between two ways of metaphor. "Epiphor" refers to the outreach and extension of meaning through comparison. "Diaphor" may stand for the creation of new meanings by juxtaposition and synthesis.

"Epiphors" express a "similarity between something relatively well known or concretely known (the semantic vehicle) and something which, although of greater worth or importance, is less known, or more obscurely known (the semantic tenor).[15] Baudelaire's metaphors are predominantly epiphoric, which is not, of course, to deny them vitality. Often they make the impression of the "déjà vu" seen again with a new twist. "De tes yeux, de tes yeux verts, / Lacs ou mon âme tremble et se voit à l'envers." — ("Le Poison"). (Of your eyes, of your green eyes, / Lakes where my soul trembles and sees itself upside down.) Lovers have often seen themselves mirrored in the pools of their ladies' eyes, but the fusion of the poisonous water with the "trembling" of the "soul upside-down" is newly suggestive.

The angel with the last trump of judgment is a common enough image, but to present "by Ganges or Seine" the human herd dancing to exhaustion, not seeing "Dans un trou de plafond la trompette de l'Ange / Sinistrement béante ainsi qu'un tromblon noir . . ." ("Danse macabre") trumpet-like the mouth of a blunderbuss gaping out of a hole in the ceiling is to work like one of the Dutch or Flemish masters of the quaint and fantastic. Or again, with Delacroix' fresco at St. Sulpice in mind—"Héliodore chassé du temple"—we return to the threatening angel in a picture that is a superb example, also, of the way in which the poet can make his line "descend." "Un Ange furieux fond du ciel comme un aigle" ("Le Rebelle"). Here the swoop is realized also by the two *f*'s and the soft *c* contrasting with the "cut" of the hard *c* and the *g* which follow.

To remind us further that metaphor is not merely a matter of relationships seen with the physical eye and the eye of the mind but becomes convincing also through sound and rhythm, consider the image of albatrosses helpless on the deck, their wings like dragging oars, "Laissent piteusement leurs grandes ailes blanches / Comme des avirons traîner à côté d'eux . . ." ("L'Albatros"). As a matter of fact, here as often, Baudelaire is not so much interested in having us *see* the bird as *feel* his plight. Thus the metaphor is "made" with that finely expansive first line with I know not what of the awkward and pathetic in the rhythm: "Laissent piteusement . . ." The "piteusement" is certainly "mathematically exact."

Or take an old phial, emptied and cast off: "Quand on m'aura jeté, vieux flacon désolé, / Décrépit, poudreux, sale, abject, visquex, fêlé . . ." ("Le Flacon"). One wonders at this monotonous piling up of adjectives of two syllables, the repetitious rhythm broken only by the pause on "sale" whose meaning, then, provides the main "sense." And then one begins to think that the adjectives model for the ear a sense of "de trop" in time and space for the desolate old flask.

The impression is confirmed when one encounters a similar situation in "Confession." The poet and his beloved, Madame Sabatier, for him the symbol of a radiant health, physical and moral, are walking arm in arm. Suddenly:

> *Une note plaintive, une note bizarre*
> *S'échappa, tout en chancelant*
> *Comme une enfant chétive, horrible, sombre, immonde,*
> *Dont sa famille rougirait,*
> *Et qu'elle aurait longtemps, pour la cacher au monde,*
> *Dans un caveau mise au secret.*

(A plaintive note, a bizarre note / escaped, tottering / like a sickly child, horrible, somber, obscene, / as if it had made her family ashamed, / and whom it had for a long time, to hide her from people, / concealed in a cellar.) Here again Baudelaire expresses, not through the choice of a single word or the apt phrase but by a kind of *mimesis* through the repeated jerkings of the rhythm, something horrible he cannot get out of his mind. At other times he can make his metaphor come true with a single word. How often is music likened to the sea! It is the "prend" in his line that "takes" us: "La musique souvent me prend comme une mer!" The echoing "ent" "end," and the hum of the *m* sound from beginning to end of course also play their part.

We have mentioned the frequent use of "comme," but even "ainsi que" is not uncommon. Baudelaire will sometimes use the conjunction to bring all the more conviction because he seems to pretend to no more than a "figure" of speech. Evoking cats, the poet writes ("Les Chats"):

Leurs reins féconds sont pleins d'étincelles magiques,
Et des parcelles d'or, ainsi qu'un sable fin,
Etoilent vaguement leurs prunelles mystiques.

Since he is praising the "magic" in the loins of cats, he gives his metaphor a realistic base by making the bits of gold explicitly similar to "a fine sand," and then from this "ground" he launches what seems like a *vers donné*: "In their mystic pupils a scattering of stars." Or the poet will use his "ainsi que" without batting an eyelash to give us confidence in a preposterous comparison. Does the heart ever fly ("Moesta et errabunda") —

> *Loin du noir océan de l'immonde cité,*
> *Vers un autre océan où la splendeur éclate,*
> *Bleu, clair, profond, ainsi que la virginité?*

"Virginity" is presented as light, color and depth, perhaps unconsciously through the mediation of paintings or statues of the Virgin Mary! On the other hand, in this same poem, the metaphor of innocent bliss will be revitalized almost unobtrusively through the adjective "green:" "Mais le vert paradis des amours enfantines . . ."

vi

We have been considering as examples of Baudelaire's "epiphors" chiefly passages where the terms of comparison need not have taken even the readers of the poet's own day unpleasantly by surprise. But what of that more radical use of metaphor Wheelwright calls "diaphor," which produces new meaning by juxtaposition alone, which is found most purely in abstract painting and in nonimitative music? A characteristic aspect of Baudelaire's Symbolisme is the richly metaphoric texture of his poetry. Yet it helps to mark the place of Baudelaire in the movement of Symbolisme to observe that it is easier to find examples of the diaphoric metaphor in Mallarmé and Rimbaud than in *Les Fleurs du mal*. "Et le splendide bain de cheveux disparaît / Dans les clartés et les frissons, o pierreries!" ("L'Après-midi d'un faune"). To begin with a less radical example from Mallarmé of juxtaposition as creative of metaphor, the cry, "o pierreries!", bursting forth next to the "brightness" and the "shivers" of the water as the nymphs plunge into it, invites us to fuse "clartés, frissons" and "pierreries" in one image: light, the feeling of movement, and the brilliant preciousness of diamonds in a shimmer of r's. What the Faun is presented as seeing is not the splendid hair that disappears but the "splendid bath" of hair that disappears. For ordinary logic the "bath" does not come until after the nymphs are immersed; but we are being made to see beforehand the splendor that will actually take form amid the abstractions of "clartés" and "frissons." The poet presents simultaneously and abstractly what in reality occurred successively in concrete time—an effect sought by later abstractionist painters.

Let us consider a more puzzling example of such "juxtaposition" from 'Toast funèbre," Mallarmé's masterpiece in eulogy of poetry and of the dead Théophile Gautier. The ideal duty, the speaker has been saying, growing for us like the Rose or the Lily in the "gardens of our star," is to make survive

pour l'honneur du tranquille désastre
Une agitation solennelle par l'air
De paroles, pourpre ivre et grand calice clair,
Que pluie et diamant, le regard diaphane
Resté là sur ces fleurs dont nulle ne se fane,
Isole parmi l'heure et le rayon du jour!

(. . . in honor of the quiet disaster / a solemn agitation through air / of words, intoxicating red and great clear chalice, / that, rain and diamond, the diaphanous gaze, / remaining in repose on those flowers, of which none ever fades, / isolates amid time and the light of day!)

The reader is reminded that, about ten lines earlier, the poet had spoken rather mysteriously of the Master who alone in Eden had evoked the Rose and the Lily through the mystery of giving them names. Thus when "pourpre ivre et grand calice clair," suggesting the flowers, are juxtaposed to the "solemn agitation through air of words," the static being set next to the vibrant, the reader will observe the connection. But what of "pluie et diamant"? Are "rain" and "diamond" in apposition to the vibrancy of the "red" and the brilliance of the "chalice," and are they the object of that diaphanous glance that isolates them among the unfading flowers? Or is the "diaphanous gaze" itself a rain falling upon these flowers and bringing them to life? Is it the transparency of that gaze which gives the diamond quality to its object? "Dia-phanous" and "dia-mond" (which came, perhaps, from the Greek *dia-phanes*) both suggest a "piercing through," perhaps by the gaze which penetrates to the essence as diamond and waters what it contemplates into unfading flower as rain. Adding some plausibility to this interpretation is the fact that Mallarmé, as in his "Prose pour des Esseintes," entertains the hypothesis of artistic vision as creative of a world which is more than hypothetical.

What we would point out is that in Mallarmé a linguistic element faces both backward and forward—as does "pluie et diamant"—and can have a meaning in each direction. "Diaphoric" in this poet is a dynamic apposition which is well adapted to the poet's sense of the many meanings of any one item. His poetry aims to present not the "rose" in its concreteness but sufficient suggestion of a "rose" so that it becomes a center radiating outwards to as many other ideas of objects as possible. Mallarmé pushes the idea of analogy farther than Baudelaire. Whereas Baudelaire's objects tend even in the spiritual world of analogy to retain as much flesh as is suggested in Dante's souls in the *Inferno* and in *Purgatorio,* Mallarmé's seem structured in intellectual light as in the *Paradiso.*

It is in Rimbaud that the diaphoric is more purely a matter of juxtaposition. An extreme example like "Mystique" from *Les Illuminations* may serve to contrast the general effect of metaphor with that in Baudelaire and in Mallarmé.

> *Sur la pente du talus, les anges tournent leurs robes de laine dans les herbages d'acier et d'émeraude.*
>
> *Des prés de flammes bondissent jusqu'au sommet du mamelon. A gauche le terreau de l'arête est piétiné par tous les homicides et toutes les batailles, et tous les bruits désastreux filent leur courbe. Derrière l'arête de droite a ligne des orients, des progrès.*
>
> *Et, tandis que la bande en haut du tableau est formée de la rumeur tournante et bondissante des conques des mers et des nuits humaines,*
>
> *La douceur fleurie des étoiles et du ciel et du reste descend en face du talus, comme un panier,—contre notre face, et fait l'abîme fleurant et bleu là-dessous.*

(On the slope of the hillock, angels whirl their woolen robes, in the grasses of steel and emerald. / Meadows of flame leap up to the top of the mound. On the left, the earth mold of the ridge is trampled upon by all murders and all battles, and all the disastrous noises race along their own orbit. Behind the crest on the right, the line of orients, of progress. / And, while the strip at the top of the picture is made of the whirling and leaping murmur of conch shells of the seas and of human nights, / The flowery softness of the stars, of the sky and of all else comes down opposite the bank like a basket—close to our faces, and marks the abyss flowering and blue below.)

A slope—angels whirling woolen robes—the grass is emerald. But why also "steely"? The rest of the poem has to do with war. Is it the smoke of battle in its rapid convolutions that suggests the woolen robes, while "angels" evoke in us a sense of intangible dynamism? From below the slope where the "angels" whirl, whole prairies of flame leap upward in assault to the very top of the mound. On the left wing the ridge, indeed its earth-mold, is trampled by furious abstractions: "all murders and all battles" and all "disastrous noises" (of wars and rumor of wars) follow along their slope to the top. Beyond the ridge on the right, the line of "orients" (the fabled East, the direction of the rising sun, the source of creation) of "progress." Is the battle's objective to attain to this line of progress?

But now for the first time we are told that what we have seen is a "tableau." This is starting *in medias res* with a vengeance! Is the poet describing, or evoking a picture seen, or is he imagining one? At any rate the top of the picture is formed by the whirling and leaping murmur of "conch shells" and the "human nights." Here "tournant" sets up the motion of the angels, the "bondissent" that of the flames. One can see how conch-shells "whirl" or how whirling conch-shells may suggest angels. Can it be that the poet is seeing the same kind of motion up there which he commends as "angels" and "conch shells"? (The sea for Rimbaud in "Le Bateau ivre" is a place of bliss, if unsustained and transitory). One catches the sexual suggestion in the relation of "bondissante" and "nuits humaines." Should one extend it to the "prés de flammes" which bound up to the "sommet du mamelon"? Is war to be seen in terms of the fury of sex? In the older poetry a thought developed, the simpler growing more complex, the motion being linear; but the poetry of the Symbolistes can be circular in effect, early suggestions waiting for illumination by later meanings. At any rate, while all this is going on "up there," opposite the bank, close to our faces, there comes a sweet flowering of stars and heaven (and of "the rest," as though Rimbaud had grown suddenly impatient and afraid of sentiment) like a basket, right against our faces, and we are enveloped in a abyss flowering and blue below.

We will run the risks of allegory and sentimentality by suggesting a kind of total vision, arranged in planes as in a picture, of heaven and hell, of strife and peace somehow to be taken in at once and harmonized in a mystic unity. Certainly never before had the attempt been made to convey a "vision" of this kind so absolutely in terms of things, movements, colors, and abstractions—"angels," "homicides," "battles," "a sweet flowering of stars." But is it correct to speak of "conveying"? When Goethe speaks of symbol as originating in a situation or an object that seems an "eminent instance," when Baudelaire feels a certain heightening and deepening of responses to existence in certain happy moments which turn objects into "symbols," we get the impression that meaning is implicit as a burning *core*, which we can discern more or less in spite of its myriad radiations. In poems like "Mystique," the lines of radiation, the directions of radiation are so bright, the suffusion everywhere so dazzling that we have difficulty in locating the focus of meaning. Now even for Rimbaud a poem must have "meaning"; in this poem that seems made up of juxtapositions of visual images below, above, left, right and back, at the very top, opposite and below, it is insinuated by the value-words which after all make at least enough "sense" to suggest an attitude— "anges," "homicides," "batailles," "bruits désastreux," "des progrès," "la douceur fleurie des étoiles," "l'abîme fleurant et bleu," "gauche," "droite." Here sensations themselves have meaning not only as sensations but as value.

Thus what characterizes Rimbaud where he is most different from Baudelaire, and working in the direction of "voyance" which he admits the older poet unconsciously possesses, is the radically "presentational" nature of his poetry. Here he seems to be seeking a music of movement, stress and color that is nevertheless meaningful, and one is tempted to apply to it the term that Susanne Langer applies to music, "an unconsummated symbol." [16]

In "Le Bâteau ivre," to take an apparently more conventional poem, the boat-as-speaker narrates a voyage on the water, under the water and in the skies, in which the boat saw whatever man had ever seen and perhaps could conceivably see. Among the objects that the boat saw, dreamed, followed, even hit, were the "incredible Floridas," the enormous rotting of Leviathan, space cataracting into the abyss, hideous shipwrecks and, finally, snakes devoured by vermin falling from twisted trees in a cloud of black odors.

Are these visual images organized in order to convey a quality of experience which is their meaning, even though conceived *in* and *through* them? Or are these images offered only for their local excitement in succession as in kaleidoscopic views? Is the poet talking about one reality in terms of other realities or imagined aspects of reality? Is he using symbol? Baudelaire, as we shall see, in a poem seeking to convey his vision of bliss, will generally aid the reader through a concise directive such as "féconde-paresse" in "La Chevelure." "That" is the state of bliss he enjoys in the hair. In the case of Rimbaud we never can be quite sure whether his sensory presentations are meant to be valuable solely as stimuli to sensation, to feeling and to imagination without further direction, or whether in and through this presentation, the reader, made strong by the poet's "dérèglement de tous les sens" will also see what is not hallucination but the ultimate reality of an epiphany. If the latter is true, as Rimbaud seems to have hoped, we have the immediacy of mysticism. In that case, as with the mystic, who must remain mute, or be satisfied like a Hindu *guru* with a "neti! neti!" "not quite that! not quite that!" Rimbaud is left speechless, or rather, articulating words whose meaning, focused in sensation, blazes in a gesture toward the ineffable.[17]

vii

In his use of metaphor and symbol, then, Baudelaire is the most conservative of the three poets. His thought "emerges" from the "matrix" relatively more readily, and it is easier to distinguish between "tenor" and "vehicle." In him the combination of epiphoric and diaphoric elements which is to be found, according to Wheelwright, in the most interesting and effective cases of metaphor favors the epiphoric.[18] Even the linking of metaphor to metaphor follows a pattern in raised relief. In contrast, as Deborah Aish has pointed out, metaphors in Mallarmé's later poems are involved simultaneously in the matrix so that one is implicated in the other and the second is needed to explain the first.[19] To illustrate the effect of unified continuity of metaphors in Baudelaire, let us consider "La Mort des pauvres":

> C'est la mort qui console, hélas! et qui fait vivre;
> C'est le but de la vie, et c'est le seul espoir
> Qui, comme un élixir, nous monte et nous enivre,
> Et nous donne le coeur de marcher jusqu'au soir;
>
> A travers la tempête, et la neige, et le givre,
> C'est la clarté vibrante à notre horizon noir;
> C'est l'auberge fameuse inscrite sur le livre,
> Où l'on pourra manger, et dormir, et s'asseoir;
>
> C'est un ange qui tient dans ses doigts magnétiques
> Le sommeil et le don des rêves extatiques,
> Et qui refait le lit des gens pauvres et nus.
>
> C'est la gloire des Dieux, c'est le grenier mystique,
> C'est la bourse du pauvre et sa patrie antique,
> C'est le portique ouvert sur les Cieux inconnus!

(It is Death that consoles, alas! and that keeps us alive; / it is the goal of life, and it is the only hope / which, like an elixir, sets us up and makes us drunk, / and gives us the courage to go on until evening; / / through tempest, snow, and frost / it is the brightness vibrating on our black horizon; / it is the famous inn written on the book, / where one can eat and drink and sit down; / / it is an Angel who holds in his magnetic fingers / sleep and the gift of ecstatic dreams, / and who remakes the beds of poor and naked folk; / / it is the glory of the Gods, it is the mystic attic, / it is the poor man's pouch and his native land, / it is the portico open on unknown skies.)

This sonnet is a poem of not uncommon type where the epiphoric element is the theme of Death, which holds together the various attributes: "It is this, it is that . . ." But observe how Baudelaire integrates internally. Death gives us the courage to march on until nightfall through storm and cold toward the light on the dark horizon which is the inn. Here, by a reversal of the expected, the image is not that of writing in the book when one arrives at the inn, but of the famous inn written in the book of life, so sure can we be that we shall at last have a place to receive us. In the tercets the poet brings in the other world. How maintain the central earthy metaphor of the inn, to which symbolic value has accrued, and yet introduce the beyond? The Angel "remakes" the bed; it is his "magnetic" fingers, as it were, which have the halo, and he has it in his hands to give sleep and the dreams that raise us beyond ourselves. And now death has become the "glory of the Gods," while still maintaining the simplicity of house and home. It is the "mystic attic." What the poor man carries in his pouch to pay for his keep at the inn is the promise of death, and he has come home. Then the final suggestion: a touch of grandeur to fit the "glory of the Gods," a "portico" with columns opening on unknown skies.

Thus Baudelaire's strong sense of the "tenor" of poetry keeps him close to the epiphor. His need to personify has the same result. One of the most frequent types of metaphor in Baudelaire revitalizes allegory and sometimes achieves the effect of the mythic. In "Le Crépuscule du matin,"

> *L'aurore grelottante en robe rose et verte*
> *S'avançait lentement sur la Seine déserte,*
> *Et le sombre Paris, en se frottant les yeux,*
> *Empoignait ses outils, vieillard laborieux.*

Above the modern city it is no "rosy-fingered dawn" that appears but a shivering house-wife in a rose and green dressing-gown, while gloomy old Paris grabs his tools, rubbing his eyes! It is hard to say by what mythic sensibility the poet succeeds in making us accept in connection with modern Paris such a figure as "Pluviôse, irrité contre la ville entière / De son urne à grands flots verse un froid ténébreux" ("Spleen," LXXV). Here not only do we have the season turned god, we even have the traditional urn! Yet the effect is very "modern." This is a barefaced imposition of imaginative power.

For Baudelaire's "frisson nouveau" consists in his giving to beauty a "modern" flavor tart with the disillusionments of realism. We have seen how his metaphors renew the old, as it were, by taking a second look; how the transfer of meaning, and the fact that such a transfer is intended, is rather clearly intimated. Yet the poet achieves the "presentational" quality that is the aesthetic virtue of "juxtaposition" in his own fashion: by introducing surprising and even shocking new terms of comparison taken from modern life in the city. What Middleton Murry noted as an effect of "exacerbation of the image" in Baudelaire is really the result of such modernism. To illustrate with images selected by Murry himself: the nights that oppress the heart "like paper being crumpled"; the sky as the "black lid of a vast pot" where humanity boils; a heart "smoked like a ham," night "growing thick like a partition wall," pleasure taking flight "like a sylph behind the stage." [20] Erich Auerbach refers to Baudelaire's mixture of the base and contemptible with the sublime as a symbolic use of realistic horror. Hence such lines as: "Mais l'amour n'est pour moi, qu'un matelas d'aiguilles / Fait pour donner à boire à ces cruelles filles" ("La Fontaine de sang"), where the "mattress of needles" is not only a "low" image but an example of the famous catechresis, or mixed metaphor in Baudelaire. To try to see the image literally as a blood-stained mattress from which "ces cruelles filles" drank would pose some problems. The mixed nature or the purity of the metaphor is no longer a criterion once one accepts the idea of synaesthesia, or the idea of metaphor as juxtaposing sensations or atmospheres intuitively judged to "go together, take it or leave it," to use Wheelwright's phrase, if only for a split second in a particular context. "Comme un sanglot coupé par un sang écuméux, / Le chant du coq au loin déchirait l'air brumeux" ("Le Crépuscule du matin"). That gurgle and catching of breath giving way to the piercing quality of the rooster's cry, the image of blood being emphasized by the suggestion of "sang" in "sanglot" and by the idea of "cutting" in both "coupé" and "déchirait," make an impression of indissoluble unity and create the atmosphere of that city dawn.

Nor does Baudelaire lack the courage of a very modern humor in the presentation of his feeling, no matter how it looks, and how "appropriate" the metaphor may seem ("Le serpent qui danse"):

> *Sous le fardeau de ta paresse*
> *Ta tête d'enfant*
> *Se balance avec la mollesse*
> *D'un jeune elephant.*

Here impressions of weight, youth, a lazy sway of motion that Baudelaire loved in his women and in ships, fuse together in an image that would exploit even the slightly comic effect of a young woman with an elephant head. But the discerning reader must not dwell upon it. In any "modern" metaphor the intersection of meanings must be adroitly handled.

Erich Auerbach, in *Mimesis*, has made the important point that the great innovation in literary Realism consisted in the acceptance, forced upon the reader by the genius of Flaubert and others, of certain kinds of people, acts, and thoughts once considered incapable of bearing tragic import. Baudelaire did something similar for subject matter and the idea of "what could be compared with what." Readers accepted the flies around the Homeric milkpails; would they accept Prostitution as a "worm"? "Elle remue au sein de la cité de fange / Comme un ver qui dérobe à l'homme ce qu'il mange" ("Le Crépuscule du soir"). Would they accept as an image for the classic idea of the untrustworthiness of the human heart ("Confession"):

> *Que bâtir sur les coeurs est une chose sotte;*
> *Que tout craque, amour et beauté,*
> *Jusqu'à ce que l'Oubli les jette dans sa hotte*
> *Pour les rendre à l'Eternité . . .*

Here the image of the plasterer is maintained in the "bâtir," "craque," and "hotte," and Forgetfulness becomes a mason carrying back debris in a hod to the Eternity whence it came.

Baudelaire's abstract nouns in these contexts are powers sometimes violently physical. Thus "nightmare" is said to have drowned the "music" "with despotic and mutinous fist" ("La Muse Malade"). "Le Vertige" seizes the soul and "la pousse à deux mains" toward the gulf ("Le Flacon"). We see "La Muse Vénale" on snowy evenings lacking a fire to warm her "deux pieds violets." "Sentant ta bourse à sec autant que ton palais, / Récolteras-tu l'or des voûtes azurées?" Very Baudelairean is the juxtaposition of the Muse's "dry" purse and "dry" palate with the classical beauty of that harvest of "gold" in the vaults of heaven. Nor does the sting of irony impair the beauty.

The vices and the virtues are always a stimulus to the poet's imagination. "Nos péchés sont têtus, nos repentirs sont lâches" ("Au lecteur"); here "headstrong," personifying "sin," brings the latter into the workaday world. We hear the "old flag" of the flesh flapping to the wind of concupiscence among the misdirected infinites of Lesbianism in "Delphine et Hippolyte": "Et le vent furibond de la concupiscence / Fait claquer votre chair ainsi qu'un vieux drapeau." The poet has such mastery of his world of moral powers that he can afford to smile at Ennui that "monstre délicat," growing sentimental over a dream of carnage ("Au lecteur"):

> *C'est l'Ennui! — l'oeil chargé d'un pleur involontaire,*
> *Il rêve d'échafauds en fumant son huka.*
> *Tu le connais, lecteur, ce monstre délicat . . .*

Baudelaire in his very "Satanism" belongs to the breed that created the medieval Moralities. He has the genius that can recover infancy at will.[21] It is a childlike, and not senile Baudelaire, who will write conscientiously in his journal under the caption "Hygiène. Conduite. Méthode: 'Faire tous les matins ma prière à Dieu, réservoir de toute force et de toute justice, à mon père, à Mariette, et à Poe, comme intercesseurs . . .'" He has a child's scruples at the thought of loved ones dead. In "La servante au grand coeur dont vous étiez jalouse," something primitive in the imagination of the poet conveys its *Schaudern*. He sees the dead in their graves as bodies

> *dévorés de noires songeries,*
> *Sans compagnons de lit, sans bonnes causeries,*
> *Vieux squelettes gelés, travaillés par le ver,*
> *Ils sentent s'égoutter les neiges de l'hiver*
> *Et le siècle s'écouler . . .*

(Devoured by gloomy dreams, / without bedfellows, without good chitchats, / freezing old skeletons worked over by worms, / they feel the snows of winter drop by drop, / and the times flow away . . .)

The world that the Latin word "pius" evokes is in the last two lines where the poet, thinking that the old family servant who loved him might come and sit at his fireside, asks himself with a child's directness and concern: Que pourrais-je répondre à cette âme pieuse, / Voyant tomber des pleurs de sa paupière creuse?" The tendency to personify is one of the earliest sources of metaphor. Baudelaire, more authentically than any of the Symbolistes, even than Verlaine, can be a primitive, with more than the vocabulary of the primitive.

viii

The vitally metaphoric quality of Baudelaire's imagination and its preoccupation with "inner" reality even when it seems to be dealing with the external can be tested by examining the use of one of his pervasive adjectives "vaste." Gaston Bachelard has called "vaste" one of the most Baudelairean of words, marking "le plus naturellement l'infini de l'espace intime." [22] Whenever greatness is attached to a thing, a thought, a dream, the word "vaste" occurs. The real meaning of "vaste" is related to the expansion and depth by which Baudelaire characterizes those almost supernatural states in which the symbol is born. But, basing his view perhaps too exclusively on such lines as "vaste comme la nuit et comme la clarté" which characterizes the "ténébreuse et profonde unité" of "Correspondances," the French critic and psychologist considers "vaste" a "mot de la suprême synthese," uniting opposites, and always invoking "un calme, une paix, une sérénité."

The majority of examples supports Bachelard's interpretation, but in matters of art, word-count is a very shaky crutch. In dealing with poetic realities one might argue that a word used only once in a poetically effective context is more to be trusted as an index of the poet's imaginative world, than a word used ten times in lines poetically less potent. Questions involving contexts would have to be considered; in other words, the usual imponderables would defeat the science of number. Nevertheless let us follow our present clue to see what it is worth. "Vaste" in Baudelaire is associated with the lucid mind: "Et les vastes éclairs de son esprit lucide" ("Bénédiction"); with the albatross, a commendatory image, one of "les vastes oiseaux des mers" ("L'Albatros"); with the sea "La mer, la vaste mer, console nos labeurs" ("Moesta et errabunda"); with the "vastes portiques" of "La Vie antérieure," where certainly it refers to the vastness of ideal inner space; with music as a sea where "Sous un plafond de brume ou dans un vaste éther, Je mets à la voile"; with "les vastes cieux enchantés" of "Le Jet d'eau"; and finally, in the last poem of *Les Fleurs du mal*, "Le Voyage," the "vaste appétit" of the child, in love with maps and prints, and with the "vastes voluptés, changeantes, inconnues." Bachelard seems amply to have made his case.

But there are telling negative instances; not, assuredly, in "Nos deux coeurs seront deux vastes tombeaux" of "La

Mort des amants," where the context shows, if anything, that the spiritual comfort in "vaste" can even absorb the idea of the tomb, but in "Derrière les ennuis et les vastes chagrins" of "Elévation," where "vaste" is given importance by the very fact that a power is celebrated that can carry beyond even the vastness of earthly troubles. Again, in "Harmonie du soir," as we shall see, the very heart of the poet's meaning is suggested by the line, "Un coeur tendre qui hait le néant vaste et noir." "Le néant" is that "gouffre," that "grand trou" by which the poet envisages even sleep.

In our view, then, this pervasive adjective, whose repetition makes it not only a major metaphor but a symbol in *Les Fleurs du mal,* brings us back to the dualism of Baudelaire, the simultaneous postulation between both God and Satan, each one rewarding with pleasures in its kind. In the presence both of the diabolic and the divine Baudelaire feels this vastitude which is also one of the inner signs that the way is open for poetry. The two elements in literature for Baudelaire are "surnaturalisme" and "ironie," and the sense of the vast comprehends them both. Satan, in moments of the poet's impatience with the hidden God, becomes the symbol of that infinite to which he responds more than to either of the theological entities. So Satan will have his "Litanies" and the race of Cain be exalted over that of Abel, identified with the prudent hypocrisy of the bourgeoisie. But Baudelaire knows that a will vaporized by Satan, "ce savant chimiste," cannot turn mud into gold. In "Le Voyage" death can even be an escape from the boredom of Satanism, "from humanity with its big talk, drunk with its genius, and as of old, crying out, furious in the throes of its suffering: O thou my peer, my master, I curse thee!"

That the "simultaneous postulations" in Baudelaire are not entirely matters of conscious theory is evidenced by another recurrent image in the poet, the image in the verbs "mordre," "ronger." If "le vaste" suggests the sometimes ecstatic, sometimes appalling sense of immensity which elevates or engulfs the soul, "mordre" and "ronger" also have a certain ambivalence and their contrasting infinites. "Et le ver rongera ta peau comme un remords" of "Remords postume" is an almost inevitable beginning, since "mordre" is reiterated in "remords," and the poet tends to connect "le ver" with the process of remorse as in "Au lecteur." In the present poem the worm gnaws "the skin" of "la belle ténébreuse" because this "courtisane imparfaite" has not even known how to serve the senses to which she is dedicated.

Ennui, too, is something that bites ("Une Martyre"):

> *Son âme exaspérée*
> *Et ses sens par l'ennui mordus*
> *S'étaient-ils entr'ouverts à la meute altérée*
> *Des désirs errants et perdus?*

Here *ennui* seems the first bite that opens the way to a pack of errant desires attracted by blood. In "Le Cygne," the swan is ridiculous but also sublime because it is "rongé" by unremitting desire. But the bite can be that of "la vorace Ironie" in the poet's voice, in his blood, reflecting itself in him, the "vampire" of his heart. "Je suis la plaie et le couteau": the wound calls for the knife and the knife for the wound. In "L'Héautontimoroumenos" the poet sings the personal cost of his vision. He is

> *Un de ces grands abandonnés*
> *Au rire éternel condamnés,*
> *Et qui ne peuvent plus sourire!*

What is worse than to be condemned to irony when one has lost the stomach for it! Thus the poet is "un faux accord, Dans la divine symphonie." Baudelaire's fidelity to his ironic vision, exaggerated sometimes to the *outrance* of a certain heroism, resulted in the "Litanies de Satan," and a world turned topsy-turvy. But now and then the poet recognizes the game for what it is.

But there is a fundamental remorse, "le long Remords" of "L'Irréparable," pictured again as a "worm" that feeds upon us, as a patient "ant," as a "termite" that saps foundations with his "accursed tooth." Such remorse, "destructeur et gourmand comme la courtisane," is the remorse of martyrs who have taken the wrong way to the "Inn" where the Devil has extinguished "l'espérance." The poet knows of a play where the "adorable Sorcière" (Marie Daubrun), winged with gauze like a fairy, brought to earth, "L'énorme Satan." The poet's heart, however, "never visited by ecstasy," is like a theatre waiting always in vain for the appearance of "l'être aux ailes de gaze." Here the "bite" cuts as deep as the "nevermore" of a life disappointed in its expectations. It is the satanic world that is irreparable, and Satan is the enemy.

What bites deepest and eats life up, growing powerful at man's expense, is Time ("L'Ennemi"):

> O douleur! ô douleur! Le Temps mange la vie,
> Et l'obscur Ennemi qui nous ronge le coeur
> Du sang que nous perdons croît et se fortifie!

The symbol in the poem is a garden ravaged by storms in the spring and that with autumn the poet must rake over, covering up holes as deep as tombs. The poet in anguish asks himself whether on this pebbly rain-washed soil he can ever grow the flowers he dreams. Will any of "le mystique aliment" be left? For all his voluntarism, Baudelaire knows that some powers are irretrievable because they have been given; nothing "bites" more deeply than the fears of the loss of unearthly radiance in his *Fleurs du mal*. As Georges Poulet remarks, remorse is the consciousness of an "absolute discontinuity" between our present and an indestructible past. "Like Coleridge's Mariner, we carry a cadaver around our neck . . . Our punishment is that of enduring ourselves." [23] And yet there is always room, especially in Baudelaire, for a certain opposite, as in such poems as "Le Balcon," "La Chevelure," "Harmonie du soir," which present a "breakthrough" by memory in certain "happy moments." Time has its voice in the clock and the bell. As auxiliary, reminding man of his duties in his sensual pleasures and of his mortality in his creative work, it is "L'Avertisseur." It is "un serpent jaune," "la Dent." Experience for Baudelaire seems to be something that bites into sensibility, tears it, threatens to annihilate it.

Even the ideal can be "rongeur," an experience that gnaws. In the poem "L'Aube spirituelle," "L'Idéal rongeur" enters with the dawn into the life of débauchés and, by the operation of a "mystery of vengeance," it awakens an "angel" in the "dormant brute." But then the heaven of the spirit in its inaccessible blue draws the soul with the dreaded magnetism of the gulf itself.

> Des Cieux Spirituels l'inaccessible azur,
> Pour l'homme terrassé qui rêve et qui souffre,
> S'ouvre et s'enfonce avec l'attirance du gouffre.

Nevertheless the sun appears; it is the memory of the beloved.[24] Here the beloved clings to memory like perfume to a discarded phial, where it is still potent enough for its bite to bring both life and death.

In a similar context "mordre" is used with the greatest audacity. In "Le Poison" the poet has been celebrating the effects of wine and opium. Wine can furnish the most sordid holes and erect fabulous porticos of gold:

> Et fait surgir plus d'un portique fabuleux
> Dans l'or de sa vapeur rouge,
> Comme un soleil couchant dans un ciel nébuleux.

A similar image of "vastes portiques" in a sunset reflected by the waves occurs in the ideal landscape of "La Vie antérieure." The effect of opium is related to both images of porticos, themselves suggesting a kind of infinite:

> L'opium agrandit ce qui n'a pas de bornes,
> Allonge l'illimité,
> Approfondit le temps, creuse la volupté . . .

Yet there is a "bite" whose "terrible prodigy," surpassing wine or opium, can plunge the soul into an "oblivion without remorse" and wash it up unconscious upon the very shores of death: it is "ta salive qui mord." There is a penetration that in its effects can rival vastitude. Thus extremes meet, each producing an ecstasy that is the supreme attraction and the supreme dread of the poet.

The study of the ideas of "vaste" and of "mordre," even

if not carried beyond their immediate semantic relationships, suggests, because of the number of poems drawn in and the rich texture of meaning accruing, that we are in a symbolic field. We find it necessary to read each poem not only with the knowledge of the "ideas" of other poems, but also with a vivid memory of the images and gestures of sense and feeling which are also essential "vocabulary" of the poet. This would be the proof that a given poet has his "world." Whatever its resemblance to the world of "nature," the essence of a poet's world is a distinctive quality or Gestalt of qualities. The poetry which we call Symboliste may in this respect only carry further what had been implicit in all poetry. But Symbolisme and the idea of poetry leading to it and deriving from it have the merit of opening up to us another way into the Greek dramatists and Virgil, into Ronsard, into Scève and the English "Metaphysicals" by their explorations in the field of poetic essences.

ix

In our effort, through the study of Baudelaire's use of metaphor, to show what is Symboliste in the poet's imagination, we have also illustrated the process by which an adjective like "vaste," and a verb like "mordre," pass from metaphor into symbol. Let us focus attention on this development. Common usage even on the part of good critics often confuses metaphor with symbol. But, as Wheelwright points out, "when an image is employed as metaphor only once, in a unique flash of insight, it cannot accurately be said to function symbolically. It acquires a symbolic nature when, with whatever modifications, it undergoes or is considered capable of undergoing recurrence." [25] Robert Penn Warren in his volume on Coleridge's "Ancient Mariner" [26] points out that symbol is "focal," bringing together the idea and the special complex of feelings associated with that idea; that it is "massive," having the quality the psychologists call "condensation," and standing for a body or sequence of ideas fused in it which may be explored discursively; that it must partake of the reality which it renders intelligible, that "reality" being found rooted in our universal natural experience, such as the "wind" in the poem under discussion, or being validated by manipulation of the artist in a special context, as in the case of "Byzantium" in the work of Yeats. The real symbol thus has a deeper relation to the total structure of meaning than is warranted by its mechanical place in plot, situation, or discourse.

This is all to the good, provided that we remember also Yeats' remark that "metaphors are not profound enough to be moving, when they are not symbols." [27] "Massiveness," "permanence," "repeatability," in the case of the symbol are themselves really metaphors for "energy-tension." And one of the dangers of the "repeatable" even for the poet himself is that with repetition his "symbol" will freeze into "allegory," for even the relatively "unique" must be kept alive as it is grafted into new and living wholes.

Yet some symbols are marked by greater stability and permanence than others, and these can have a wide-ranging power of suggestion and evocation. We shall continue to follow Wheelwright as he summarizes "five main grades of comprehensiveness, or breadth of appeal," comparing with them as we go Baudelaire's practice:

A symbol may be "the presiding image of a single poem," as in the case of Mallarmé's "Faun" or Hart Crane's "Bridge," where the meaning has to be drawn from many images, with their half-suggestions of idea. These idea-images are related with various degrees of affinity and contrast, the latter amounting occasionally to paradox.[28] Many, and some of them the finest, of Baudelaire's poems, as we shall see, are of this type.

Our discussions of "vaste" and "mordre" have indicated that Baudelaire has "personal symbols," that is, those which have "continuing vitality and relevance for the poet's imagination and perhaps actual life."

In Baudelaire are to be found symbols of "ancestral vitality," that is, "those that are lifted by one poet, for his own creative purposes, from earlier written sources." Vivier's *L'Originalité de Baudelaire* is a mine for such symbols. But the French poet does not utilize the added resource of allusiveness with the same degree of system as does T. S. Eliot.

As for symbols of "cultural range," Baudelaire, too, used the Bible, the symbols of the Christian cult, pagan mythology, and made a rich resource especially of his interest in painting.

But what of "archetypal symbols," that is, "those which carry the same or very similar meanings for a large portion, if not all, of mankind, such as sky father and earth mother, light, blood, up-down, the axis of a wheel?" Certainly in the poetry of Baudelaire, as we have already seen, the up-down image is a pervasive one, specialized in the sense of "le gouffre" and lending itself to personification in the figure of Satan. The archetypal symbol, blood—"of an unusually tensive and paradoxical character"—with its ramifications would not be hard to follow in Baudelaire. As for "light, not merely as permitting visibility, but as heat, wisdom, enthusiasm," the "feu clair qui remplit les espaces limpides" ("Elévation"), we shall study this image in "La Chevelure." The pairs light-dark, male-female, life-death, are everywhere in *Les Fleurs du mal*, but with a special ambivalence, the "dark" mistress bringing at times both death and life, Satan sometimes seeming to deserve a prayer, death itself being invoked for the sake of the unknown and the new. The archetypal symbol, the Word, tending to become an "auditory image symbolizing rightness," the "What-Ought," the Logos, is presented in Baudelaire neither as thunderbolt nor as rushing wind; the mystic voice he hears in the temple of nature speaks the language of "les correspondances," the new "word," faith in which gave him his language as a poet.

The "Logos" for Baudelaire is born to a mother who feels not blessed among women but accursed, an object of disgust for her husband ("Bénédiction"). Not understanding the purposes of the Eternal, she vows to prevent the opening of the buds of the "wretched tree." The child, part Ishmael, part John the Baptist, with something also of the little Jesus carrying his cross, plays with the winds and talks with the cloud. He is feared or hated by everyone. His wife contemptuously subjects him to an idolatry of herself; she will eventually tear out his heart to feed it to the dogs. But the poet, seeing a splendid throne in the skies, and with the aid of the "vastes éclairs de son esprit lucide," blesses God for suffering, which is the "divine remedy" for our impurities and the purest essence to prepare the strong for the "sainte volupté": "Je sais que la douleur est la noblesse unique / Où ne mordront jamais la terre et les enfers . . ." From primitive rays drawn from the heart of light, a diadem is being made for the poet, and of its splendor mortal eyes are only "dim and plaintive mirrors." Baudelaire was not always willing to accept suffering as the divine remedy for our impurities; at times, like Ivan Karamazov, he was ready to hand back his ticket. All the more then did the poet remain for him the "Word," standing for man and between man and his fate. No French poet, not even Mallarmé, was to have such a sense of vocation.

The "Logos," as symbol, has its Baudelairean twist, as will other symbols. Water is not for him the cleansing agent and the sustainer of life, symbolizing purity and new life, except after his own fashion. Rimbaud who had not seen the sea when he wrote "Le Bâteau ivre" nevertheless made the sea a cleansing agent thanks to which the voyager could see "le poème de la mer" and be swept toward what might be epiphany. For Baudelaire water was the sea and, in his memories if not in his dreams, it meant the open air full of light and joy, the graceful, measured movement of the ship which in his youth had borne him to what in memory became paradise. The final cry in *Les Fleurs du mal* is for a ship to weigh anchor and to bear him into the Unknown to find the new.

As for the Circle, according to Wheelwright, "the most philosophically mature of the great archetypal symbols . . . together with its most frequent imagistic concretion of the Wheel," the "voyage" is too much Baudelaire's mode of response for any vision of the "still center." As we shall see, the nearest he came to stillness in his poetry is in the "infinis bercements du loisir embaumé"—the infinite lulling motion of a leisure perfume-fraught evoked in "La Chevelure." In Baudelaire the constant self-exhortation to centralize the self, the scorn of "prostitution" in every sense, in short the fear of dispersion of self, betray the man who is all exposed nerve-ends, with no "wise-passiveness" and, as Charles Du Bos said, no "entre-deux," no "normal vegetative life." [29] The nearest he came to a "still center" is an effect in his poetry of static lyricism.

WE HAVE MEASURED Baudelaire against theories of the
symbol in order to illustrate their meaning and to assess his
contribution. We have discovered that, like a Monsieur
Jourdain, he had practiced a mode of expression in
ignorance of the terminology. Although we could continue
our study by interrelating major and minor themes in his
poetry: despair, *ennui*, remorse, the abyss, hope, love,
death, the sea, the cemetery, Paris, the prison, bells,
spiders, etc., we should only be repeating what can be
found elsewhere in the literature on the poet. Most of
these themes we shall have touched upon in various
contexts before we finish.

Another side of our subject invites treatment. Certainly
an important aspect of "suggestiveness" is that tendency
of poetry since Baudelaire to defy, or to enlarge, the
classical conception of poetic unity, by stressing what the
poet himself described as "le thyrse." In the "moral and
poetic sense the thyrsis is a sacerdotal emblem," in the
physical sense a stick around which "in capricious mean-
ders stems and flowers play and frolic, the former sinuous
and evasive, the latter leaning like bells or cups upside
down." The stick is the masculine will, "straight, firm, and
unshakeable"; the flowers are the feminine element, "exe-
cuting around the male prestidigious pirouettes." And who
will be so bold as to declare which is made for the sake of
the other? [1]

Some students have more than taken Baudelaire at his

word, and Symbolisme has been connected especially with a growth of natural detail along the line of march, the "vehicle" sometimes like a float over-flowing with vines and flowers advancing slowly along the "tenor" of a path which is seems to overgrow. Empson has added in our day his acute consciousness of "ambiguity"; and the realization that "paraphraseable meaning" is only a major thrust of meaning has given rise in some circles to the idea of a literary structure as a set of themes holding one another in suspension by mutual opposition. These are said to form a "pattern"; but it is sometimes forgotten that any real "pattern" in order to have meaning must always require subordination of parts to a dominant effect.

"Ambiguity" in Baudelaire deserves its study, and it has received full and subtle attention in a book by Judd Hubert [2] on *L'Esthétique des Fleurs du mal*. We ourselves do not think that ambiguities are so many or matter so much if we keep the stick firmly in view while we enjoy the *fioriture* of the vine. In Baudelaire the "tenor," it seems to us, governs the "vehicle" firmly. His practice of "symbolisme" here too is conservative, and "ambiguity" is what Wheelwright calls more exactly "plurisignation." What is most "classical" in Baudelaire is that strict unity which he diversifies, sometimes riskily, but which he seems anxious to regain even at the cost of an awkward straining.

But even this aspect of the poet's work we shall touch upon, at least, in our final enterprise: to study the structure of his poems in order to observe the various ways in which music, suggestiveness, synaesthesia, and metaphor are organized into unity. From this study we shall hope to approximate a little more exactly a definition of the Baudelairean symbol.

i

A study of the structures in *Les Fleurs du mal* to determine how Baudelaire actually uses *le symbole* might well begin with a major instance, "Le Balcon." It is a poem based upon a "happy moment"; indeed the speaker, carried away by his experience, even boasts of his power to evoke such moments: "Je sais l'art d'évoquer les minutes heureuses." Snuggling close to his mistress' knees, he can recall "la beauté des caresses," "le charme des soirs," lit by the warmth of the coals from the grate as darkness thickens into a partition enclosing them in a tender intimacy: "Et tes pieds s'endormaient dans mes mains fraternelles." In such moments, "Que l'espace est profond! que le coeur est puissant!" These are indeed moments, to revert from the poem to the well-known passage in *Fusées*, "when time and space are deeper, and the feeling of existence is immensely increased," moments when "the depth of life is revealed completely in the spectacle . . . which one has before one's eyes."

What was the spectacle, in this instance? His mistress in her gentleness and goodness to the lover. It was the time for the saying of "imperishable things." Synaesthesia in Baudelaire's poetry has seldom been more appropriate than in the sentence: "Je croyais respirer le parfum de ton sang." To breathe in the perfume of her blood, to guess in the darkness at her pupils, to drink in her breath, "ô douceur! ô poison!" In this poem of the most tender intimacy of body and mind, only that O *poison!* hints at the usual Baudelairean ambivalence, as a tart but momentary reminder of passage from the ecstasy of the heart's power to the ecstasy of destruction. But for the moment, and because of such moments, the beloved, modeled after Jeanne Duval, Baudelaire's quadroon mistress and usually celebrated in a "demonic" context, is "mère des souvenirs, maîtresse des maîtresses," maternity and mastery, the source of the lover's pleasures and of his "duties."

What is the "symbol" in this poem? Certainly there is no "symbol as component," no dominant metaphor or cluster of metaphors, no core of meaning requiring special attention or interpretation within the poem as a whole as its real substance distinguishable from the apparent substance. The poem is an evocation of experiences of consummation, "les soirs au balcon," in the presence of the "mother of memories." The poem "has" no symbol; it is symbol in the Goethean sense, that is, it is the evocation

and the perpetuation in language of an experience capable
in the creative energies it can release in the shaping poet
and the sympathetic reader, of suggesting the "universal."
It becomes itself as a poem an "eminent instance" of the
ideal fullness of human love finding its ideal language in
an experience of the infinite. "O serments! ô parfums! ô
baisers infinis!"

At the very end the poet asks the seemingly inevitable
question, asked before him by Lamartine and after him by
Proust: "What happens to our experiences, even our high
moments when they are gone?" Proust's Marcel was to
imagine that they are ever with us, but dependent for their
evocation upon the chance sensation and the artistic
heroism that will not let the exceptional moment go
without wresting from it its secret. The lover in Lamartine's "Le Lac" will argue himself into an at least
provisional belief that high moments of love become part
of the very texture of "nature" that has been privileged to
witness them. Baudelaire's lover merely asks whether they
will rise from an abyss not to be plumbed, just as the sun
rises, renewed, from its washing in the depths of the sea?
One of the poet's almost obsessive images is that of
le gouffre, that falling away of everything, and of the
self, into nothingness. But here he does not press the
point. His mood is different from that of Lamartine's
lover, who takes his mind off the experience of love even as
he seeks to honor it by some extraordinary perpetuation.
Baudelaire's is not even the mood of impassioned meditation, but the more "musical" mood that wonders where
high experiences go only in order to enjoy for a moment
the feeling of their transiency and the imagined triumph,
held as bare possibility, of their return with the sun in its
daily renewal. "O serments! ô parfums! ô baisers infinis!"

Thus, as we shall see, though a majority of Baudelaire's
poems have symbols as components, a good number of
them, including some of his best, coming from all periods
in his production, are symbols in what we have called the
"Goethean" sense.[3] Yet the passage from the poem as
symbol in the Goethean sense—in which any successful

poem is "symbol" — to the ordinary sense of a "symbolic" poem can be a subtle one, concerning which not all competent readers will agree. Let us examine two poems from the *Tableaux Parisiens* whose apparent similarity in "realistic" base will make their differences more instructive. In "Les Petites Vieilles" the structure is anticipated in the speaker's observation that in the "sinuous folds of ancient capitals" like Paris, everything "even horror, turns into enchantment." Cases in point are some old ladies, who are "souls," after all, that we must love (the poem is dedicated to Victor Hugo), though they look like "monstres disloqués." The poet's description of their physical activity accents the animal and the mechanical in their movements, summing up with an image of bells to whose cord "a Demon hangs without pity."

The moral silhouette which follows plays again on the pathos of dislocation: the old ladies' eyes, "piercing like gimlets" are essentially "the divine eyes of the little girl, which is amazed and laughs at anything that glitters." A quaint observation that many old ladies' coffins are of a child's size yields the thought that "Death in its wisdom puts into such coffins a symbol of a bizarre and captivating taste," as though the fragile creatures were each one "going slowly toward a new cradle." What saves the poet from sentimentality at this point is a very precise and literal-minded bit of "figuring," ironically dry in expression and angular in rhythm:

> A moins que, méditant sur la géométrie,
> Je ne cherche, à l'aspect de ces membres discords,
> Combien de fois il faut que l'ouvrier varie
> La forme de la boîte où l'on met tous ces corps.

(Unless, thinking in geometrical terms, / I begin to figure, in view of all the discords of limb, / how many times it is necessary for the workman to vary / the form of the box where they put all those bodies.)

Returning to the old ladies' eyes, which he had described before the quaint excursus as "shining like those holes where water sleeps at night," the poet uses his image in building up to his first climax:

> *Ces yeux sont des puits faits d'un million de larmes,*
> *Des creusets qu'un métal refroidi pailleta . . .*
> *Ces yeux mystérieux ont d'invincibles charmes*
> *Pour celui que l'austère Infortune allaita!*

(Those eyes are pools made of a million tears, / Crucibles that a cooling metal spangled . . . those mysterious eyes cast an invincible spell / upon him whom . . . austere Mischance took to nurse.)

The old ladies, then, have been presented as peculiarly helpless and appealing instances of the misfortune that, perhaps, is life itself; at any rate they have a particular charm and meaning for the particularly unfortunate. Thus far, there is no symbol except in the sense in which any good poem, according to Goethe, and to Coleridge, Cassirer, Urban, and Langer is "symbol." What in this poem comes closest to a component symbol of the "indirect" kind, based on a metaphor, is the meditation on the tortuousness of a small coffin to hold the shapes dislocated by life; and that impression has been forced upon us by the odd literalness of the image. At least, once the reader has "seen" the box, it is likely to "stand" in his memory as the microcosm of the poem as a whole.

In the second section the poet comes down to cases: in a few lines he disposes of two or three actresses among his old ladies, hardly remembered or completely forgotten. More memorable among these frail creatures are those who made a "honey out of sorrow" and rode Devotion's "powerful Hippogryph" to heaven. (Baudelaire's Paris, we must emphasize, is seen through a mind educated in the classics and therefore able to include in his vision the "fracas roulant de l'omnibus" and Frascati, the Vestal Virgin, the priestess of Thalia, and Tivoli.) Outstanding among the old ladies are the war-widow, the woman whose husband added to the normal load of human suffering, and that other, the "Madonna whose heart is pierced through by her son."

Section three now focuses upon a particular instance, one martial old lady with marble brow made for the laurel. When "the falling sun bloodies the skies with crimson wounds," she will listen to a military concert sitting upright, avidly sniffling up the warlike song, her eye blinking like that of an old eagle.

"Telles vous cheminez, stoïques et sans plaintes," insulted, frightened, ashamed to exist: "étranges destinées! Débris d'humanité pour l'éternité mûrs." The poet broods upon them tenderly and thoughtfully, as though he were their father, worrying about their tomorrows. His "multiplied heart" enjoys all their vices and his soul "shines resplendent" with all their virtues.

> *Ruines! ma famille! o cerveaux congénères!*
> *Je vous fais chaque soir un solennel adieu!*
> *Où serez-vous demain, Eves octogénaires,*
> *Sur qui pèse la griffe effroyable de Dieu?*

(Ruins! my family! O congenerate minds! / Each night I bid you a solemn adieu! / Where will you be tomorrow, octogenarian Eves, / upon whom presses God's frightful claw?)

Yet these are not the "rejects" of blind process, but the daughters of Eve. Herein consists their Pascalian "grandeur" and "bassesse," that "across the chaos of living cities," such souls should travel, from little cradle to little coffins hard to shape to the distortions of life, suffering but uncomplaining, yet under judgment. Grace and glory forgotton, they have no friend, no father but the eye of the poet, and he sees them dispassionately, even ironically, but not merely as victims. They are "pour l'éternité mûrs," and Baudelaire's eternity is never a neutral timelessness but the symbol of an absolute value.

Obviously in such a poem the "realism" in depiction of city and character adds the touch of "modern" beauty with its sense of evil seeming to outweigh the sense of God, without whose imagined indifference that evil nevertheless would lack its characteristic poignancy. These ladies and their lives are not symbols except in the sense in which all poetry may be "symbol." One group among the big city's unfortunates, in its activity and its fate, is made to "look like" life and to universalize life's meaning. Thus the literary symbol existed, as concrete universal, even when Homer represented his gods as looking upon one human battlefield and as marvelling at the strange pitiableness of the human lot. Poetry in the symbol as concrete universal presents a particular instance with only the inevitable indirection of fiction and of its own representative nature; it presents a "universe" which we then translate in our own interpretation more or less immediately and more or less credulously into a universal.

What distinguishes a Symboliste is a radically metaphorical vision abstracting not the "common sense" aspect of objects but their special sense, propitiously revealed. The language which grasps and expresses may depart in varying degrees, but more than in other poetry, from the patterns of "discourse." Compare another poem of Paris appearing with the one just discussed in the *Revue contemporaine* for September 15, 1859 and later added to *Les Fleurs du mal*, whose first edition had been of 1857. In "Les Sept Vieillards," again the setting is Paris, "fourmillante cité, cité pleine de rêves," and the eerie quality of experience in the city receives even greater stress than in "Les Petites Vieilles." Here the "specter in full daylight hooks on to the passer-by" and "mysteries everywhere flow like the sap of things in the narrow canals of the powerful colossus." The poet is in a state of nerves and what he sees comes through a dirty yellow fog. He spies an old man whose rags imitate the color of the rainy sky, with "Judas-beard, stiff as a sword," a glance keener than frost from an eye dipped in bitterness, and wickedness ashine in his eyes. His spine appears broken and at right angles to his feet, and his stick seems an extension of his face as he walks. The "baroque" specter stumbles through mud and snow, as though crushing the dead under his worn-out shoes and "hostile to the universe rather than indifferent." And when (like Macbeth) the poet sees not one but *seven* of these figures marching "toward an unknown goal" the "hideous monsters" having about them an "eternal air," no wonder he flees, locking his door, feverish, confused and awestruck, "wounded by mystery and by absurdity."

> *Vainement ma raison voulait prendre la barre;*
> *La tempête en jouant déroutait ses efforts,*
> *Et mon âme dansait, dansait, vieille gabarre*
> *Sans mâts, sur une mer monstrueuse et sans bords.*

(Vainly did my reason seek to seize the tiller; / the tempest made a mockery of every effort, / and my soul danced, danced like an old lighter, / mastless, upon a sea monstrous and without shore.)

Everything is done to unify the experience artistically and to make it psychologically plausible. The image of the "lighter" at the end is attuned to fog and to the mystery "flowing" through the canals of the city. The poet is in a state of nerves (where one *might well* see such specters); yet, as we have insisted, special psychological conditions in the perceiver, for Baudelaire, do not necessarily invalidate the truth of what is seen. What the poet had had was a vision of evil, something seven times multiplied and eternal. These seven old men are not life's unfortunates like the old ladies, registered at the city hall in any city and from the contemplation of whose misfortunes one may be tempted to form a picture of life. They are, like Calibans, figures issuing full-born from the poet's creative imagination, needing not a model in reality but only a hint that may itself arise in a special circumstance. Baudelaire, we have seen, insists that the poet shall add something of himself to what nature offers; here he adds a maximum. In this poem Paris provides a dirty fog, a street shaken by heavy tumbrils; and as for a character of Poe's, "discutant avec mon âme déjà lasse," out of that fog evil is born, contorted, Judas-like, eternal. In "Les Sept Viellards" the atmosphere in the city fuses with the *état d'âme* of the poet to give form to figures born of the outer and the inner at once. In "Les Petites Vieilles" the atmosphere helps to account for the old ladies and supports them realistically and interpretation is based on the evidence; in the case of the old men interpretation strains toward becoming a proof by creating figures, like metaphor, at once unlike and like. The Judas-figure is born not of Paris but of the sense of evil, yet perfectly acclimated, at the moment of the poem, to Paris. We can get an inkling here of the way in which the dream, the vision, the nightmare are related to the symbol, and why a Baudelaire is fascinated by the tales of Poe, and a Novalis says that all true literature must be *märchenhaft*. For the symbol of the Symboliste, that work of an indirection beyond the normal indirection of poetry, strains toward a meaning which "reality," conceived as independently external, cannot launch by itself and which it certainly cannot support.

Thus in "Les Petites Vieilles" a certain realistic verisimilitude supports the universal significance which is suggested: old ladies are like *that*, or can be like *that*, and we go on from there. In "Les Sept Vieillards," what is offered us is hardly believable; we must in a special sense "take the poet's word for it." Where the object interpreted from our customary experience, what we call "reality," cannot be our anchor, we demand a special convincingness calling on all the resources of language, even the relevant powers of other arts. The symbol must be adequate to something which is in the highest degree, though not totally, unspecified. We require reassurance from something in the tone, in the rhythm, in the very sense of solidity impressed upon us by a maximum unity of form and content in order to believe that what is evoked is not merely "imaginary," nor "imaginative," but *real*, though needing to be translated into our language, as the eternal menace of evil was translated into the figures of the seven old men. Here we catch the meaning of "magie" and "sorcellerie évocatoire." Or, to use a contemporary image, compared to the symbol as concrete universal, the "symbole" of Baudelaire is a kind of "space-platform" created by the coming together of units in orbit, forces impelled toward a pattern located, for our ordinary geography, "nowhere."

The symbol in the Goethean sense, or as concrete universal, we may summarize, works under the guidance of a presumptive "truth to life," in order, especially in an "eminent instance," to give perception of a "higher truth." The Baudelairean "symbole," characteristically, that is, when non-Goethean, aims at truth to the deeper realities of existence; but it denies "truth" and "life" to any experience not infused with vision. The traditional "mirror" image for art uses "light" as a merely neutral element, as that without which reflection is impossible. No classicist, of course, ever takes the mirror image literally, but he does accept what it is meant to suggest: that the artist sees by an essentially neutral light, from an essentially neutral point of view in his work. The result, it is presumed, is that such an artist presents life, as Matthew Arnold would say, "as it really is."

For Baudelaire at his most characteristic, the roles of "light" and of the "reality," which it is said to illuminate, become essentially interdependent. The artist at the moment of creation does not distinguish between the so-called "external" object, which is supposedly "mirrored," and the "light" which suffuses it from the so-called internal source, the artist's own vision. That vision is an "inner" and an "outer" reality simultaneously: how can he know what he sees until he sees it? In Baudelaire's discussion of "color" in Delacroix, what is at stake in his advocacy is not that there should be more or brighter color in pictures or poems, but a fundamental principle of vision and construction. Translating from the painter's "color" into literature, the term means "music," suggestion, atmosphere, metaphor, unity of form and content—all those powers of "language-meaning" which are another name for the poet's vision suffusing and infusing that co-ordinate something, not of themselves, toward which they strain, the union with which is felt as the sense of real reality.

If we accept the idea of "symbol" at all as it developed in the nineteenth century, "light," "color," as metaphors for the effective activity of the mind and spirit in knowledge and creation, become positive factors in *all* art. But, though we are incapable of distinguishing the subtler nuances of the transition from one type to another, we can think of two types of artists and lovers of art. Artists of the first type prefer a created object whose effect upon them does not remove them uncomfortably far from what they feel confident is the "common sense" of sane men in their view of the world.[4] Those of the second, their sense of reality being dissatisfied with the "common sense," strain with every resource at their command to reach closer to the reality that beckons beyond. What we are offering at present is the main difference, perhaps, between "classic" and "romantic" as modes of vision. The classicist, in polemics, will of course insist that his "common sense," which is more than the "common sense" of his social group or of his time, reaches the eternal reality; the romantic, just as convincedly, will attribute to conservatism and convention the refusal to see the "living truth" beyond "common sense." This is perhaps the only war that is really necessary. Even here the wise man will imitate the citizens in *Aucassin et Nicolette* who cooled the enthusiasm of their youthful ally for the total destruction of their enemy.

We see Goethe, then, in those "classical" moments when he is sure that Romanticism is "disease," set up a stance like that of a fine Greek statue even as he reaches in art beyond the phenomenon to the *Ur-phänomenon*. Baudelaire, even though he can assess its cost and eventual betrayal, will try hashish for some more easily manageable foretaste of that experience of the "vast" reality, both horizontal and vertical, that is the source and the reward of poetry. For an infinite seen as an indefeasible order of essences, Mallarmé will religiously subject his own inner life, as well as language, to an excruciating <u>fastidiousness</u>. The young Rimbaud will plunge into a "dérèglement de tous les sens." Tolstoy, at least in *Anna Karenina*, will picture an artist for whom the use of "light" and "color" is so neutral that he will represent the poet's function as merely that of taking the "wrappings" off reality in order to expose its living core of meaning. Perhaps it is only to a Tolstoy, so sure of the identity of his vision and truth, that it would occur to describe the artist's function in this way. But it is clear that, despite his contempt for Racine, he is closer to Racine and Goethe in this aspect of his art than to Baudelaire. On the other hand Dostoevsky, with a theory that the extreme cases and situations convey the greatest reality and truth, reminds us of Baudelaire, who would have seen the Symbolisme in him just as he did in Balzac and Hugo. Light and color in Dostoevsky are forces so positive that he can make us take them for common day, and his evil men carry their "infini" with them like Baudelaire's, though they are more fully fleshed.

The Baudelairean *symbole*, we conclude, is based on metaphor of a radical type and is more "indirect" than the Goethean symbol. The preponderant power is in the imagination, which uses "nature" as a dictionary, and shapes it in forms that are more than an idealization or a heightening of the model of "nature" which common sense fashions. In "Les Petites Vieilles," the old women remain fundamentally what they are for common sense even as they become symbols of a universal "condition humaine." In "Les Sept Vieillards," the human shape, countenance, and attitude as understood by common sense are used more as "material" or "stuff" in order to express economically and subtly *something other* than what could be intimated by their "natural" appearance reduced to its essentials and heightened. The satanic old man is presumably "in Paris," as are the old ladies, but Paris has ceased to be geography, and the old man multiplied by seven has ceased to be human: the manifold is a "projection" of spiritual meaning. Some of us, in certain contexts, implying that we are grasping an objective character of the object, speak of a cliff as "grim" or "sinister." The poet presents the sinister quality of a man multiplied into an objective characteristic of reality. His spiritual energy requires objects of common sense less as models than as materials by which to express its insights. Thus Baudelaire's "Symbolisme," properly so-called, is at a different "remove" from "nature" than Goethe's; it is more "indirect" in the sense that the metaphor at its base

is concerned less with the "likeness to nature" of its
concrete term than to use an element of "nature" in order
to project a "second nature" which is also "reality." But
we would remind the reader that there is always something
arbitrary in differentiations and in the examples chosen to
establish them, and that the movement from the type of
symbol which we have called "Goethean" to the Baudelairean symbol is more apparent in extreme than in
intermediate instances.

ii

Goethe, as we have seen, defines allegory as a
general idea which has endowed itself with a body,
whereas the meaning of symbol is shaped in the body in
which it grows. But the distinction between the two, from
the reader's point of view, must depend on the effect of the
literary work. Thus that work is allegorical, in Goethe's
sense, which, whatever its superficial appearance, conveys
to the reader the impression that it is a thought invested
with a body, and not a body that is food for thought.
What looks like "allegory" may be symbol, and vice versa.
One of the most striking characteristics of his art, as we
have seen in Baudelaire's metaphors, is his renewal, nay
transformation, of the coldest form of "allegory," the
moral personification. In "Recueillement" the miracle is
the fusion of the greatest intimacy with seeming abstractions marked by capital letters: *Douleur, Soir, Plaisir,
Années, Regret, Soleil, Nuit.*

> *Sois sage, ô ma Douleur, et tiens-toi plus tranquille.*
> *Tu réclamais le Soir; il descend; le voici:*
> *Une atmosphère obscure enveloppe la ville,*
> *Aux uns portant la paix, aux autres le souci.*
>
> *Pendant que des mortels la multitude vile,*
> *Sous le fouet du Plaisir, ce bourreau sans merci,*
> *Va cueillir des remords dans la fête servile,*
> *Ma Douleur, donne-moi la main; viens par ici.*
>
> *Loin d'eux. Vois se pencher les défuntes Années,*
> *Sur les balcons du ciel, en robes surannées;*
> *Surgir du fond des eaux le Regret souriant;*

Le Soleil moribond s'endormir sous une arche,
Et, comme un long linceul traînant à l'Orient,
Entends, ma chère, entends la douce Nuit qui marche.

As one speaks to a restless child the poet turns to his *Douleur,* the suffering that has become so intimately the ache of existence itself. The child has been impatient for "le Soir," and now it comes bringing peace to some and cares to the base multitude, driven by the whip of Pleasure, that merciless executioner, to cull the flowers of remorse in a festival of slaves. But "Come away, give me your hand," says the poet. The image is that of a man who takes his sorrow as one would take a child to the spectacle of our mortal "show." And there, at the show, as in an ancient pageantry, appear the long-dead Years, leaning over the balconies of heaven in old-fashioned dresses, while below, Regret surges up smiling from the deep. The tender smile with which man learns to look back over a past grown dear and quaint prepares us for the quality of the climax. "Le Soleil moribond" goes to sleep under the arch of a bridge in a certain solemnity of rhythm. This prepares for the most triumphant entry in French literature in lines whose long, slow, liquid music, stiffened by the repeated nasals of "traînant," "orient," "entends, ma chère, entends" evoke the long-awaited procession of "gentle Night" with its train, both sheet and shroud, trailing grandly from the source of things.

The child has been impatient for le Soir; it is given the vision of "la douce Nuit," that gentle and majestic annulment of our human hopes, all perhaps except the final one. A poem like this, better than medieval allegories outside of Dante, would seem to support C. S. Lewis' thesis that "allegory" rose out of the Christian consciousness under the special stress of conflict between good and evil. The inner life of Baudelaire was certainly the theatre of moral powers intensifying one another by their very conflict, and it is for this reason, perhaps, that in his poetry so many moral abstractions can be capitalized and humanized. On the inner stage of "Recueillement" even *le Soir* and *le Soleil* become personages and are crowned with their capitals; yet the artist discriminates also, and there is no capital, for instance, for *paix* and *souci*. Thus allegory becomes symbol not by some external mark but by an internal creative stress. One may even speak in this connection of the "mythic," which, after all, is a vision of cosmic forces engaged in the drama that involves human life. Because of such not unusual effects in Baudelaire's poetry we have insisted on the metaphysical context in which the poet's imagination worked. The deep meaning of the theory of "analogies" and "correspondences" in Baudelaire's poetry lies here, and not merely in encouraging him to fix his eye on "nature" which supplied metaphors. It was a philosophy or explanation accepted because it helped to account for, and thus also to support, what his poetic imagination postulated by its practice.

What we have said seems as true in a poem of "spleen" as in a poem of reconciliation. "Spleen" LXXVII ("Quand le ciel bas et lourd pèse comme un couvercle") weaves together the elements of a rainy day of the spirit when the low and heavy sky weighs upon us like a "lid" and the earth is changed into a "damp dungeon," the sweeping gusts of rain imitating the "bars" of a vast prison. The "longs ennuis" weigh on the groaning spirit, with "Hope, like a bat, striking against the walls with timid wing and hitting its head against the rotten ceiling-timbers." What is worse, a "muted multitude of infamous spiders comes and stretches its nets in the very depths of our brains." Perhaps only Dostoevsky's Svidrigailov has known a grimmer spleen: "one little room, like a bath-house in the country, black and grimy and spiders in every corner, and that's all eternity is."

The unbearable pressure suddenly erupts into a leaping of bells, casting toward heaven a frightful howl "like spirits wandering and without a Country, who begin to moan and groan without let-up."

> Et de longs corbillards, sans tambours ni musique,
> Défilent lentement dans mon âme; l'Espoir,
> Vainou, pleure, et l'Angoisse atroce, despotique,
> Sur mon crâne incliné plante son drapeau noir.

(And long hearses, without music or drum, / file slowly in my soul; Hope, / vanquished, weeps, and atrocious Anguish, despotic, / on my bowed cranium implants its black flag.)

After three stanzas in which the physical image and its moral equivalent are kept parallel, a fourth stanza transforms the physical into the moral: "bells" become "wandering spirits," the "lid" image of the first line develops its ultimate implications, and *out of the soul* files the long hearse of death. The gradual transition from the outer atmosphere to the inner atmosphere where the drama has its dénouement is an accomplished piece of poetic tactics; as a result, here, in the soul, "L'Espoir" and "L'Angoisse" become moral realities, one weeping vanquished, the other, despotic in its very assertion of victory over hope, plants that unforgettable black flag. The kind of vision that sees the virtues and the vices not as names given to modes of behavior in the practical bookkeeping of the mores but as moral powers acutely distinguishable makes possible Dante's *Divine Comedy*. Baudelaire has that vision and, as in the case of Dante, his "allegory" tends to become "symbol." [5]

But let us test his practice in poems which invite allegorical treatment such as "La Beauté" (1857), "Hymne à la Beauté" (1860), and all the more since the titles promise a definition. In the first, "La Beauté," it almost seems as if the poet were transposing from an allegorical sculpture to literature. "Je suis belle, ô mortels! comme un rêve de pierre . . ." His sense of the beautiful in this sonnet is conveyed through the coolness of snow and the whiteness of swan's down, through immobility, impassibility and grandeur. It is a lapidary ideal, and he hints throughout at a figure of marble or stone. Yet, in spite of the "sphinx incompris" enthroned in the blue, and the "grandes attitudes" which Beauty seems to "borrow" from the proudest monuments, despite the mute and eternal love, like a love of "matter" that she inspires in the poet who has "bruised" himself against her breast, she is not stone but truly a "dream" of stone.

Car j'ai pour fasciner ces dociles amants,
De purs miroirs qui font toutes choses plus belles:
Mes yeux, mes larges yeux aux clartés éternelles.

"Beauty" who speaks here makes no list of attributes but describes herself in metaphor. She modulates from the effect of a statue with its unbending absolute (which is nevertheless "a dream in stone") to that of a pure mirror identified with the eyes which see in eternal clarity a beauty that is not entirely of this world. Added to the metaphors within each of the two major images, the shift from stone to light confirms the effect of symbol.

In the later *Hymne à la Beauté* (1860) the poet faces a similar problem, to belie the abstractions of his title, to give life to what will otherwise remain a string of attributes. "Viens-tu du ciel profond ou sors-tu de l'abîme, O Beauté?" Here we have the intimacy of familiar and direct address for what is problematic. The shock of such intimacy with what is, on one side at least, the infernal, the fatal, and the irresponsible—the kisses of Beauty being a "philtre," with Horror not the least charming of her "jewels," Murder a cherished "trinket" dancing amorously on her proud belly—begin to dissipate the sense of abstractness in conception. Furthermore, "Beauty," in this poem, keeps the imagination busy with her activities. Her glance, like a wine, pours indiscriminately both good and evil; she scatters fragrances like a stormy night; she has in Destiny a dog following at her heels; she sows haphazardly joy and sorrow; she walks on the dead mockingly. As in the preceding poem, the de-allegorizing by metaphor would be clinched, if necessary, by such an image as "L'Ephémère ébloui vole vers toi, chandelle, / Crépite, flambe et dit: Bénissons ce flambeau!" (The moth flies toward the candle, / crackles, flames and says: Let us bless this torch!)

The image expresses again, in addition, the essential ambiguity: Beauty, blessing or curse?

De Satan ou de Dieu, qu'importe? Ange ou Sirène,
Qu'importe, si tu rends, — fée aux yeux de velours,

> Rhythme, parfum, lueur, ô mon unique reine!—
> L'univers moins hideux et les instants moins lourds.

At the very end the poet, uniting them to the intimate magic of "fée aux yeux de velours," dares to cry out "Rhythm, perfume, light"—one can afford abstract commendations as an added poetry for what is indubitably alive!

Which of the two poems expresses Baudelaire's sense of beauty? The answer is both and neither. These are not poems in definition but responses to envisaged qualities of Beauty. In "La Beauté" her impregnable and rather forbidding immobility and the resistless invitation in her eyes of eternal light are the two sides of an awesome numen. In "Hymne à la Beauté," she is still "rhythme, parfum, lueur," in spite of sufferings which, like a demonic creature, she exacts as the price of the antidote against the ugliness of life and the dreadful weight of *ennui*.

We would suggest also that the earlier poem expresses the postulation toward heaven, with its analogue in life the kind of feeling inspired in the poet by the beauty of a Madame Sabatier. The later poem, coming a year after "Le Voyage" (1859) and with a similar élan, "Anywhere out of this world," be it the heaven or hell of Beauty, expresses the postulation toward hell and has its analogue in what the poet felt for a Jeanne Duval or a Marie Daubrun. Modern beauty must have something of "ironie" and of "diabolisme." At any rate these poems are not bodies devised for definitions but atmospheres of love that initiate into the intimacies of total response to what Baudelaire idolizes. Both poems have one element in common, the awe of the worshipper as one who fears and yet finds joy in what he fears.

iii

Related to "allegory" are those poems in which Baudelaire seeks to revitalize or renew images which have become part of the cultural domain, which therefore tend with time to lose their full symbolic or mythic force and to become terms of reference or "allusions." The "Muse" and figures from Greek or Roman mythology, "Satan" (or the "Demon") or the "Angel," the "Madonna," characters from the Old and New Testament, can become counters which merely "stand for" or are "equivalent to" certain ideas of moral and religious importance.

Not so obviously related to allegory are those ideas, images, and forms which a poet may borrow from works of art already created. Apart from questions of literary property, the real objection to a poet's use of these materials stems from the danger of "allegory." What the poet borrows he is tempted to use as concept or illustration, as a mechanical technique not completely assimilated in creation.

Robert Vivier has indicated that a large number of Baudelaire's poems draw upon the fine arts and from the poet's reading of other poems and writings. Though Jean Prévost has retorted quite properly that it is not what the poet uses that matters but how he uses it and what he makes of it, the subject deserves further discussion in our present context. Let us grant that in some sense a poem makes use of "life." But our idea of "life" is always an interpretation based in part upon our "temperament," that is, upon a characteristic rigidity in our response to experience, upon our social, religious and economic circumstances, upon the reading, including the reading of literature, that may have affected our thought, our emotions and associations, our actions.

The point is that Baudelaire brought to bear upon experience not only a temperament mystical in a number of respects, but a love for, and an early training in, looking at prints and pictures. To these he added a considerable literary, but not merely literary, culture. He has been for many par excellence the poet of "modern life" because he insisted upon the modern element in beauty, because he had a quadroon mistress, stupid and treacherous but obsessional, because he wrote of Paris the big city with its heartless mystery, with its prostitutes, its Lesbians and its drug addicts, because he came closer than Job to carrying out the advice, "Curse God and die," and because these and other forms of the "frisson nouveau" came together explosively in a volume whose very title was a challenge to respectability and even sanity, *Les Fleurs du mal*. Nevertheless, the first discerning reader might have glimpsed what subsequent studies have brought into the light. What characterizes Baudelaire is not his portrayal of life, which, whatever the word may mean for aesthetics, he shares with all other good poets, but that he did exactly what he said he would do. In an age when realism imagined the artist as an impassive recorder, he brought consciously a personal and ineluctible point of view to bear upon phases of life whose expression had hitherto been denied clearance as serious literature.

That personal and ineluctible point of view was "cultured," that is, it envisioned every experience, no matter how trivial and how sordid, in terms of the great "myth" of humanity that is classical and Christian tradition. What is more, these traditions retained still for Baudelaire, to a greater degree than for Mallarmé, their mythic power. It was a brilliant adolescent, Rimbaud, in radical revolt, seeking to make himself something other than Western man, who was to declare like a voice in Revelations, "Behold, I make all things new" and who, though he thought Baudelaire a "god" and a real "voyant" found his form a bit trivial. What is exciting and exemplary in *Les Illuminations* is the effort of the newly declared young "god" to create a language of his own for a transcendent vision of his own achieved through the discipline of debauch. The voice of the God of the old Testament has been mediated through a human tradition, "Moses and the prophets"; the voice of the new "god" was to fix images, in the god's own hand, on his own "painted plates" in *Les Illuminations*, or to speak in tongues of fire.

But Baudelaire could not see a swan escaped from a Parisian circus waddling helplessly in the dust without thought of Andromache ("Le Cygne") and he interpreted even Lesbianism as a Christian might but a Greek would not, that is, as a misguided effort to assuage the thirst for the infinite. His insistence upon a modern quality in beauty is not to be taken as a rejection of either Virgil or Racine. What is shocking in his subject matter is tempered and distanced by inevitability of form, and the intensified aesthetic values satisfy the need of the ideal which in the older poetry was met by moral values positively expressed. Baudelaire transforms all his material through a mind in which culture itself is a living force, and this establishes a new "correspondence," and revitalizes or renews what has already been made. Thus in "La Malade," the muse becomes a woman with hollow eyes who has had bad dreams, and what is gained in intimacy is not lost in imaginative force. In "Don Juan aux Enfers," the hero of Tirso de Molina, of Molière and of Byron, in his cold contempt in the other world for those who even in that world remain bound to him by love or hate, becomes the symbol of the Baudelairean "dandy." In "Bohémiens en voyage" we are in the Bible and out of the Bible as we follow the long line of "the prophetic tribe with ardent gaze," for whom the rock gushes water, the desert blooms, for whom, even as it looks dejectedly to heaven, remembering the chimeras of the past, there is opened "the familiar Empire of shadows to come." "Le Reniement de St. Pierre" with its "Saint Pierre a renié Jesus. Il a bien fait," uses blasphemy to dramatize the Baudelairean, and characteristically modern impatience which, demanding a heaven here and now, is exasperated by the slow-working paradoxes of suffering and self-sacrifice. In "A une Madone. Ex voto dans le goût espagnol," the poet makes for his "madonna," a "crown" of verse, his Jealousy furnishing a mantle embroidered with tears, his Desire a robe of kisses, his Respect, satin slippers, his stormy spirit, an incense, etc. What saves the poem as vision are the seven sharp knives of the cardinal sins (or of the sufferings of the Virgin) that the poet, with a kind of baroque savagery, and in order to "complete her role of Marie," aiming at the depths of her love, will plant "dans ton coeur pantelant, dans ton coeur sanglotant, dans ton coeur ruisselant." Is the poem a heavily stylized revenge, as has been suggested, upon Marie Daubrun for abandoning him for Banville? At any rate the poet has personalized an established symbol in a monument of imaginative sadism.

The most suggestive example in a major poem of Baudelaire's treatment, not so much of paintings as of the imaginative world of painters, is "Les Phares." Here the problem for the poet is fourfold: (a) He must not describe the work of a painter but evoke his world.

> *Leonard de Vinci, miroir profond et sombre,*
> *Où des anges charmants, avec un doux souris*
> *Tout chargé de mystère, apparaissent à l'ombre*
> *Des glaciers et des pins qui ferment leur pays;*

(Leonardi da Vinci, deep and somber mirror, / where charming angels, with a gentle smile / fraught with mystery, appear in the shadow / of glaciers and pines which seal off their country.) The painter's mirror, it is suggested, is no neutral reflector, but one "deep and somber," his own personal vision. Leonardo's world is presented as essentially that of the "Virgin and Child and St. Anne." The vision of the poet who is interpreting the painter is likewise creative and symbolic.

b) At the same time the poet must reconcile the needs of the poem being made, his vision of another artist, and the general consensus concerning that artist's vision. Baudelaire satisfies the first two requirements at the expense of the third:

> *Rembrandt, triste hôpital tout rempli de murmures,*
> *Et d'un grand crucifix décoré seulement,*
> *Où la prière en pleurs s'exhale des ordures,*
> *Et d'un rayon d'hiver traversé brusquement;*

(Rembrandt, sad hospital full of murmurs, / and decorated only with a large crucifix, / where prayer in tears rises out of ordures, / and which is suddenly traversed by a wintry ray.) But is this the Rembrandt of the "Night Watch" or even of the "Anatomy Lesson"? Only one aspect of the painter becomes "Rembrandt" for the poem.

c) Whatever the poet "sees" in the painters he must

relate in his poem in some kind of pattern. Thus the lethargy of the very excess of animal health, the flow of physical life in Rubens, give way to the subtle mystery of the spirit in Leonardo, which is followed by the "sad hospital" of Rembrandt and, in the same tonality, by Michelangelo's waste lands where Christs and Hercules mingle and powerful phantoms rise upright, with outstretched fingers tearing their shrouds. Transition is thus effected to Puget, "melancholy emperor of convicts sentenced to hard labor," creator of the "rages of boxers and faun-like impudence." Then the imagination and feelings are revived by the sudden contrast of the airy rhythms of the Watteau stanza: Watteau, "ce carnival," where hearts like butterflies wander aflame, where all is lighted by chandeliers, "qui versent la folie à ce bal tournoyant." Then we are in for the horrors of Goya, "cauchemar plein de choses inconnues, de foetus qu'on fait cuire au milieu des sabbats," and also of dreadful old ladies at the mirror and nude little girls prostituted to the demons of sex. Saved for the climax is the Delacroix stanza:

> *Delacroix, lac de sang hanté des mauvais anges,*
> *Ombragé par un bois de sapins toujours verts,*
> *Où, sous un ciel chagrin, des fanfares étranges*
> *Passent, comme un soupir étouffé de Weber.*

(Delacroix, lake of blood haunted by evil angels, / shaded by a wood of sapins evergreen, / where, under an angry sky, strange fanfares / pass, like a muffled sigh from Weber.)

Baudelaire himself quoted and commented upon this stanza in his "Exposition Universelle de 1855." He had been pointing out that, even seen from a distance too great for understanding or analysis of the subject, a Delacroix painting already produced upon the soul "une impression riche, heureuse ou mélancolique," and this because of a pre-established harmony in the mind of the painter between color and subject. "Il semble que cette couleur . . . pense par elle-même, indépendamment des objets qu'elle habille." One thinks of "harmonic et mélodie" in the presence of such an accord of colors, "et l'impression qu'on emporte de ses tableaux est souvent quasi musicale." [6]

The accord of image, rhythm and mood is to be found in Baudelaire's own poem, where the painters have been presented not in chronological order but in a blending of the synaesthesized senses with atmosphere. The stanza on Delacroix is especially noteworthy for the contrast of complementary colors, red and green, of their associations—lake of blood haunted by evil angels against the hope of sapins ever green—and what Baudelaire tells us himself is the romantic music of the horn, muffled like a sigh, against an angry heaven.

d) But the drift of single stanzas, of varied images and tones, working toward a kind of climax in what is, after all, only another stanza, requires a summary of the whole. Baudelaire knows this, and taking advantage of the tonality of the Delacroix stanza, he makes transition to

> Ces malédictions, ces blasphèmes, ces plaintes,
> Ces ecstases, ces cris, ces pleurs, ces Te Deum,
> Sont un écho redit par mille labyrinthes,
> C'est pour les coeurs mortels un divin opium.

It will be observed that the voices of lamentation and malediction are not the sole voices of art: there are ecstasies and Te Deums. And all these voices are an opium, indeed a "divine opium." But to present the meaning of a summary through abstractions will never do in a poem up to this point metaphorical throughout. The poet, picking up the "echoes" repeated from "labyrinthine" sources, creates the symbol of art itself: a militant cry of warning:

> C'est un cri répété par mille sentinelles,
> Un ordre renvoyé par mille porte-voix;
> C'est un phare allumé sur mille citadelles,
> Un appel de chasseurs perdus dans les grands bois!

Observe what happens to the title image as an illustration of the problem of blending, which Baudelaire in this instance does not solve with perfect success. "Un phare" is not in its immediate context a beacon light, as on a lighthouse, warning those at sea of danger. It is a beacon on land, or rather it is a thousand beacons lit on the citadels of human existence, a call for help, like a hunter's call in the deep woods. And this interpretation of the image is confirmed by the final stanza:

> Car c'est vraiment, Seigneur, le meilleur témoignage
> Que nous puissions donner de notre dignité
> Que cet ardent sanglot qui roule d'âge en âge
> Et vient mourir au bord de votre éternité.

It is the "ardent sanglot," the sob of an anguish, at once an order and an appeal, that is the best witness of our human dignity. It is man's reproach of God justified by his inborn aspiration toward the Infinite. "Le phare" is an image of this appeal and this reproach. But the appeal rolls from age to age, like a sea, and spends itself upon the shores of eternity. And the beacon, by poetic contamination, and thanks to the original meaning of Pharos, preserved in French, becomes the "lighthouse," and the poet the source of light and leading. But many forget that it is by the quality of his sorrow that the poet commends himself and humanity to the Eternal.[7]

Baudelaire's "transpositions" of the poetic personality of painters are thus made in fact to serve the poet's own vision of art in a poem of his own. We need have no fear of an imitation that becomes allegory. He is in fact most "painterly" not in his subject matter but in his effort to achieve color and music through language. What happens when the poet takes images and ideas not from paintings but from works of literature? Is the result a pastiche, a mosaic, or have the remembered elements become new words in the "dictionary" of art? Observe an extreme example in "Le Guignon."

The modern American reader, for whom Gray's "Elegy in a Country Churchyard" and Longfellow's "Psalm of Life," despite their difference in quality, share the double disadvantage of the scholastic and the edifying, needs to give "Le Guignon" a sharp reading in order to catch the Baudelairean twist. "Art is long and time is fleeting," wrote Longfellow after Hippocrates, but the soul has time in heaven. What Baudelaire sees is a graveyard, far removed from famous tombs, and the human heart like a muffled drum beating funereal marches toward the grave. The artist's enemy is not futility but time. This is to reinterpret Sisyphus. The image of the cemetery is retained in the tercets. Gray's "gem of purest ray serene" born in the "dark, unfathomed caves of ocean" is an image eloquently sad compared to Baudelaire's, "Maint joyau dort enseveli / Dans les ténèbres et l'oubli, / Bien loin des pioches et des sondes . . ." The pick-axe and plumb-line deny the jewel that lies buried in darkness and oblivion all the lusher consolations of poetry. The rose, "born to blush unseen, and waste its fragrance on the desert air," is an image of a magnificent waste. In contrast we have the quiet intimacy of Baudelaire's "Mainte fleur épanche à regret / Son parfum doux comme un secret / Dans les solitudes profondes." We would not, in spite of Verlaine's injunction, take Gray's "eloquence" in this instance and "twist its neck." Yet the "parfum doux comme un secret" has the magic of Verlaine's finest simplicity, and in this context, "les solitudes profondes" belong to the Baudelairean vastitude and to his infinite. Time with its incessant heart-beat toward the grave and sorrow sweet as a secret, tend to lead toward the very heart of Baudelairean intimacy. Whatever hints the poet has received from other writers, the poem is authentically his.

Finally let us examine the poet's handling of a major image where the symbol, because of constant use, has dwindled to allegory. The favorite Romantic endearment for woman, as Baudelaire pointed out derisively, was "ange." Yet he himself used the term, for which a set of religious connotations had long been established, for the woman whom he refused to love as a woman, Mme Sabatier.[8] For Baudelaire knew the Beatrice experience both as an absence and as a presence. As a negation "La

Béatrice" appears in the poem by that name amid a cloud of vicious demons. She stops with them to consider coldly "this caricature, this shadow of Hamlet imitating his posture, his glance undecisive and his hair in the wind," this "bon vivant," this "histrion on vacation" of a poet who, because he plays his role as an artist, would interest all Nature in his sorrows. And she laughs with them at his somber distress, and bestows upon them occasionally "a dirty caress."

Mme Sabatier ("Tout entière") whose eyes with their "mystic clarity" a "very expert angel no doubt has magnetized," is a Beatrice-figure in the positive. The angel for Baudelaire betokens awakening and renewal, but it is the "perfume of angels" that bathes her "spiritual flesh," while her eye "clothes us with a garment of light." Even when the Demon asks the poet to state his preference "among the black or rosy objects which constitute her charming body," he can only cry out:

> O *métamorphose mystique*
> *De tous mes sens fondus en un!*
> *Son haleine fait la musique*
> *Comme sa voix fait le parfum.*

The mystic metamorphosis which comes of the fusion of all the senses into one takes us into the region of correspondences where "Nature is a temple" because of this very interpenetration of sensations in mystical fashion. Baudelaire's mysticism has two aspects, one of them dualistic, in its sense of life as battle of spiritual forces, divine and satanic; the other, more "naturistic," demanding an ecstasy of all faculties of sense fused into unity. Perhaps his conviction of the "fall" was based more often on the denial of this "mystic metamorphosis" by ordinary experience of life than by an aspiration to "holiness."

Here a comparison with Dante may be revealing. Dante's Beatrice stands on the other side of the refining fire through which the body must finally pass. The senses must somehow be superseded and transcended despite the anguished hesitation of Dante's pilgrim. Baudelaire's Beatrice-experience is expressed through clarity, light, music, perfume; but these images are not used to suggest something beyond. What there is of the "beyond" is contained in their fusion.

The ineradicable sensuous quality of Baudelaire's spirituality, discernible even in images of the woman with whom he rejects sensual relations, can be illuminated further from "Correspondances." Baudelaire's temple, where man passes by living pillars and through "forests of symbols" which know him, evidently, even better than he knows them, is a place of "responses" of perfumes, colors and sounds. But two kinds of perfumes are singled out for celebration in the tercets:

> Il est des parfums frais comme des chairs d'enfants,
> Doux comme les hautbois, verts comme les prairies,
> —Et d'autres, corrompus, riches et triomphants,

> Ayant l'expansion des choses infinies,
> Comme l'ambre, le musc, le benjoin et l'encens,
> Qui chantent less transports de l'esprit et des sens.

Of these two types, the perfumes which "sing" (the image of "responses" in a church being maintained) "the transports of mind and sense" and which have "the expansion of infinite things" are those perfumes which are "corrupt, rich and triumphant." We need not make too much of their "corruption." We observe, nevertheless, that they are not "pure" and that they sing the transports of mind united with body, of volupté and connaissance. In Baudelaire and in Novalis, but not in Dante, the spirituality, at least for an orthodox Western mysticism, has a disturbing element of sense: it is a volupté. The flesh of Baudelaire's Beatrice may be spiritual, and its perfume may be that of the angels, but it is perfume, connected with an olfactory sense traditionally held to be less spiritual than sight or hearing.

Even in his cult of his "angel," then, Baudelaire cannot, in all honesty, forget the simultaneous "postulation" of the human soul toward God and Satan. In "L'Aube spirituelle," another poem addressed to Mme Sabatier, the poet considers how a dawn white and vermilion—together with the Ideal which also can "eat" into the soul—effect a mystery of "vengeance" so that in "the dormant brute an angel is awakened." For "the inaccessible azure" (of which Mallarmé will make a theme), "opens up and hollows out a depth with all the attraction of the abyss," *le gouffre*. In the present context *l'azur* suggests a certain ambivalence, and this certainly was not lacking on other levels in Baudelaire's attitude toward his "angel." "Ange pleine de gaieté," full also of beauty and health and happiness, and joy and light, "Connaissez-vous l'angoisse?" the poet asks his mistress. Is she acquainted with vengeance and hate and the "Fevers" which drag along the ashen hospital walls like exiles "seeking a rare sun and mumbling to themselves"? ("Réversibilité"). Shall he love her, therefore, or hate her, "folle dont je suis affolé," with her dazzling health and her dresses like "ballets of flowers"? And punishing upon her as he would punish upon a flower the "insolence of Nature," he feels the sadistic impulse to "infuse her with his poison," all the monotony and lifelessness of his spleen. If "Harmonie du soir" does indeed belong to the Mme Sabatier cycle, and if it is the last of the cycle, it seems appropriate that the memory of the "angel" should shine like a "monstrance" and suggest a sacrifice.[9]

"Angel," then, for Baudelaire is an ancient image that takes on new life in his poetry. The brightness of the angel is shadowed by doubt arising like a pall from human sin; the spirituality of the angel is transmitted into a perfume, an attar of sense. In Baudelaire, as in Novalis, the spiritual comes closer to a sublimation of sense than its transcendence as in Dante or Plato. The Paradisial experience is sought *hic et nunc*.

iv

We have attempted, in the preceding section, to distinguish between the "Goethean" and the Baudelairean symbol as structures. We have seen that symbol in the first sense is less than in the second sense a *coup d'état* of the poet's vision, which is metaphoric in a more thoroughgoing way. "Metaphoric" here is synonymous with the emphasis on music, suggestiveness, synaesthesia, atmosphere. We have sought, furthermore, to show, on the basis of the poet's handling of materials that might, because of their status in art and tradition, impose their weight coercively upon him, how the poet's vision, in its authenticity, achieves its triumphs. Poetic thought in Baudelaire, though relatively "emergent," is seldom distinct from metaphor and symbol. Let us now in poems where the symbol is the Baudelairean *symbole*, where it is "component" in varying ways, finally to become fully generative, study the poet's methods of synthesizing his materials as he seeks to bring the "whole soul of man into activity," to infuse his work with the "color" that is another name for Imagination as "queen" ruling everywhere.

There is the simplest type of symbolic structure verging on the allegory in the directness of its comparisons and "message." Its best-known example in *Les Fleurs du mal* is "L'Albatros" where a vast sea-bird is shown as "king" in the air and as awkward and pitiful cripple on the deck, the butt of the sailors' cruel humor. The "vehicle" is a single image and its "tenor" is explained: such is the fate of the poet in exile on earth. "Ses ailes de géant l'empêchent de marcher."

Poems of this type are not infrequent in Baudelaire and have, of course, their slight variations. "Le Chat" begins "Viens, mon beau chat, sur mon coeur amoureux"; but the poet soon falls into explicit comparison of the animal with his beloved who has similar qualities—especially that deep, cold gaze "qui coupe et fend comme un dard." In "Les Aveugles" the poet's soul is asked to contemplate blind men who walk like mannekins and somnambulists, their eyes raised toward a distant heaven with its eternal silence: "Vois, je me traîne aussi." Or we have two warriors in their combat changing from swords to teeth and nails, then rolling into a ravine infested with wild animals; but, 'ce gouffre c'est l'enfer, de nos amis peuplé." The sex-conflict is clearly identified in this "Duellum" with the challenge to the "Amazone inhumaine" to roll without remorse into the same abyss as the lover in order to give eternity to the ardor of mutual hate. Or, in poems like "L'Homme et la mer," man and sea in their similarity and contrast as "lutteurs fraternels" and "frères implacables" are compared item by item.

Another structure evokes the fundamental image through contrast with what it is not. Thus "Spleen" ("Je suis le roi d'un pays pluvieux") develops through examples of the usual royal distractions which, in this case, do not succeed. Even the "alchemist" who had made gold for the king must fail to warm him in Roman baths of blood. For in this deathlike body the blood is "l'eau verte de Léthé." [10]

There is a goodly number of poems composed of various images which the poet seems able neither to juxtapose nor to co-ordinate rigorously. The perils of this type are evident in "L'Héautontimoroumenos" where the very subject invites a certain dispersion. To be the "vampire" of one's heart makes for every destructive ambivalence within the personality, those of wound and knife, slap and cheek, limb and wheel, victim and executioner. When Irony makes the poet a false note in the "divine symphony," the reader must expect certain discords. Yet those tears that, as in the case of Moses' striking the rock, gush from the beloved like the sea upon which the sadist's ship will sail can hardly become the "drum" that beats the charge. The poem, despite Baudelaire's striving for a maximum unity, is as tortured as its subject.

More successful is the variety of structure represented by "La Causerie," beginning in fine style: "Vous-êtes un beau ciel d'automne, clair et rose, / Mais la tristesse en moi monte comme la mer." For the lover's bosom is a "place sacked by woman's claw and ferocious tooth." His heart has been devoured by animals. Or again, the bosom is a "palace" blighted by a drunken, bloodthirsty crowd. Yet Beauty demands submission and the poet offers what is left of his heart (thus picking up an earlier image) to be "calcined" by her "eyes of fire, shining like festivals." Here the poet seeks a return to the first line, to the light of a beautiful autumn sky attributed to Beauty. "Festivals" at the end of the poem may even be in the spirit of the crowd's licence; certainly it suggests the feast due to Beauty with the human heart as burnt-offering. The memorable portion of the poem is in the first four lines, and in the rest Baudelaire fails to maintain his level. Yet relatively imperfect poems like "La Causerie," where the garment of art shows the seams and the bulge or the tightness here and there, reveal how pervasively metaphorical Baudelaire's art is and how strong is the will to unify.[11]

In "L'Irrémédiable" we have perhaps a hint of the obstacle to unity. What are the "emblêmes nets, tableau parfait" of an "irrémédiable fortune" which shows that "what the Devil does, he does well"? A heavenly Idea, Form, or Being fallen into the leaden, muddy Styx, an Angel tempted by the love of the deformed and swimming in the whirlpool of an enormous nightmare; some bewitched unfortunate groping vainly, in a place full of snakes, for light and key; some damned soul descending without a lamp along a bottomless pit known by its dank smell alone, where viscous monsters make night even more dark with their phosphorescent eyes. But why did Baudelaire present as the final emblem a ship caught in the polar sea as in a crystal trap, and seeking its way out of the prison? Immersed more deeply in his soul than the rather forced images preceding, was the ship so invariably evoked with felicity both in Baudelaire's poetry and in his prose. Thus in *Fusées* there is reference to "those fine big ships, imperceptibly rocking . . . on tranquil waters, those robust ships, with their idle and nostalgic air, do they not say to us in their mute language: When shall we sail for happiness?" [12] Perhaps no image in the poem gives us more of an insight into the "irrémédiable" than the ship, sails spread for happiness, imprisoned in the ice (Mallarmé will present a swan frozen there), but we see the ship perhaps too well to give full poetic faith to the preceding emblems.

Perhaps the most instructive illustration of Baudelaire's art of suggestive interweaving in poems where the strands are several and apparently of a different stuff, needing to be far fetched, is "Le Cygne." The poem was sent with a letter to Victor Hugo on December 7, 1859, explaining that what had been important for the poet "was to say quickly all that an accident, an image, can contain in the way of suggestions, and how the view of an animal suffering makes us turn our minds toward all those we love, who are absent, and who suffer."

> *Andromaque, je pense à vous! Ce petit fleuve,*
> *Pauvre et triste miroir où jadis resplendit*
> *L'immense majesté de vos douleurs de veuve,*
> *Ce Simoïs menteur qui par vos pleurs grandit,*
>
> *A fécondé soudain ma mémoire fertile,*
> *Comme je traversais le nouveau Carrousel.*

The links of association seem to hook on in the following order: the poet is crossing the new Carrousel bridge over the Seine, feeling a bit "dépaysé" amid the changes that have destroyed the old Paris. Suddenly he thinks of another river, of another stranger, Andromache, *falsi Simoentis ad undam* (*Aeneid*, III, 302) shedding her tears not into . . . her native Simoïs but into a little stream at Buthrotum. Out of the synthesis of Seine, false Simoïs, and the sense of strangeness and suffering the poem begins to take shape. From the "fecundation" of memory are born the images of the section of old Paris with its shacks, abandoned columns, confused bric-a-brac and that menagerie where, early one morning, the poet had seen

> *Un cygne qui s'était évadé de sa cage,*
> *Et de ses pieds palmés frottant le pavé sec,*
> *Sur le sol raboteux traînait son blanc plumage.*
> *Près d'un ruisseau sans eau la bête ouvrant le bec*
>
> *Baignait nerveusement ses ailes dans la poudre,*
> *Et disait, le coeur plein de son beau lac natal:*
> *"Eau, quand donc pleuvras-tu? quand tonneras-tu, foudre?"*

(A swan which had escaped its cage, / and rubbing the dry pavement with its webbed feet, / dragged its white plumage over the bumpy ground. / Near a rivulet without water the animal, opening its beak, / bathed its wings nervously in the dust, / and said, its heart full of its beautiful natal lake: / "Water, when will you rain, then? and bolt, where is your thunder?") Though the sequence of events in the poem is presented dramatically and not chronologically, it is hard not to believe that this poem had its "origin in emotion recollected in tranquillity." The feelings, developing obscurely in the poet since he saw the swan, suddenly find release and a meaning as he crosses the new Carrousel over the Seine flowing past alien structures on its banks.

In the swan Baudelaire's "L'Albatros" returns, and with many felicities. The poet, who is sometimes denied "visual" powers, can certainly evoke for eye, ear, and our sense of movement the pathetic awkwardness of his exiled creatures. The swan, like other exiles, is "ridicule et sublime"; his heart is full of his "beau lac natal"; and when he asks for thunder and rain, "Vers le ciel ironique et cruellement bleu, / Sur son cou convulsif tendant sa tête avide," the poet sees this "poor unfortunate," as a "mythe étrange et fatal." Like "l'homme d'Ovide" he was made, not like other creatures to look at the earth, but to stand up and contemplate the heavens and turn his face to the stars (*Metamorphoses* I, 82–84). But the sky promises nothing but drought and dust, even though the swan seems to address his reproach directly to God.

The sky, "ironic and coldly blue," the swan "dans l'exil inutile"—they will be major symbols for Mallarmé. An image in Virgil, an image in Ovid, "mythe étrange et fatal"—these Baudelaire fused with a swan by a waterless rivulet seen on a cold clear morning in Paris when the Highways Department "drives a sombre hurricane through the silent air," to create a symbol of "archetypal" force. The swan is the symbol of man's exile from an infinite he somehow knows and has lost. How many of the poems which we have discussed, dealing with *ennui*, spleen, "l'irrémédiable," the inversions of "les femmes damnées," the "dislocated" old ladies, the appeal of those beacons that are works of art, even the reconciliation in "Recueillement" are aspects of this same theme of *lostness!*

"Paris change!" the poet repeats as he begins the second part of the poem; but what remains unchanging is the poet's melancholy. Everything becomes "allégorie" and his memories are as heavy as rocks but not merely out of a sense of the transitory. Something, he feels, is irretrievably lost for himself and for mankind. Hence his sympathy for "quiconque a perdu ce qui ne se retrouve / Jamais, jamais!" This is the deep sense of Baudelaire's "Nevermore," not the mere passing of

> *le vert paradis des amours enfantines,*
> *Les courses, les chansons, les baisers, les bouquets,*
> *Les violons vibrant derrière les collines,*
> *Avec les brocs de vin, le soir, dans les bosquets . . .*

("Moesta et errabunda") as human experiences subject to time. What aches in the memory is the loss of a *paradise.* "O serments! o parfums! o baiscrs infinis!" ("Le Balcon"). Thus, the poet continues,

> *Devant ce grand Louvre une image m'opprime,*
> *Je pense à mon grand cygne, avec ses gestes fous,*
> *Comme les exilés, ridicule et sublime,*
> *Et rongé d'un désir sans trêve . . .*

Or the poet thinks of Andromache: "Auprès d'un tombeau vide en extase courbée / Veuve d'Hector, hélas! et femme d'Hélénus!" Her "ecstasy" before an empty tomb where she bends, suggests that Hector's widow can transform the void through the memory of her *status* when she had it. The negress seeking beyond the immense wall of the fog "Les cocotiers absents de la superbe Afrique" suffers not merely from absence in space and time but from "le secret douloureux qui me faisait languir" ("La Vie antérieure").

> *Ainsi dans la forêt où mon esprit s'exile*
> *Un vieux Souvenir sonne à plein soufflo du oor!*

Je pense aux matelots oubliés dans une île,
Aux captifs, aux vaincus! . . . à bien d'autres encore!

One would like to think that this forest of the poet's exile is the forest of "Correspondances," Nature as a forest of symbols. Certainly, at any rate, this is a poem where memory is fecundated, where all becomes, as the poet says, "allegory," (obviously meaning symbol) where the Imagination fuses Paris, Troy, and Africa. This is one of those moments when one perceives in the depths of life all meanings coinciding. Man is in exile and the sailors forgotton on an island are one with Roland and the peers of France defeated at Roncevaux. "Dieu, que le son du cor est triste au fond des bois," Vigny had sung in one of those lines of his that were really Symboliste, and we hear the same horn in Baudelaire and Mallarmé.

Hugo's letter to Baudelaire in acknowledgment of "Le Cygne" begins as follows: "Like all that you do, Sir, your Swan is an idea. Like all true ideas, it has its depths. This swan in the dust has more abysses under him than the swan on the bottomless waters of the lake of Gaube. These abysses, one glimpses them in your verses so full of shudders and starts." "Une idée . . . . profondeurs . . . abîmes"—Victor Hugo had recognized an archetypal force in "Le Cygne."

From a structure such as that of "Le Cygne" to the kind of structure exemplified in "La Chevelure," we go a full step. In the former poem, the swan corresponds in a round-about, but explicit way to Andromache, to the negress, to the sailor on the abandoned isle, to paradise lost. In the latter the meanings have more implicit and intrinsic relations which center in the woman's hair whence they are shaken forth both as perfume and as memory.

Here, too, the hair as "forêt aromatique" becomes "in its depth" a forest of symbols bespeaking correspondences between tropical sea and port and the dream of bliss.

O toison, moutonnant jusque sur l'encolure!
O boucles! O parfum chargé de nonchaloir!

Extase! Pour peupler ce soir l'alcôve obscure
Des souvenirs ardents dormant dans cette chevelure,
Je la veux agiter dans l'ombre comme un mouchoir.

O *fleece*, and the image that follows is of what the English call "white horses" of the waves breaking over the neck and withers of the animal. In French the picture is of an end-less herd of sheep, and this carries out the suggestion, in fleece, of the "golden fleece," of the "Argonauts." Thus a poem of "voyage" is inaugurated, of *ecstasy*, a going out of oneself. But it will be in connection with the *frizzy hair* of a quadroon mistress and its *perfume charged with non-chalance*. In this poem the motion is most like that of a dance, a going out that at the same time "stays put" in a balance that is perfect ease and enjoyment. "To people tonight the obscure alcove with memories sleeping in that head of hair, I want to shake it in the air like a handker-chief." The "fleece" becomes a "handkerchief," from which the poet will shake out memories, the "classical" image becomes familiar and modern. And the principal agent of travel will be the perfume of memories and asso-ciations hidden in the hair.

La langoureuse Asie et la brûlante Afrique,
Tout un monde lointain, absent, presque défunt,
Vit dans tes profondeurs, forêt aromatique!
Comme d'autres esprits voguent sur la musique,
Le mien, ô mon amour! nage sur ton parfum.

(Langorous Asia and burning Africa, / a whole world, gone by, almost defunct, / lives in your depths, aromatic forest! / As other spirits row on music, / mine, o my love, swims on your perfume.) The key expression here is "forêts aromatiques." We seem to go back to the sonnet "Correspondances," where man passes through "des forêts de symboles," where the various senses call to each other but where nevertheless it is the language of perfume that is celebrated. Here Asia and Africa are not geography but states of soul buried deep and to which the poet will "swim" on perfume, with more "nonchaloir" perhaps

than those who "row" on music. At any rate, be it by row-
ing or swimming, the travel theme is set in motion.)

> J'irai là-bas où l'arbre et l'homme, pleins de sève,
> Se pâment longuement sous l'ardeur des climats;
> Fortes tresses, soyez la houle qui m'enlève!
> Tu contiens, mer d'ébène, un éblouissant rêve
> De voiles, de rameurs, de flammes et de mâts:

I shall go down where tree and man, with sap replete, in a
long languor / swoon under these ardent climes; [The
swooning is as in Keats' "Nightingale," a matter of
plethora of blood. And strength is in the rhythm of the
next line.] Strong tresses, be the surge that carries me! /
You contain, sea of ebony, a dazzling dream of sails and
rowers, of flags and masts;)

> Un port retentissant où mon âme peut boire
> A grands flots le parfum, le son et la couleur;
> Où les vaisseaux, glissant dans l'or et dans la moire,
> Ouvrent leurs vastes bras pour embrasser la gloire
> D'un ciel pur où frémit l'éternelle chaleur.

(A resounding port where my soul can drink / large drafts
of perfume, sound, and color; / where ships, gliding in the
gold and the moire, open their vast arms to embrace the
glory / of a pure sky where quivers an eternal heat.) The
poet has reached port, and it is a consummation. Here
there is maximum of sound, the drafts of the synaesthetic
are drunk deep, and the vessels in their silk and velvet gliding encompass the whole sky as if in an embrace of human arms ("bras" and "embrasser"). What they take in is
a quivering purity of eternal heat. This is the image of
bliss: a sky pure, but not cold, and alive with warmth.
Baudelaire will repeat the image, for the poem has reached
a plateau of richness to be exploited.

> Je plongerai ma tête amoureuse d'ivresse
> Dans ce noir océan où l'autre est enfermé;
> Et mon esprit subtil que le roulis caresse
> Saura vous retrouver, ô féconde paresse!
> Infinis bercements du loisir embaumé!

The movement of the poem suggests that up-and-down-motion where there is no real progression. "I shall plunge my head in love with intoxication / into the black ocean where that other [the ocean of my remembered bliss] is enclosed; / and my subtle spirit that the roll caresses / will learn how to find you, o fruitful idling! / infinite cradlings of leisure perfume-fraught!" Here language strains every resource to convey the quality of an infinite, a state in the absence of which, as we have seen, Satan seems to the poet to have taken over the world, time is at a stop and the heart is dead in lifeless spleen broken only by spasms of cruelty to others and to oneself. *Féconde paresse* is a *volupté* never settling into the inert but kept alive by *connaissance*. The "esprit" is "subtil" and never is more active than under the caressing roll of this sea, the inner "ocean" contained within the physical "ocean" on which Baudelaire at twenty traveled toward a Calcutta he never reached on a Pâquebot-des-mers-du-Sud. What "la mer" means when it is really a symbol in his poetry is never far removed from the "infinis bercements" that accompany and stimulate a "volupté" of mind and sense together. The ideal is "ordre et beauté, luxe, calme et volupté," but the critical and self-critical mind, mercilessly active in Baudelaire, perceives all too clearly the dreadful sameness of so many forms of failure to achieve an infinite in existence. No wonder that the poet is at the end ready to plunge, with Death as captain "Au fond de l'Inconnu pour trouver du nouveau" ("Le Voyage"). But Baudelaire is not a dynamic seeker of "experiences." Like Dante he seeks an experience "perfect" because it is at the same time satisfaction and stimulus where the satisfaction is its own inherent stimulus—the experience of Dante's pilgrim in the vision of God. Baudelaire demands its first fruits at least here and now, "infinis bercements du loisir embaumé." The experience is more positive then that of "honied indolence" in Keats' Ode; one thinks of a contemplation where the mind is not like an eye but a sensitive and discriminating nostril. Dante's pilgrim said "I saw." Olfactory images may not be as numerous by actual count in Baudelaire as was once thought; but the number of instances does not determine intensity and importance. "Cheveux bleus, pavillon de ténèbres tendues, / Vous me rendez l'azur du ciel immense et rond"; (Blue tresses, pennant of darknesses stretched taut, / you give me back the blue of the sky immense and round;). The "féconde paresse" is possible only under the azure of an immense round sky, a pure blue heat, to which the blue-black pennant points, taut in the wind. Once more happiness comes in a heady fragrance in a land where man and trees are "full of sap."

> Sur les bords duvetés de vos mêches tordues
> Je m'enivre ardemment des senteurs confondues
> De l'huile de coco, du musc et du goudron.

(On the downy tips of your twisted locks / I intoxicate myself ardently with the commingled scents / of cocoanut oil, musk and pitch.)

> Longtemps! toujours! ma main dans ta crinière lourde
> Sèmera le rubis, la perle et le saphir,
> Afin qu'à mon désir tu ne sois jamais sourde!
> N'est-tu pas l'oasis où je rêve, et la gourde
> Où je hume à longs traits le vin du souvenir!

(A long time, forever! my hand in your heavy mane / will sow the ruby, pearl and sapphire, / in order that you may never be deaf to my desire! / Are you not the oasis where I dream, and the gourd / from which I breathe in large drafts of the wine of memory.)

After the "féconde paresse" and the "infinite cradlings" that the subtle mind will learn how to recapture within that inner ocean, the poet returns with masculine vigor to the outer ocean, to the source of all that bliss. What intoxicates his ardor is a rather strong mixture of odors; and there is something of the animal in his mistress' mane, and she will have to be placated perhaps with precious stones in her hair. But the last image is again one of peace: an oasis where one dreams, the gourd containing the intoxicating wine of memory. The final image also suggests travel, but by land and not by sea, or rather a stasis, the end of travel with an intoxication one breathes in like a perfume. So our poem ends at rest; this "voyage" is not for the sake of voyaging; it has reached the "golden fleece" with its perpetual promise of remembrance.[13]

A poem like "La Chevelure" strains the concept of "symbol as component." Such a poem not only is symbol in the Goethean sense, having its origin not in an idea, but in an object of perception which opens toward some universal of paradisial bliss. Not only does it contain a metaphor that is focal, massive, repeatable, "la chevelure," through whose properties *as developed in the poem* beyond a mere heightening of the observable, the bliss is conceived. The component symbol *covers the expanse of, and coincides with the poem itself. Les Fleurs du mal* contains a number of such poems where the "radical" metaphor generates a poem. A woman's hair becomes a fleece, and through associated images conveys a paradisial state characterized in its essence through sensuous imagery: "infinis bercements du loisir embaumé." This paradisial state is further qualified in more abstract language as a "féconde paresse." But even an abstraction like "féconde paresse" says very little to the individual who has not entered into the world of the poem. Statements in Baudelaire can become song, and of the most intimate kind. "Là tout n'est qu'ordre et beauté, Luxe, calme et volupté"—the poet enumerates five abstractions, but their very function as refrain turns them into song in their context. What is the world qualified in such ideal terms in "L'Invitation au voyage"? It is a world "là-bas" where there is "douceur," where one loves at leisure and yet where the mind is ever active because of the beautiful mystery of "humid" suns, of skies "a tangle of fog," casting the spell "De tes traîtres yeux, / Brillant à travers leurs larmes."

It is a world where exotic flowers and perfumes mingle with the antiquity of polished furniture, with deep mirrors and rich ceilings, the oriental splendor speaking secretly to the heart its sweet native tongue. In the ships that are asleep, though their humor is "vagabond," Baudelaire again associates the ideal bliss with a motion that is also rest in a world also asleep in the warmth of a sun enduing it with garments of hyacinth and gold.

Yet the quality of bliss presented both by "La Cheve-lure" and by "L'Invitation au voyage," is interpreted for the reader by the poet's brief abstractions, however musical: "féconde paresse," in the first poem, and a refrain of abstractions in the second. But Baudelaire in some poems will go further and present an experience qualified with a very minimum of abstraction and a very maximum of sensation.

"Harmonie du soir" is a famous example of this type of structure. "Here and in a few similar poems," Henri Peyre writes, "Baudelaire, anticipating the oft-quoted claim of Mallarmé and of Valéry, attempted to recapture from music the subtle and rich orchestration that it had exclusively appropriated." [14] Jean Prévost feels that the poetic emotion of this poem sets up a "danse intérieure" within the reader, each movement with its sounds and images aiming only to succeed the preceding or to establish a balance with it, and having no other aim than harmony and perfection. [15] We would add that this harmony and perfection characterize the presentation of the quality of a lover's memory of the beloved, with an almost complete absence of interpretation and definition within the poem itself. Thus the lyric poem approaches the very limits of the condition of music.

> Voici venir les temps où vibrant sur sa tige
> Chaque fleur s'évapore ainsi qu'un encensoir;
> Les sons et les parfums tournent dans l'air du soir;
> Valse mélancolique et langoureux vertige!

The poem opens with a religious image, the swinging of the censer that aids combustion of the incense, and "les temps" like the Biblical "in those days" enhances the suggestion. This is a poem of "recueillement." ("Behold the time is come when vibrant on its stem, / each flower breathes out its vapor like a censer; / sounds and perfumes whirl in the evening air; / melancholy waltz and langorous vertigo!" The *v* sounds in the first line combining with the *r*'s and the strong *t* at each of the pauses ("temps" and "tige") suggest the energy for the swing of the censer and prepare for the letting out of scent at the next two caesuras in *s'évapore* and en*censoir*. In the third line that same energy is concentrated on *tournent* (echoed by "vertige" in the next line) which the reader holds for about as long as he does the next four syllables. The final line in a syllabic pattern of $2:4 - 4:2$ suggests the balanced swing of the waltz.)

The metrical form of the *Pantoum* requires the repetition of a line at the beginning of the second stanza and also of a rhyme. Observe that Baudelaire's rhyme word is *encensoir* which then will be matched with *reposoir* and finally *ostensoir,* all of them belonging to religious cult. Now it happens that rhyming with them throughout the poem are *soir* and *noir,* words meaning or evoking "darkness." And we are told in lines ten and thirteen that *noir* is hateful. Thus the "religious" images seem to be contrasted with the "night" and "nothingness" images.

> *Chaque fleur s'évapore ainsi qu'un encensoir;*
> *Le violon frémit comme un coeur qu'on afflige;*
> *Valse mélancolique et langoureux vertige!*
> *Le ciel est triste et beau comme un grand reposoir.*

(Each flower breathes out its vapor like a censer; / the violin quivers like a heart brought to grief; / melancholy waltz and langorous vertigo; / the sky is sad and beautiful like a great altar.) Here the progression in the *Pantoum* should be observed. The form withholds and then more than restores. In the first stanza there was mention of "sounds" without their source, of "melancholy" motivated only by "evening" and perhaps by the spending of scent by flower and censer. The quality of sound is now traced to the violin, to the sadness of evening, and to the grief of a human heart. Sadness will descend more and more upon the poem, until the end. The sunset is "sad and beautiful" like an altar upon which the sacred host will rest. Religious associations grow in suggestiveness.

As for "triste et beau," they are indeed examples not so much of the so-called "abstract" qualitites of Baudelaire's adjectives as of the renewal of the hackneyed in the new bath of life that is effected by every line of real poetry. These are indeed words impossible to translate though they may be given in the first five lessons in French. Striking adjectives call attention to themselves; but words like "sad" and "beautiful," so common that their meaning has passed into unconscious feeling, can be transformed into "musical notes." Verlaine knows the secret in "Clair de lune": "Au calme clair de lune triste et beau . . ." His most characteristic "music" is that of "simple" things which, because we think we know their meaning in the familiarity of old use, astonish us, once they are revived. They are like people whom we have long taken for granted until one day we discover that time and habit have become powers and sanctities.

> Un coeur tendre, qui hait le néant vaste et noir.
> Le ciel est triste et beau comme un grand reposoir;
> Le violon frémit comme un coeur qu'on afflige
> Le soleil s'est noyé dans son sang qui se fige.

(The violin quivers like a heart brought to grief, / a tender heart which hates the void vast and dark! / The sky is sad and beautiful like a great altar; / the sun has drowned in its own congealing blood.) It is only now that we are sure that the "sorrow" suggested from the very beginning is due to evening. "Tu réclamais le soir, il descend. Le voici" ("Recueillement"). And the beauty and sadness of evening is associated with an archetypal image, as if some god had drowned in his own blood.

"See, see, where Christ's blood streams in the firmament!" (Marlow, *Doctor Faustus*, Scene 1).[16]

> Un coeur tendre, qui hait le néant vaste et noir,
> Du passé lumineux recueille tout vestige!
> Le soleil s'est noyé dans son sang qui se fige . . .
> Ton souvenir en moi luit comme un ostensoir!

(A tender heart, which hates the void vast and dark, / garners every vestige of the luminous past! / The sun has drowned in its own congealing blood . . . / Your memory shines within me like a monstrance.) A monstrance is a receptacle in which sacred relics are exposed to view; in the Catholic Mass it exhibits the Host. We have seen how the image has been emerging very gradually in the poem. We still feel the movement of the "valse mélancolique," just as in "La Chevelure" the highest bliss is associated with the movement of "bercements infinis"; but it is a background music for what advances steadily to the fore and shines in splendor at the end. What is that triumphs for the tender heart over the hateful void? "Ton souvenir," a memory of woman coming out of the sadness, and beauty with its suggestion of a sacred death. Whatever death may do, whatever love may be or become, demonic or angelic (for "Le Balcon" and "La Chevelure" seem to "belong" to Jeanne Duval and "L'Harmonie du soir" to Madame Sabatier), whatever Baudelaire may write in his diaries about the love between man and woman as the deliberate enjoyment of the diabolic, the poet has succeeded in redeeming love in a memory that makes his finest music. The ambiguities, nay the violent contradictions of Baudelaire's attitude toward women, may perhaps be transcended in the poem thanks to the influence of an archetypal symbol which is here of a characteristically paradoxical character. For blood may connote "life" but also death, which makes it taboo, or the horrible penalties believed to be connected with the violation of an oath, and in general the "rites de passage," that simultaneous birth and death.

A poem like "Harmonie du soir," with its slow, undulatory progression like one of Baudelaire's women, "Quand elle marche, il paraît qu'elle danse," the refrains and repetitions of Poe adapted to a higher use, the repeated contrast of the two rhymes in "ige" and "oir," (which Henri Peyre tells us are rare in French) —these and other aspects of the poem which we have not brought out in our analysis are distinguishably "musical." What is profoundly "musical" in this poem we can best appreciate through contrast with the poetic structures which we have already considered. In poems like "Harmonie du soir," what the symbol symbolizes has all the definiteness and indefiniteness of an image, where image means an immediate fusion of sense, thought, and feeling that resists paraphrase almost to the degree that a sensation of "red" for instance, resists paraphrase. All that the reader has for meaning is the symbol almost in the sense in which it could be said of one listening to a sonata, "All that he has is the music."

In a poem like "La Chevelure," the symbol creates the state of soul which is envisaged in and through the symbol of "hair," but the poet helps to define the area of vision through the "abstraction" of "féconde paresse," itself to some extent musical because it is really conceivable only through what it helps to define. The theme is like a tangent being drawn to a circle, the straight line becoming in a flash one with the curve even though, both before and after the contact, it resumes its own nature—a linear discursiveness.

In "Harmonie du soir," what emerges out of a rich sorrow whose motive is itself defined, the tender heart's hatred of "le néant vaste et noir," is an "ostensoir," a vessel of gold containing the Host, and to be exhibited triumphantly when the mystery of redemption is once accomplished. "Ostensoir," prepared by "encensoir," "reposoir," and by the poem as a whole, is therefore the central symbol and not merely an effective closing metaphor. Though it has meaning for the Catholic which an informed person could interpret in discursive language, this meaning is presented immediately and dramatically in a shining vessel which, as it were, has absorbed meaning into itself so that the outward and the inward become one. As symbol it is "indefinite," not as the vague is indefinite, but as something concentrated and brilliant absorbs outline in dazzlement.

In "La Chevelure" the poet himself reduced to its epitome what the total symbol transcended: the statement of a quality of bliss like "the infinite lulling of leisure perfume-fraught" ("infinis bercements du loisir embaumé"), or, with even greater discursive precision, "féconde paresse," an idleness rich in *volupté et connaissance*. And though these phrases were "musicalized" in their context, the "ostensoir," because not specifically interpreted with respect to the feeling it was meant to convey, speaks for itself in a sense closer to what happens in music. If one were to ask wherein the "Harmonie du soir" consisted, one could almost present it in that "ostensoir," the embodied quality of the poet's memory of the beloved, much as one might reply to a question about the "meaning" of a piece of music by playing it over again.

Yet even to determine the central image in a poem is to abstract, for, as we have shown in our analysis, "ostensoir" is itself the climax of a scheme of sound and sense in which verbal meanings approach the "condition of music." But what is the "condition of music"? Unfortunately the experts disagree; but let us turn, for one opinion especially relevant at this point, to the suggestive eighth chapter of Mrs. Langer's *Philosophy in a New Key*:

> The assignment of meanings is a shifting, kaleidoscopic play, probably below the threshold of consciousness, certainly outside the pale of discursive thinking. The imagination that responds to music is personal and associative and logical, tinged with affect, tinged with bodily rhythm, tinged with dream, but *concerned* with a wealth of formulations for its wealth of wordless knowledge, its whole knowledge of emotional and organic experience, of vital impulse, balance, conflict, the *ways* of living and dying and feeling. Because no assignment of meaning is conventional, none is permanent beyond the sound that passes; yet the brief association was a flash of understanding. The lasting effect is, like the first effect of speech on the development of the mind, to *make things conceivable* rather than to store up propositions. Not communication but insight is the gift of music; in very naive phrase, a "knowledge of how feelings go."

Nevertheless even a knowledge of "how feelings go" defines by indicating a speed or a direction if not a contour or an essence. *Adagio, accelerando* are at least elementary gestures of commitment, like "up" or "down." They are more than sheerly directional: thus "up" may mean what

"Heaven" means and "down" what "Hell" means, and they may become symbols of the "lost" or of what must be regained or restored, as we have seen in certain of Baudelaire's poems. For poetry, like music, to be said to have "import" rather than meaning seems to be a purely verbal escape from the irreducible conceptual element in meaning. Yet, as we have shown in Baudelaire, especially in his more "musical" poetry, there is the kind whose meaning seems to call for such a term as "import." In our opinion, we must distinguish here only between more and less. "Féconde paresse" has more meaning of a conceptual kind than "ostensoir"; yet "ostensoir," presented in a more direct and dramatic fashion, still depends for its "meaning" on other meanings, those of the Catholic mass, which themselves combine direct and intuitional elements with discursive elements. Poetry, we think, because of its verbal element, cannot completely avoid *representing*, but it can *present* what it represents in structures of language that point, in varying degrees, *inward*, toward the created world of the poem, "intransitively," to use Vivas' word. The more "intransitive," the more "suggestive." But Walter Pater's phrase, in our opinion, should be used heuristically and as a norm *within* kinds. Different kinds of poems approach the "condition of music" only after their fashion, and poems of a certain general kind should be compared with each other, allowing for whatever can be meaningful in their so-called "uniqueness," which should also be treated heuristically. Mallarmé's roses and lilies are flowers, and each rose or lily is different from every other specimen, yet a wise criticism will seek to compare only rose with rose and lily with lily.

We have seen that Baudelaire presents wholes composed of different elements in different ways. Some of these wholes, as in "La Chevelure" and "Harmonie du soir," can be differentiated, not absolutely but usefully, from other wholes, because they seek to convey in words the quality of a feeling rather than the quality of a thought. They can also be differentiated from each other. Poems of their type are rarer in Baudelaire than in Mallarmé who in his later style might be said to seek to make intellectual essences

presentational. Verlaine, in *Romances sans paroles* especially, with his ideal, "De la musique avant toute chose,"
approaches the "condition of music" in his own way. He
attempts, as we shall see, through a simplicity and transparency of language to make an effect of naive objectivity
thanks to a vision that depends on the external world less
than Baudelaire's. As for Rimbaud—and we have illustrated this point in "Mystique"—sheer persentation seems
the aim, so that it is difficult to distinguish between
sensation itself and that "vision" which presumably is
conveyed in and through his structures.

In order to indicate the breadth of that class of poems to
which "La Chevelure" and "Harmonie du soir" belong, let
us consider several other poems. "Elévation," in thought,
imagery, rhythm, and general movement may be called an
"up" poem. The poet, like a masculine swimmer, aswoon
with *volupté*, is carried up into the "air supérieur," where
upper air also has moral implications. He drinks of the
clear fire of interstellar spaces after passing from *ennui*
into a luminous air. But such a soaring "above" life is also
an image of a penetration into life, for it enables the poet
to understand without effort "le langage des fleurs et des
choses muettes." Upward motion here is a rendering in
kinaesthetic terms of liberation and of sympathy with
life.

To turn to a poem whose subject, Baudelaire said,
should be subordinated to an "intention plastique,"[17]
"Les Bijoux," we find that the plastic rendering of a nude
clad only in jewels, and who invokes a world of sound and
light as she moves achieves other than a sculptural effect.
For though the beloved sits on a divan as on a "rock of
crystal" with the vague and dreamy air of a tamed tiger,
trying poses of a "candeur unie à la lubricité," our
attention is attracted by the movement toward her of the
lover's affection, a sea mounting toward a cliff. The poem
ends with a stanza which is of the very essence of
suggestion:

> Et la lampe s'étant résignée à mourir,
> Comme le foyer seul illuminait la chambre,

Chaque fois qu'il poussait un flamboyant soupir,
Il inondait de sang cette peau couleur d'ambre.

(And the lamp having resigned itself to die, / since the hearth alone illuminated the room, / each time that it flamed into a sigh, / it inundated with blood this amber-colored skin.)

We shall not dwell on phallic and religious hints in "death" in this context, nor on the similarity at this point between "Les Bijoux" and "Harmonie du soir." To repeat, the poem conveys the figure of an aspiration, a motion of love from "down" to "up" which is duplicated at the end by the hearth whose "flaming sigh" inundates the beloved's skin like a rush of blood. What does this poem "say"? It is almost as if one asked this question of a piece of music.[18]

We have seen, then, that Baudelaire, in his effort to present a vision of his own personal "color" ranges from the Goethean symbol to a *symbole* of a markedly "musical" character. His structures vary even as they extend from the presentation of an object which, as concrete universal, directs the mind from what common sense calls "nature" to the intuition of a not otherwise apprehensible "higher law," to the presentation of an object, person, situation, or state seized initially through a metaphor whose development becomes the poem. We have poems like "L'Albatros," where the symbol is offered and then explained; like "La Chevelure," where our interpretation of the symbol is guided tersely by a discursive statement in the form of an ejaculation; we have poems where the symbol offers itself to a maximum degree unaided.

The common element in all these symbolic structures is Baudelair's firm will to an internal unity. He works as if the interweaving of an internal logic could by itself insure the poet's access to an objective realm, which is the real meaning of his faith in analogies and correspondences. Goethe in his famous letter to Schiller of August 17, 1797 said of symbolic objects that from *within* as well as from without they claim a certain oneness and universality. Baudelaire concentrates on internal relations as if thereby to guarantee objectivity and truth.

The critic in Baudelaire would have consented to Valéry's idea that meaning in poetry should be concealed, "like nourishment in a peach." Of atheism he writes in a review of *Prométhée Délivré* by Louis Ménard: "Fine, and we would like nothing better than to subscribe to it if it were gay, pleasing, seductive, and nourishing." [19] But, he cries, "La grande poésie est essentiellement *bête*, elle *croit*, et c'est ce qui fait sa gloire et sa force." The context makes it clear that Baudelaire expects beliefs in poetry—and will tolerate even antipathetic beliefs. Of utmost importance, however, is the way in which these beliefs are held, and therefore presented. Poetry is made not of the "fantômes de la raison," which are "des équations," but of "fantômes de l'imagination," which are "des êtres et des souvenirs."

The question of the truth of poetry to a presumed state of affairs, whether in nature, history, or feeling, may properly arise; but what creates true poetry is a fusion of elements dramatized and nourishing mind, imagination, and sensibility together. Baudelaire's poems do make assertions, which we cannot believe were for him merely "materials" or "subjects" or "scenarios." The assertions in different areas are presented in different ways. There are assertions about human destiny and the power of evil in "Les Petites Vieilles," and "Les Sept Vieillards," in "Le Reniement de Saint-Pierre," in "Les Litanies de Satan" and "Abel et Caïn," and generally in all poems where Satan figures. "La Beauté" and "L'Hymne à la Beauté" if certainly not to be read as "definitions" of Beauty, present responses of the poet to the beautiful which accord with his characterizations of Beauty in his critical writings. "Correspondances" asserts a belief about a certain relation between man and nature. "Les Phares" seeks to situate the imaginative works of man with relation to the divine. "Bénédiction" presents the poet's individual relation to the divine and, with "L'Albatros," pictures the poet in society.

In poems of this type the Baudelairean *symbole* seems, at least, to support W. M. Urban's definition: it "lends intuition to the concept." In this classical post-Kantian and Hegelian view, the symbol in general is "the indirect representation of the concept through the intuition." And Urban quotes Harald Höffding: "It is characteristic of all symbols that images and ideas are taken from the narrower and more intuitible relations and used as expressions for more universal and ideal relations which, because of their pervasiveness and ideality, cannot be directly expressed." [20]

But what of the poems which aim to present a quality of feeling, an *état d'âme* not motivated by thoughts which seek conclusions about human destiny, the power of evil, the nature of beauty, the role of art, the relation of the poet to society? These poems, to refer only to those which we have discussed, seem to present for our cognition qualities of emotion and states of emotion: "spleen," a sardonic bitterness ("Le Guignon"), various kinds of despair ("L'Irréparable," "L'Irrémédiable," "Le Voyage"), sympathy with defeat and the defeated ("Le Cygne"), ecstasies of a number of kinds ("Elévation," "L'Invitation au voyage"), resignation ("Recueillement"), and the sentiment of love in its tenderness ("Le Balcon"), in sadistic vengefulness ("A une madone"), in its adoration of sensual beauty ("Les Bijoux"), in its submission to destruction ("La Causerie"), in its association with ideal happiness ("La Chevelure"), in its martyrdom to an infinite which it seeks in the satanic ("Un Voyage à Cythère" and poems in the "Femmes Damnées" series).

To be sure these poems are none the less motivated by thoughts even if they are not thoughts *about* philosophical questions. Among these poems even those like "La Chevelure," where the state is interpreted by phrases like "féconde paresse," intuition seems "lent" to the concept. But, in the latter case, the "concept" seems to tell us relatively less apart from the intuition. For "féconde paresse" to have real meaning for us, and not merely as designation of an abstraction, we must have apprehended the quality of the *état d'âme* presented. Whereas statements about human fate, the Satanic, art, poetry are *relatively more significant* when detached from the poem. Let us not be misunderstood: it is only as part and parcel of the poem that such statements have their *full* modality. Yet they seem more detachable from the concrete whole because, we think, their ideas achieved the status of "beings" and "memories," without, for that reason, being expected to give up citizenship in the community of thought.

On the other hand, in poems like "Harmonie du soir," for reasons already discussed, it seems more appropriate to say with Yeats: "How can you 'tell the dancer from the dance' "? It is in connection with a situation of this type that Susanne Langer seems justified in her objection to W. M. Urban's demand for a "more adequate rendering" of meaning through paraphrase.[21] Certainly, as we have pointed out, such poems seem more amenable to a theory for which the symbol conveys knowledge of a pattern of emotion into which all seeming statements are transmuted. Let us repeat, such distinctions cannot be absolute: there is no road by which a poem conveys knowledge of feeling, however subtly and "musically," that must not pass through words whose "dictionary meaning" cannot be completely ignored. Different poetic subjects, offering different materials, call for a different rendering. Just as a sculptor may be said to see in terms of stone, the poet sees not merely in terms of characters, situation, and rhythms, but also in terms of the painterly or plastic possibilities inherent in thoughts. A satisfactory theory of the symbol must accommodate many nuances.

We have sought to study in Baudelaire what kinds of situations give rise to symbol, by what uses of language and in what shapes of poetry he presents a beauty which, though fully true only in "another world," must nevertheless here below, through analogies and correspondences, participate in the structures of that other world. We have found no evidence, apart from abandonment of poems of the "Albatros" type, of any evolution toward exclusive use of structures of the type of "Harmonie du soir." Perhaps for the poet, within the confines of a general theory, solutions were strictly *ad hoc*, the structure of the poem being determined by the kind of content. No doubt, only that aesthetic of the symbol would be philosophically satisfactory to some aestheticians which could account convincingly for all shapes of the literary symbol. The shapes of Baudelaire's poems are varied enough to seem to lend support now to one theory of the symbol, now to another. One may conclude, therefore, that we probably need more analyses of poetic structures and strategies before we are ready for an all-inclusive theory of the symbol in relation to meaning. Perhaps the best theory of the symbol in literature might seek the formulation of an ideal, defined not as an absolute but as a direction; which, avoiding the bagginess of a mere eclecticism, could give a theoretic account of such modes of relation between theme, structure, and meaning as we find in a modern poetry like Baudelaire's.

BAUDELAIRE,
LES SYMBOLISTES, AND
MODERN THEORIES

WHAT IS THE RELATION of Baudelaire to the other "'te-trarchs," as Thibaudet called them, Mallarmé, Rimbaud, Verlaine, and to the Symbolist movement of 1885? How do the aims and achievements of that movement compare with the poet's? Our vantage point on Baudelaire has been modern theory of the symbol which, though anthropological, linguistic, and philosophical in its interests, has also been working on a rationale for modern poetry. What is the situation, within this enlarged prospect and with particular reference to the modern English-speaking world, of Baudelaire?

From Baudelaire's poetic experience, according to Guy Michaud's comprehensive study in *Le Message du Symbolisme*, three roads emerged. Verlaine followed the master's example in the effort to seize the "resonances of the world" in his soul by an almost mystical ecstasy. Rimbaud investigated *sorcellerie évocatoire* in his search for a verbal alchemy and a poetic image that in its strangeness and intensity would be immediate metaphysical vision. But Baudelaire laid out a path for Mallarmé and the Symbolistes especially in his intuition of correspondences and universal analogies.[1]

That path for Michaud continues the Neo-Platonic and esoteric tradition, and reaches a philosophical expression in Henri Bergson. Yet Michaud is hostile to another theory embracing the work of Baudelaire, Verlaine, and Mallarmé which would explain the symbol in these poets, though with Marcel Proust as exemplary culmination, in Bergsonian terms. E. Fiser in a volume, *Le Symbole littéraire*, contrasts the "classical" symbol, by which he means no more than the use of words in conceptual thought in "static" fashion, with "le symbole dynamique." Henri Bergson's attacks upon the "symbole" were directed only at the former, according to Fiser, and his writings on the question, contemporaneous with the Symbolist movement and culminating in *Le Rire* that appeared in the *Revue de Paris* in 1899, really present the theory of the "dynamic symbol." For if words used as concepts are counters valuable only in the exchanges of practical knowledge in our social and scientific pursuits, they can nevertheless be so organized and rhythmed, so animated with an original life that they will express through *suggestion* states of soul which ordinary language does not convey. The "symbole dynamique," then, is both the key to the philosopher's aesthetics and to that of the Symbolist movement, and before Bergson, Fiser holds, such ideas had been expressed by Baudelaire, Mallarmé, and Wagner.[2]

The feelings which we know directly in life can, according to this theory, if suggested, become a source of beauty, the words employed being bathed in a new atmosphere. Some poems make contact not only with what is individual and particular but with the universe itself. Only those images through which flows the current of changing meanings and the memory which remains alive in them because every nuance has been lived, can symbolize through concrete suggestion the melody of the inner life of consciousness. No one of these images alone can replace the intuition of our experience as *durée*, that is, as a living unity fusing past, present and future beyond possibility of analysis; nevertheless, if one chooses images from various orders of things and focuses the consciousness upon the point where each in some aspect converges upon all the others, then one can enter into the heart of the melody.

Such a theory, presented in Bergson's *La Pensée et le mouvant*, can explain the difference, Fiser believes, between the symbol of Baudelaire and the Symbolistes and that of other French poets. The latter make use of objective symbols which do not analyze but illustrate; in their work "pain, desire, forgetfulness, the calm of passion spent are treated like things, that is, like realities projected into language and whose story they tell as one would of the hero of the novel . . ." The "new symbolism" seeks metaphors which cause us to participate in affective states for which words do not suffice; it does not seek to translate "philosophical ideas or emotional data preconceived, but the data of the inner life, and in this data that which is most personal and most mysterious." [3]

Developing the suggestions of Bergson along the lines indicated in Proust's *A la recherche du temps perdu*, Fiser seeks further to characterize the "dynamic symbol." What distinguishes it, first, is the new combinations of words and ideas which we have already described. The second mark is an interplay of analogies between the new combination of symbols and the "durée profonde" of life which they symbolize. The third is the emotion arising from the discovery of such analogies between the "durée" of things and a moment of the "durée" of the spirit in the atmosphere of poetic revery. Finally, the symbol utilizes in a special way the past which is the poet's quarry.

Unfortunately, Fiser's attempt to apply his four criteria drawn from Proust to the poetry of Baudelaire and Mallarmé, after some forcing of the texts, ends with the admission that in neither of the poets does one find as complete and as striking examples of the "dynamic symbol" as in the novelist. In the work of both Mallarmé and Baudelaire "les véritables symboles dynamiques sont rares." He concludes that Baudelaire "only indicated the path taken by the following generation, and in Mallarmé the symbol is so veiled that it can lend itself to the most contradictory interpretations."

ii

Yet the idea of the "dynamic symbol" is worth investigating further, especially if it be relieved of the

Proustian burden. Thus Bergson and Mallarmé may be said to have in common the rejection of what the poet called the "reportorial" aspect of language. For Bergson it was the tension between concepts that elicited the spark of intuition of a living reality. In Mallarmé, by a tightly linked and yet circuitous ceremony of language the poet evoked, not the living reality of the "rose" but the idea of the rose "absent from all bouquets." Language properly attenuated touched the rose with sense at the last moment before it vanished into what Mallarmé's doubtful Faun thought might be, in the case of the song he piped, a "vaine, sonore et monotone ligne."

"To name an object," wrote Mallarmé for the *Enquête* of Jules Huret, "is to suppress three quarters of the enjoyment of the poem which is made up of the happiness of divining something little by little; to suggest, that is our dream. It is the perfect use of this mystery which constitutes the symbol: to evoke an object little by little in order to show a state of soul, or, *inversely*, to choose an object, and disengage from it the state of soul by a series of decipherings." [4]

We can attribute it to Mallarmé's special humor that he makes the reading of a poem sound like a guessing game. The "enjoyment," the "happiness" is witness to the creative activity in the reader as he participates in the dramatic detection. Moreover, if the poet induces the reader to breathe out the name of the object before it quite takes shape, then a deadening abstractness can be avoided. For, even before he encounters the final hint that would reveal the name withheld, the reader has experienced what constitutes its idea and therefore "cela va sans dire." The state of soul can only be glimpsed in its essence, can subject itself to externalization only indirectly through images of objects so interrelated that each one loses individual consistency as it combines with the others.

If, on the other hand, the poet starts from an object, then by asking repeatedly, "What does it mean?" and noting the appropriate images it evokes in him, he can direct the co-operative reader to a glimpse of something ultimate in a state of soul. For just as the physicality of objects is reduced to a purity, so is the pyschological grossness of the state of soul purified to an essence. Here we come to the main point of contrast. For Mallarmé what seems to rise out of the net of language for a moment is an essence, slight and indestructible; for Bergson what flows through the net of language is a patterned movement, a melody.

In his reply to the same *Enquête,* Mallarmé adds: "Poetry consisting in creating, we must seize in the human soul states, gleams of such absolute purity, that well sung and well brought to light, they will constitute the jewels of man: *there we have the symbol, there we have creation and the word takes on its meaning:* it is, in short, the only creation possible for human beings. And indeed, unless the precious stones with which we adorn ourselves manifest a state of soul, we are not justified in adorning ourselves." The sole creativity available to man, the "making" that is poetry, is likened to providing a setting for what then becomes fully visible as a jewel. As an essence, it is hard to make manifest because of its purity and not because of its mobility. Mallarmé's symbol is a special way, through an aloof indirection, of "elaborating essence," as Coleridge said, "into existence." That symbol, like Shelley's star, is "pinnacled dim in the intense inane," where, of course, the "intense inane" means mere vacuity only for those who do not see.

In contrast, the emphasis in Baudelaire seems to be upon the symbolic *object.* It is the object, we remember, which in states of soul almost supernatural reveals the depths of life and becomes the symbol. The object is no more for Baudelaire than for Mallarmé the so-called "real" object, nor the object of "imitation." Nevertheless Baudelaire's handling of the object seems to intensify an effect of *presence.* Mallarmé does everything he can to *distance:* through alliteration, plurisignation, punning, interanimation, the juxtapositions and appositions of metaphor, through effects of rhythm and even of rhyme, of a "music" that is symphonic rather than melodic, spatial rather than temporal, and by shaping even the blank spaces upon the page and the types of print so that the poem may evolve into a form of ideal meaningfulness. He never intends to give up the denotation of words, for it is one of the marks of poetry's superiority to music, but he does want to restore to language its original power and mystery, and this through the pressures of poetic distillation.[5] If he seems in his last poems to have no pity on the reader it is because Mallarmé can easily mistake intensity white-hot for clarity.

Baudelaire, on the other hand, can save appearances for the objects, people, events, the life of Paris, and yet make them function as analogy. The relationship between himself, as representative of man, and life in its higher meaning, he can present in poetic structures where the quality of assertion is a central, directive energy of the poem which is diffused, but not lost in something wholly other. Here the "state of soul" is conditioned by what he wants to say about man and the world. But he can, secondly, compose poems like "Recueillement" where the state of soul in that poem, resignation, also bespeaks, though more indirectly, *la condition humaine*. Finally, there are poems like "La Chevelure," "Harmonie du soir," which offer not so much a response to the world which qualifies the world but a response to some aspect of experience that qualifies the self in the world. The distinction between the second and third kind of poems is even less sharp than that between the last two kinds and the first. It is in poems of the third type that Baudelaire opened a path for Verlaine along which the author of *Romances sans paroles* and of *Sagesse* developed his own originality, and it is comparison of the two poets in poems of this type that will help, as a final touch, to define the achievement of the author of *Les Fleurs du mal*.

The comparison is all the more interesting because it is to poems that might seem to reveal a very "personal" state of soul that Fiser's "dynamic symbol" could naturally apply. The "best definition" of that symbol, according to the same author, is Georges Bonneau's: "The symbol is a concrete analogy set up as a guide-mark by the poet as far as possible along the current of his consciousness." Or, in other words, the symbol is "an analogical image along the path of intuition." [6]

As we have observed in the case of suggestion of an "essence" by Mallarmé, the poet, through delay in presenting the image until the last moment, takes advantage of the reader's creative tension and limits to a minimum degree an arrest of meaning by the final stage of the image. The poet's and the reader's knowledge are intuitive. Such a poem must, of course, use words which "refer," since they have dictionary meanings, but it aims through associations of words and the strategy of the withheld image to create responses of "feeling-knowledge" and attitude. Verlaine's *Romances sans paroles* would then be the ideal title of all such poetry, "songs without words," or words which have become the direction of a melody and are known as a song is known.

Thus, commenting on a famous line from Baudelaire's "Spleen" (LXXVI), "Je suis un cimetière abhorré de la lune," Bonneau imagines the poet descending to the depths of his soul and coming upon a cemetery whose desolation was so much his own desolation that he could not say where the cemetery finished and his own soul began.[7] Unfortunately, the poem does not seem to have the fluid suggestiveness that Bonneau's *symbole dynamique* would seem to require. Analysis will show that in this poem Baudelaire, not content with the marvelous and truly suggestive first line, "J'ai plus de souvenirs que si j'avais mille ans," sets it off and then proceeds to construct an amplification. "Memory" and "time" are the cues. The residues of memory are love letters, verses, etc., associated with receipts and balance sheets, or they are "les pastels plaintifs et les pâles Boucher," with their fragrance of a phial uncorked. But the very quantity of memories suggests a pile, or a deep container, and they become respectively "une pyramide" (which will suggest "un vieux sphinx ignoré du monde insoucieux" at the end of the poem), and a "caveau" or "cimetière." The idea of memory itself is associated not only with death but a death accursed—"un cimetière abhorré de la lune" and "un granit entouré d'un vague épouvante." Finally, time itself becomes horrible with its "boiteuses journées" and "les lourds flocons des neigeuses années," when *Ennui* takes on the proportions of immortality.

Now it would be possible to argue that the "dynamic symbol" is at work in this poem because of the way in which massive elements of imagery offset or redirect each other and yet converge toward the meaning of "spleen," intuitively grasped. "Dynamic," it could be said, is always relative to the mass of what is moving: the Mississippi is fluid and so is the trickle of a hidden brook. This we would grant. On the other hand we would point out that dynamism is not confined to the Bergsonian symbol; the symbol of Schelling, the Schlegels and Coleridge enables us to apprehend and work like *natura naturans* and not merely *natura naturata*. We have already suggested that Baudelaire shares the Romantic sense of the mobile, and it is the basis for his "realism" and his theory of a "modern" beauty. Yet there seems to be a difference between the dynamism of his symbol and that of the "dynamic symbol."

To illustrate, we have at hand an example which Fiser himself draws from Verlaine's volume, *Sagesse*:

> *Un grand sommeil noir*
> *Tombe sur ma vie:*
> *Dormez, tout espoir,*
> *Dormez, toute envie!*
>
> *Je ne vois plus rien,*
> *Je perds la mémoire*
> *Du mal et du bien* . . .
> *O la triste histoire!*
>
> *Je suis un berceau*
> *Qu'une main balance*
> *Au creux d'un caveau:*
> *Silence, silence.*

(A great black slumber / falls on my life, / sleep, every hope, / sleep every desire. [Here the blackness of sleep suggests in "tombe," in anticipation of the image at the end, also a "tomb."] I see nothing any more, / I lose the memory / of good and evil . . . / What a sorry state of affairs! / [where "triste," used apparently in a familiar sense, gives a twisted-smile effect to what follows] I am a cradle / that a hand is rocking / deep in some underground: / Silence! silence! [Here "caveau" can mean a small wine cellar and also a burial vault. "Creux" also suggests the "hollowed out," the "darkness," and prepares for the plurisignation of "Silence! silence!" which may be interpreted as a request not to wake the child or as an ironic commentary—with the "dormez, dormez" of the first stanza—on the whole situation.])

Thus the idea of sleep and loss, suggested from the very beginning of the poem, is intensified toward the end by the image of a cradle rocking in an implausible place. It is as if a child returned into the darkness whence it came, rocked into oblivion by a fatal hand. Especially in the last stanza, Fiser points out, each of the words has a precise, conventional and stable meaning "which has nothing to do with that which the poet attributes to them in these verses. The poem indicates no precision, no stability. It is a movement of the soul, in its momentary fluidity. It is an indication of the direction which the poet invites us to follow, but where he himself will not follow us." [8]

In a poem of this type Verlaine uses a vocabulary drawn from our elementary relations to experience—sleep, hope, desire, good, evil, story, hollow, cellar, cradle—nouns without adjectives (the only three are "grand," "noir," "triste") because the nouns are already rich in connotation, indeed can almost be considered adjectival because their import is so largely affective. Allegorical elements pass unperceived: "Dormez, tout espoir, dormez, toute envie! . . . Je perds la mémoire Du mal et du bien." The symbol, too, seems drawn from the most natural relations—"un berceau."

Yet attempt to detach that "berceau . . . au creux d'un

caveau," and to make it "stand," not as an allegorical equivalent, but in the sense in which even a symbol must stand for some reality in whose apprehension man can participate with the feeling that he is bound to other men. It is convincing *in its context* — or so we are persuaded — but somehow it does not reach beyond, so that it would seem natural for men to quote it, or think of conveying their state of despair through its image. Here one quotes the whole poem or nothing.

Some writers, we know, define symbol in contrast with allegory by its efficacy only in a given context. Evidently they are equating symbol with the "dynamic symbol." But the point at issue is whether, granting that meaning is always in some context, and that the symbol makes a special use of context, it does not persuade us of a meaning in a context broader than the one given. Goethe's "eminent instance" is a convenient example. Within any species there are magnificent specimens which, though they are structured like every other member, "stand out" in their capacity to call attention to that structure and to represent it.

We have reason, then, to affirm that the Baudelairean symbol, even in those poems where the poet comes closest to the kind of structure which is most original in Verlaine, makes the effect of apprehending more fundamental patterns of human feeling in their response to what is fundamental in the world. This is true, we think, even in those images that some would disparage or explain away as "Gothic" — for instance: "Je suis un cimetière abhorré de la lune." Or we might pick from the same poem ("Spleen" LXXVI) such lines as:

> Rien n'égale en longueur les boiteuses journées,
> Quand sous les lourds floçons des neigeuses années
> L'ennui, fruit de la morne incuriosité,
> Prend les proportions de l'immortalité. . . .

> Désormais tu n'es plus, o matière vivante!
> Qu'un granit entouré d'une vague épouvante . . .

The very fact that, as we have indicated, even in poems like "La Chevelure" the individual *état d'âme* is massive enough to invite a concept, "féconde paresse," which is used as a kind of climax of the song, offers evidence for our contention. In "Harmonie du soir," as we have shown, there is no similar statement but the mood concentrates upon a traditional symbol, "ostensoir," which has long stood for meanings partly personal but sufficiently universal to make it the focus of communal worship.

As evidence of the possibility that, even in poems of the type we are discussing, Baudelaire uses the symbol as more than the "objective correlative" of private feelings, we offer, finally, "L'Invitation au voyage." What poem could appear more indubitably a concrete attitude which is inseparable from its words, their meanings, sound, rhythms, images, the total formal construct—an *état d'âme* become a *paysage d'âme*. The poem was published in the *Revue des Deux Mondes* for June 1, 1855. Two years later a prose poem, "L'Invitation au voyage," appeared in "Le Présent" for August 24, 1857. There the poet invited his beloved to a land "singular, superior to others, as Art is to Nature, where the latter is reformed by *le rêve*, where it is corrected, embellished, melted into a new form."

> Fleur incomparable, tulipe retrouvée, allégorique dahlia, c'est là, n'est-ce pas, dans ce beau pays si calme et si rêveur, qu'il faudrait aller vivre et fleurir? Ne serais-tu pas encadrée dans ton analogie, et ne pourrais-tu pas te mirer, pour parler comme les mystiques, dans ta propre *correspondance.*

(Incomparable flower, tulip lost and found, allegorical dahlia, it is there, is it not, in that beautiful land so calm in its dream, that we should go to live and reach our flower. Would you not be framed in your analogy, and could you not be mirrored, to speak like the mystics, in your own *correspondence?*)[9]

Thus a love poem with its landscape suggesting the beloved can offer the perception of an aspect of the universal harmony. The idea of "correspondances" for Baudelaire was not merely the "myth" organizing his activities as a poet creating; to achieve the effect of a "correspondance" may also have served as the test of depth and the breadth of his outreach and as the measure of his success as a poet.

We can understand, then, why Guy Michaud, with the pages of Fiser in mind, rejects the "dynamic symbol": "True symbolism, of which Baudelaire has already given us a foretaste, is something very different, the search for a fundamental correspondence, of a real and constitutive analogy between our soul and the universe; and this idea will be more sharply defined later"—by the Symbolistes.[10] Sometimes, he adds, Verlaine discovered it instinctively, and he quotes from *Romances sans paroles* a few lines of a poem worth examining in its entirety:

> *Dans l'interminable*
> *Ennui de la plaine,*
> *La neige incertaine*
> *Luit comme du sable.*
>
> *Le ciel est de cuivre*
> *Sans lueur aucune,*
> *On croirait vivre*
> *Et mourir la lune.*
>
> *Comme des nuées*
> *Flottent les chênes*
> *Des forêts prochaines*
> *Parmi les buées.*
>
> *Le ciel est de cuivre*
> *Sans lueur aucune,*
> *On croirait vivre*
> *Et mourir la lune.*
>
> *Corneille poussive*
> *Et vous, les loups maigres,*
> *Par ces bises aigres*
> *Quoi donc vous arrive?*

Dans l'interminable
Ennui de la plaine,
La neige incertaine
Luit comme du sable.

(In the interminable / tedium of the plain, / the fitful snow / glistens like sand. / / The sky is of copper / without glimmer of light, / one would say a moon comes alive and dies. / / Like clouds / the oaks in the forest nearby float gray / among the mists. / / The sky is of copper / without glimmer of light, / one would say a moon comes alive and dies. / / Wheezy crow, / and you, skinny wolves, / in these raw north winds, / what happens to you? / / In the interminable / tedium of the plain, / the fitful snow / glistens like sand.)

The essential *paysage* in this poem is the interminable flatness of a plain with a ghostly motion of sand and moon within the dull tedium of earth and sky. The image is twice repeated, making up four of the six stanzas. The only positive movement is that of oaks, of all trees, it would seem, most earthbound; but they have become clouds and they float, gray blurs among the mists.

The poem would be an impressionistic word-painting were it not for the sudden inquiry about the fate of the "corneille poussive" and "les loups maigres." With subtle indirection the poet is judging his world, and it is not purely "his" but universal enough to be shared with menaced animals—and men. Guy Michaud does not give a reason for setting off this poem—according to Henri Peyre "among the few perfect examples of pure poetry in the French language" [11]—against seemingly similar poems of Verlaine which he appears to accept as examples of the "dynamic symbol." He describes Verlaine's poetry as a fusion of consciousness and the world, creating "le pittoresque-état d'âme." Very appositely he quotes one of the best examples of what, in the case of this poet, could not be called "pathetic fallacy" because the tears of hopelessness are not *attributed* to the foliage of trees, but *identified* with them as in the lines "Et que tristes pleuraient, dans les hautes feuillées / Tes espérances noyées" ("Ariettes oubliées, IX").

Verlaine's great discovery, according to Michaud, and the chief source of his influence on the Symbolistes of 1885, lies in a "poésie-musique" which he bears in himself, a kind of dream vision in which language evaporates into melody, where logical meaning is swallowed up "by a suggested impression, totally internal and intuitive," following the lines of a song, unreasoningly sad, the last form of the "mal du siècle." [12] To judge by this account, Verlaine, except occasionally in poems like "Dans l'interminable . . ." and in the religious sonnets of *Sagesse*, does not achieve the constitutive symbol.

How, then, differentiate between what appears to be and is not a symbol, the "dynamic symbol," and the "constitutive symbol"? For the poem under discussion we have already suggested the reason for a certain sense of universality. The world presented is the world that both wolves and men are "up against." Such an effect is strengthened by a certain consistency in the landscape, however delicately etched, attained by repetition. Yet we must admit that these are matters where one gives reasons as only a kind of external check upon the real reason—an immediate perception. Baudelaire, we recall, stated that the recognition of a symbol depends upon the clairvoyance and good will of the spectator. Mrs. Langer speaks of "the forms of feeling—nameless forms, but recognizable when they appear in sensuous replica," and she quotes approvingly W. M. Urban's statement that artistic forms should be designated as "*adequate* or *inadequate* to the ideas they embody." [13] That is, there is no fully persuasive way of demonstrating that what is being conveyed by an aesthetic structure of words is "fundamental" enough to be constitutive. The "burning bush" with all its meaning for Moses, is for another man only a peculiarly striking effect of sunlight on foliage.

Thus, Fritz Strich, exponent of what we have called the "Goethean symbol," denies that the *symbole* of the Symbolistes is a symbol at all. Basing his discussion of the symbol on Goethe's delicate lyric, "Wanderer's Nachtlied," he will deny to Verlaine's "La lune blanche,"

(*La Bonne Chanson*) anything more than the quality of
"Suggestionskunst."

> La lune blanche
> Luit dans les bois:
> De chaque branche
> Part une voix
> Sous la ramée . . .

> O bien-aimée.

> L'étang reflète,
> Profond miroir,
> La silhouette
> Du saule noir
> Où le vent pleure . . .

> Rêvons: c'est l'heure.

> Un vaste et tendre
> Apaisement
> Semble descendre
> Du firmament
> Que l'astre irise . . .

> C'est l'heure exquise.

In this poem the voice issuing from under the branches in
the white moonlight becomes one in a special way with
the lover's cry: it "says" what the lover's cry "means."

Again, the reflection by the pool like a deep mirror of
the black willow where the wind weeps has the image and
the tonality of a dream. The vast and tender calm seeming
to descend from the firmament—an essentially moral
image—is nevertheless given a sensuous accent by an
iridescence of moonlight. "C'est l'heure exquise!" Here
the sharp *i* sounds of "irise" and "exquise" against the
veiled sonority of the nasals work the magic of a culmination.

In a poem like this one, Strich comments, the solitary

poet succeeds through suggestion in imparting his experience to others, freeing himself thereby. But it is an insinuation almost against the will of the reader. Whereas in a poem like "Uber allen Gipfeln ist Ruh" the poet feels something universal in himself and it is received willingly as a universal by the reader.[14]

The moment evoked by Verlaine is certainly very special—in the literal sense of "exquise" (Latin *exquaesitus*). The state of soul cannot be dissociated, it seems, from a quality of light, a chorus of bird songs, the reflection of a black willow in a pool. "O bien-aimée," "Rêvons, c'est l'heure," "C'est l'heure exquise"—each ejaculation set off from its stanza insinuates itself not so much as the consequence but as the equivalent of the particular aspect of the landscape. A white moon and bird-song, through a romantic association previously established in culture, readily suggests love's call. A pool reflecting the silhouette of a dark willow where the wind weeps does not so inevitably suggest dreaming: "Rêvons, c'est l'heure!" In the last stanza the "vaste et tendre apaisement" *seems* to descend from heaven, to be appreciated in the exclamation, "C'est l'heure exquise!"

As a matter of fact, the strategy of these poems consists in throwing an affective coloring backward on the landscape through the ejaculations. The landscape seems to be the "objective correlative" of the *état d'âme*, but in reality the state of soul does not so much *find* its equivalent in a *paysage* as subject the landscape to the power of a mood. In contrast, in "Dans l'interminable ennui de la plaine," it is the nature of the landscape itself with its chill and coppery dullness that motivates a concern for crows, wolves, and men. The images there seem to endow the poem with the feeling that is *in them*.

We know that we are speaking metaphorically, though we are trying to convey objective differences in quality. Consider again Baudelaire's "Le Balcon," which also evokes "les minutes heureuses." There the landscape is the background of feeling, accompanies the feeling, tends to become the equivalent of the feeling: "Que les soleils sont beaux dans les chaudes soirées / Que l'espace est profond!

que le coeur est puissant!" But the volume of feeling seems to be attached to a total situation to which we can attribute these effects even after we have been surprised by poetry's "fine excess." The poet's *coup d'état*, which Baudelaire recommends, but in a context of objective analogies, makes a conquest, in the case of Verlaine, of a domain created by the poet himself.

The same mode of poetic creation is observable in poems where Verlaine uses the most common elements of a landscape—"ciel," "arbre," "oiseau"—as in the celebrated "Le ciel est par-dessus le toit"—and forces them to subjection to his mood by his magic. Sky and tree, bell and bird, become symbols of the great simplicities of life which a young man has squandered—but only by a kind of psychological *coup d'état* in a context created by the ejaculation of the last two lines: "Dis, qu'as tu fait, toi que voilà, / De ta jeunesse?"

This anatomy of butterfly wings may be excusable if it helps to outline a distinction between two forms of symbol. In the first form, the symbol is a structure of language through which the poet conveys to the reader cognition of a quality of feeling so private that, though the poet uses nature as a "dictionary," the preponderant power is that of his personal mood. Yet this mood is not so purely private that it cannot be presented as cognition in its special focus and under a special pressure of language. The symbol in its second form also uses nature as a "dictionary," but the poet seems to be discovering as he creates and the reader has the feeling that he participates in the knowledge of constitutive forms. The first type of symbol is Verlaine's, while Baudelaire, even in such poems as "Harmonie du soir," attains to the second type.

Let us observe Verlaine even in his religious sonnets, in which Michaud sees authentic constitutive symbols. Yet with great acuteness he points out that in the ten sonnets at the end of the second part of *Sagesse*, in those "intuitions of a truly mystical poetry," we have the "melancholy incantation" of the *Romances sans paroles* transmuted into murmur of a prayer. Nevertheless one could go farther in emphasis on Verlaine's effort to shape the dominant intonations of the Catholic faith to his own voice. "Le génie," said Baudelaire, "c'est l'enfance retrouvée à volonté," but a distinction must be drawn between childlikeness and childishness. Even at the heart of his religious poems one sometimes catches a note not of true childlikeness but of the spoiled child Verlaine had been. He seems to have merely transposed instead of transmuting his own experience into Christian symbols. The bibulous poet will drink a wine from the "unchanging vine, whose power, whose sweetness, whose goodness, will cause [his] blood to ferment toward immortality" (Sonnet VII). The friend of Rimbaud will seek on the heart of Jesus which was the human heart, "the place where the head of the apostle reposed" (Sonnet VI). His sufferings merge with those of the Christ, and he hopes to be rewarded by an ecstasy "better than the caress where only the old Adam is embraced." Baudelaire would remind us that human sin can express an exasperated demand for the infinite. Perhaps so, but we find more suggestion of that infinite in his own poetry of revolt than in some of the better examples of Verlaine's poetry of faith. *Sagesse* shows the power of a temperament to transpose to the all-too-human an established symbolism.

iii

We can well believe, then, with Guy Michaud, that Verlaine, "in spite of Baudelaire . . . never even suspected" the constitutive symbol, "leaving to others . . . the trouble of drawing from his work the consequences of the aesthetic that it contained implicitly." These others were *les Symbolistes*. "Le Symbolisme" and "les Symbolistes," terms first used of a French literary movement by Jean Moréas in the "Manifeste" of 1886, have proved to be a prolific source of confusion. The nonspecialist, especially outside of France, and the specialist bowing to current usage, uses them to refer to the poetic achievements and theories of Baudelaire, Mallarmé, Verlaine and Rimbaud. Yet technically the terms belong to a movement of young poets and pamphleteers that gathered around Mallarmé late in his life and around Verlaine, sometimes setting one off against the other. Baudelaire had died nineteen years before, knowing nothing of these descendents to whom he was to contribute an essential *charisma* and an example and doctrine which they interpreted in their own fashion. Rimbaud in 1886 was in Abyssinia, ignorant of the movement and content to be ignored; rediscovery was to begin with his return to France in 1891 to die in that year.

Thus we may speak, as Henri Peyre suggests,[15] of three groups, the first spanning the period between 1821, Baudelaire's date of birth, and 1854, Rimbaud's date, Mallarmé and Verlaine having been born respectively in 1842 and 1844. Theirs was the major poetic achievement which was to cast a luster on the movement that followed; in all of them, too, if we count the Verlaine of the religious sonnets of *Sagesse*, poetic expression aspires to make known or to construct a metaphysical reality. The second and third group consist of poets and writers born as early as 1855 and as late as around 1870 (Claudel, Gide, Proust and Valéry) for whom the symbol was, at one time or another, connected with some idea of a metaphysical depth or supra-natural outreach which seemed to require and justify a poetic language distinct from the language ordinarily used among men. One hardly knows how to mark the end of the movement, which some place in 1905, for Claudel, Gide and Valéry are our contemporaries of yesterday and Proust of the day before yesterday, and our problems with Symbolisme and even with symbolism are their problems. Proust and Claudel in different ways represent the "mystical" current; Gide and Valéry tend, as we have said, to reduce the "miracle" to the effect of the miraculous to be achieved by a modern poetry fully aware of its means and fully disciplined.

Thus Baudelaire and the three great poets who followed him can be called "precursors" of the movement only if one holds with Guy Michaud that the meaning of the whole process lay in the fuller definition of the constitutive, analogical symbol which was achieved by the theorists of the later groups, and in the culmination both of the theory and of the poetry in Paul Claudel.

iv

Let us pursue such an interpretation for the sake of a later comparison and contrast. For Guy Michaud "le Symbolisme" as a movement is characterized, first of all, by the use of poetry itself as a means of attaining to a higher reality than can be known by sense, reason, or emotion in themselves or in any fusion that is not poetic.[16] Ideas are to be grasped not in themselves but in their relations. These relations, furthermore, are to be perceived from a point of view that is "human," and within the focus of emotion; in this sense, and only in this sense, they may be called "subjective." For the poetic attitude is at once cognitive and emotional. Such a mode of knowledge is "supra-rational"; it is the equivalent of "le coeur" for Pascal. This point of view, already suggested by Mallarmé and by René Ghil and other poets and critics, will not be elucidated philosophically until after 1891 in Bergson's theory of "intuition." But of course it had for ages been implied in mysticism and asserted explicitly by some of the mystics.

Yet Symboliste poetry is inevitably communicative in the sense that it functions in and through language which, whatever may be its uses as confession, incantation, or prophecy, also has its "message." Nevertheless—and this is the crux of the philosophical problem of knowledge—the "knowledge" communicated is not discursive. For it is the result of a state of *illumination* in the poet, a state (or at least its equivalent) which he must in turn create in the reader. This state is ineffable; and in order to give the reader the memory of something never seen before, the poet must *suggest*. The idea of "suggestion" was already in Verlaine's "Art Poétique" (1882) and the Symbolistes soon took it over. Mallarmé will affirm that the poet must "retain only the suggestion of anything." But to use language in order to "suggest," indeed to imply that suggestion is its original and certainly its purer use, is to propose a whole theory of language. And this, according to Guy Michaud was "the real discovery of Symbolisme."

Moreover as Verlaine saw, and the Symbolistes after him, such a suggestive language had affinities with music. It must take back the powers that suggestive language lost to its discursive uses, powers that had been exploited by music. But the Symbolistes, here following Mallarmé and not, according to Michaud, the different theory of the nature of "music" in Verlaine, held that the poet in a moment of inspiration discovers for his vision "the necessary form, not so much an instinctive music but an essential music, not a melody any more, but a harmony." When language rediscovers at least a part of its powers, the "real Symbol" is born.

The true Symbolistes, Michaud insists, are therefore more exacting than a Jean Moréas seemed to be inclined to say. For the latter "symbol" meant "metaphor," and he let the matter rest there. Whereas the Symbolistes, in accordance with the tradition of the Kabbala and the "occult" philosophy, sought to make of metaphor the instrument for the discovery of truth through analogy. They accepted the ancient Tradition's "gospel of Correspondences."

> To give back to the word its role of symbol is to restore to it its primitive and central function, and to rediscover, so far as possible, primitive language in all its power and virtualities . . . The symbol is more than a crossroads; it is a center of radiation. It is more than a privileged position; it is a dynamic center whence truth is diffused in all directions and at all levels of reality. Only at such a price can the word symbol find its true power and meaning; only at this price will it be what the Symbolistes meant it to be: a synthesis.

To be a "living synthesis" the symbol must express truths valid simultaneously at every level, with multiple meanings superposed in hierarchical order and with the infinite resonance of an inescapable "music." Thus the symbol, as Maeterlinck said, is a "force of nature" and the poet must remain "passive in the symbol" and let the eternal order of the universe use him as an instrument. This is what Mallarmé meant by restoring the initiative to words, "rendre l'initiative aux mots."

Thus it is to the credit of Symbolism, according to Michaud, to have posed in definitive terms, if not to have resolved, the question whether true poetic experience may not be in some sense, an "experimental knowledge" of reality. Yet the poet does not "create" but "re-creates" life through a "fiction." He enables the reader to remember a world which is not the everyday world; it is an ideal world, the world of emotions and of the soul's dreams which are dreams of truth. The dream quality serves to protect both against the dryness of abstraction and the dazzlement of a Beyond seen face to face. Through an effect of aesthetic distance it imports a greater depth and resonance to things.

In this way the Symboliste movement, according to Michaud, rediscovered "poetic truth." Moreover it achieved self-consciousness together with its rediscovery of poetry as latent symbol expressive of the harmonious correspondences of the universe. The realization that, in the past, all true poetry had instinctively been symbol was now edged with the will to make poetry symbol. Thus Henri de Régnier, of the second generation and one of the *habitués* of Mallarmé's Tuesday night gatherings, will write for Huret's *Enquête* that, if in the past the symbol "rose up instinctively" in works of art, in our day "we make of the symbol the essential condition of art."

Nevertheless some time was to elapse before le Symbolisme attained its fulness of meaning. According to Michaud the "one far-off divine event" toward which the whole process moved is not the work of Proust who, using "the dynamic symbol," went both farther and less far than the Symbolistes, nor that of Valéry, for whom symbolism becomes in theory a kind of superior algebra, a system of signs expressing relations too subtle for translation in direct language, but the work of Paul Claudel. Reaching a conviction of the supernatural thanks to his experience of Rimbaud's *Illuminations* in 1886, learning at the *mardis* from Mallarmé to ask of everything, "Qu'est-ce que ça veut dire," making contact with medieval esoteric doctrine through his study of St. Thomas, Claudel will restate the doctrine of eternal archetypes, of macrocosm and microcosm, and of the constitutive symbol. He will seek to relate man intimately with the world through a "connaissance" interpreted as "co-naissance," the birth in mutuality of man and the world; he will reconcile dynamism and the timeless, and make of *le hasard* nothing but metaphor which is forever at work in an organic and integrated universe. Thus for Claudel as for the Kabbalist, not only is each object a symbol in relation to the constellation of other objects with which he is in intimate contact, but it is also a reality. More exactly, it permits the passage from one reality to another. Through the symbol, for Claudel, man may have access really and substantially to God. The role of man, and more particularly, of the poet, is to attain to the pure essence of things as created by God and to witness to their Maker.[17]

Thus in Claudel—at least in Michaud's view—our study of symbolism seems to have come full circle. We are back to Neo-Platonism and the Middle Ages, but with a difference. The difference is a conscious reaction to Francis Bacon's supposed destruction of analogy, and with it of symbolic knowledge, by philosophers, critics, and poets in the very century in which scientific positivism was reaching its apogee. The difference is a conception of the symbol which is more fully theorized and which takes advantage of new modes of poetic indirection, of "music" and suggestion. A novelty, too, is the promotion of poetry from the camp follower of Christian theology to an exposed position as witness, not necessarily to that theology, but to the "spirit."

v

If Guy Michaud's views of the meaning of the symbol for the heirs of Baudelaire are correct, the idea that modern poetry is essentially Symboliste poetry would need drastic revision. In contrast, Professor Lehmann's *The*

Symbolist Aesthetic in France, 1885–95 makes the most of the affiliation of the epigoni to modern poetry: the Symbolistes are "very close" to us but chiefly because, in spite of everything, they have helped us to resolve the symbol into a "literary monad." To support his advanced reductionism he brings up the heavy guns of an expressionist aesthetic.

His position, based on a linguistic philosophy that owes much to R. G. Collingwood's *Principles of Art* with its Crocean affinities, may be used for a final perspective upon the meaning of Baudelaire and the Symbolistes for a modern aesthetic. For Professor Lehmann it is not the actual achievement of the Symbolistes as systematic thinkers that counts, but their exceptional importance as artists who called for a new systematic thought. The "most striking feature" of their effort was the attempt to establish art as an autonomous branch of human activity, distinguishing it from history and science. Both Flaubert and Baudelaire had sought to refute Taine and positivism by basing the distinction on form alone; the Symbolistes with remarkable unanimity had agreed that all art is *not* science. Indeed, in their excessive separation between *Begriffen* (concepts) and *Ideen* they were to lead, in Lehmann's view, to a distortion the very opposite of Taine's—to Bergson and to Surrealism. Yet, ironically, the generation which brought the Symbolist movement into being was "solid on one point of aesthetic doctrine; namely, on this assumption which much of their detailed speculation and study tended to undermine . . . the assumption that an intellectual element, an element of reference was the fundamental mark of language under all circumstances whatever."

Thus the Symbolist movement, though it set on foot a "proper observation of the distinct facts of poetry," and was working "implicitly towards a conception of imaginative creation such as we can isolate in Valéry," with Mallarmé coming nearest in the nineteenth century to formulating this concept, proves disappointing to a linguistic philosophy. In all their labor to broaden and to refine modes of poetic expression, we may summarize, the Symbolistes had refused to give up the element of reference even in the language of poetry and had not considered such reference incompatible also with mysticism.[18] In other words, they would have found in Yeats a companion as they had in Baudelaire an ancestor.

On the whole, then, Lehmann is forced to confirm at least the general trend of Michaud's interpretation of the Symbolistes. Let us compare the two views of Baudelaire. According to Michaud, Baudelaire gave a decisive orientation to the Symbolistes at one point: the idea of a poetic state that realizes the fusion of self and not-self, an impulse he had received from Swedenborg, Poe and the esoteric tradition. Yet he never sought to analyze exactly on a metaphysical level ideas of macrocosm and microcosm but was content with the sense of the mystery of life. He did conceive of a poetry restored to its real function, to symbolize the depth of life by the evocation of a more or less external spectacle; but it was the following generations that elaborated the theory of the poetic symbol. Baudelaire was content to practice the theory instinctively, "but in the full recognition that the symbol is not the simple concrete representation of an abstract idea, as a classical rhetoric would have it, but the means, and the sole means, of creating a new world with the debris of the old." [19] He is a precursor especially through his intuition of correspondences and universal symbolism and analogy, and in his desire to decipher the mystery and the hieroglyphics of creation. In this he prepares for Mallarmé and the Symboliste generation which, no longer content with promises, "tentera décidément de dérober le Paradis d'un seul coup."

Lehmann, too, like Michaud, and unlike Lloyd Austin and Jean Prévost, will give full weight to the mystical element in Baudelaire. Thus he insists on the "uncompromisingly mystical foundation" upon which the poet rested his theory. For a Symboliste like Baudelaire, he avers, mysticism accounts for the value of art. The poet's activity was "first and foremost mystical, a-linguistic," and he never suggests that the "use of language is poetry." He did not distinguish even as clearly as Mallarmé between the language of "reportage" and the language of poetry, and he never completely brought to light the distinction between "éloquence" and what Verlaine called "littéra-ture." Words to him are symbolic in the ordinary sense they may have in science and philosophy, as names or concepts; it is the "experiences they signify" which are "symbols in the mystic's special sense." Thus Baudelaire limits the term symbol by excluding words and language, which are the poet's material, from the realm of symbols.

Here Professor Lehmann overstates his grievance. It is, to be sure, the "spectacle" or object before one's eyes in certain states of soul almost supernatural that becomes the symbol of the depth of life. But in our discussion of Baudelaire's notes: "De la langue et de l'écriture, prises comme opérations magiques, sorcellerie évocatoire," and "Le surnaturel comprend la couleur générale et l'accent, c'est-à-dire intensité, sonorité, limpidité, vibrativité . . ." we stressed the poet's *voluntarism*—that is the realization that the symbol is not evoked without a concentrated effort of expression that includes language, atmosphere, and music united in an objective perfection. And Lehmann himself concludes that Baudelaire's conception of "le rêve," was a contribution to the future—"staying awake and working hard: composing poetry." [20]

Baudelaire, in his theory and practice, we would suggest, being concerned with gathering up the threads that are woven into a poetry where *volupté* of a number of kinds is one with *connaissance* on a number of levels, did not discern and would have been temperamentally and philo-sophically incapable of untangling the snarl in their remoter reaches. But can we say even in our time that the major problem, the relation of knowledge to a special state and a special language, has been solved, we who are beginning to witness an offensive in favor of the very position held untenable by critics like Lehmann—a re-assessment and restatement within the context of a sym-bolic theory of poetry, of the referential capacities of poetry? After Baudelaire and Mallarmé, the Symbolist

Movement found it even more difficult to avoid confusion because of the greater intricacy of the developing web. Lehmann suggests eight meanings of the word "symbol," each more or less interrelated and ranging from allegory, artistically highly wrought, and the "eminent instance" in the Goethean sense or something suggesting a Platonic idea, to representations embodying attitudes of special emotional power, sometimes attributed to supernatural sources, and finally to "any work of art at all, considered as a formal unity, or embodying an aspiration to formal unity (Gide)." In the case of Baudelaire, the symbol meant "any isolable member of the external world or any quality which bears witness (to the mystic) of a supernatural unity and 'universal analogy' in the world." The Mallarméan symbol as any sensible thing or any word so far as it suggests "the Platonic idea immanent in it," according to Lehmann, "shades" into the Baudelairean type and is "virtually identical" with the Yeatsian type defined as "any representation serving as a sign of a general attitude which either tradition or supernatural decree has invested with powerful emotional resources."

Yet Baudelaire, whose "mystical" intention in the symbol Lehmann has maximized, is said to have "pointed to" the symbol as a "fragment of highly organized and expressive speech," that is, as "literary monad," and to symbol in the sense of "the aesthetic unity of created art—which is indifferently unity of form and unity of content." [21] This would be true if we added to "pointed" the adverbial phrase "at quite a distance." No doubt the symbol came to mean this for some theorists, though we have strong doubts that any poet, even when provided with a "phrase donnée" or with a rhythm at the beginning, is motivated by visions of the cool self-reflection of a "literary monad." It is possible to abstract from the totality of Baudelairean poetry certain procedures or techniques, such as indirectness. Lloyd Austin is quite correct in rejecting the "literary monad" because, with Cazamian, he feels that the term "symbol" should emphasize "la présentation indirecte des valeurs." [22] But, as we have seen, he would make of the symbol no more than an "objective correlative."

When we have come to the point where the symbol means nothing more distinctive than the "aesthetic unity of created art," or even such a unity distinguished by indirection of presentation, we might ask whether we still have a useful term. At any rate we have attempted to show why Baudelaire should not be considered the source of a modern "Symbolism" conceived after this fashion. Professor Wellek warns us against the dangers of mysticism and intellectualism for the doctrine of the symbol. But mysticism, as we have shown, was an essential part of the context in which the idea of "symbol" developed. Is there no danger that "symbolism," completely abstracted from that context may become, as did classical mythology until it was given a new and suggestive reality by modern symbolic and mythical theory, merely an ornament or a device? An interest in "mysticism" or "truth," we will acknowledge, tends to distract the reader from appreciations and judgments of aesthetic quality. Yet Baudelaire and Mallarmé never expected their poetry to be read for its mystical "truth" rather than for its "beauty," although each poet, in a different way, entertained the hope that beauty itself might be the seal marking the passage through their poetry of a higher reality. We can understand the methodological impulse in any aesthetics or theory of literature to make of poetry purely "this" and "not that"; yet we suspect that in the case of poetry, in its dangers both for religion and from religion, we are faced with the eminently human choice between killing the goose and spoiling the egg.

vi

A light is thrown on our entire journey *From Symbolism to Baudelaire* by the late Renato Poggioli in an excellent volume on *Poets of Russia*, 1890–1930. Looking beyond the French to the German Romantics and Novalis, the three leaders of Russian Symbolism, Vjacheslav Ivanov, Andrej Belyj, and Aleksandr Blok, according to

Professor Poggioli, "made the bold attempt to supply Russian Symbolism with that mystical intuition and metaphysical insight which, all their theoretical declarations notwithstanding, earlier Symbolists both Russian and Western, perhaps with the exception of Baudelaire, had conspicuously lacked." Ivanov, the only one who succeeded in keeping faith with the Symbolist ideal, though acknowledging that the modern poet is attracted to Symbolism by his extreme subjectivity, had hoped to go beyond the "new-fangled Symbolism" through Novalis and Goethe, back to "the great anagogic poetry of Dante and of his predecessors." Even Baudelaire's symbolism seemed to Ivanov to be in "improper combination" with the "new-fangled symbolism," no doubt because of its relation to subjective idealism. For the Russian aimed at a symbolology "exclusively intent on revealing within the objects it represents their full ontological significance and the seal of their value." The symbol would thus acquire its genuine meaning and imply "an ascent *a realibus ad realiora.*"

Thus, even in the case of the Russian symbolists, symbolism was attached to mysticism, though it might be a personal and private mysticism that brought them close to Stefan George, Rainer Maria Rilke, Hofmannsthal, and Yeats. Our purpose is broad enough to accommodate even Poggioli's opinion that, "while some good Symbolist poetry was written in the illusion that the Holy Grail was within reach, far better poetry was written out of fear that the quest would fail, or even the realization that it led to a dead end." [23] We should like only to repeat that, even then, it was the "Holy Grail" that cast the spell.

The idea of symbol from the Neo-Platonists to Baudelaire, as we have seen, has been connected with the manifestation of a "higher reality" conceived either in traditional religious language or, as in the case of Goethe's unfathomable *Urphänomenon*, in a metaphysical language with religious overtones. Symbol, then, has been a term with a metaphysic or the metaphysical attached. The poetry of Baudelaire, Mallarmé, Rimbaud, and Verlaine was implicated in different ways, which it is important to differentiate, within this context. In Baudelaire a sense of the symbol seeking to fuse both old and new combined with a sharp consciousness (and conscience) of art. Poems appeared in which the symbol as component played a dominant role, providing examples of what common usage means when it calls poetry "symbolic." The other side of vision in terms of metaphor-symbol was an expressive language which, called "suggestive" or "musical," pointed steadily toward a radical differentiation between the language of poetry and the language of ordinary discourse.

Once the belief in such a special, and even specialized, "language of poetry" had been established, the inevitable temptation was what we have called the "Valéryan shift" after its most brilliant and famous French exponent. The new language was subtly extracted from its native context, that context, in the case of Baudelaire and Mallarmé, as perhaps also in that of Yeats, being shrugged off politely. Yet something of the native mystery of the symbol still accrues, as in the tone of those modern accounts of poetry that make its *raison d'être* its penetration into the "mysterious" depths or intricacies supposedly beyond the reach of psychological science. Given such words as "life" and "feeling" modern religiosity speedily finds itself *en plein mystère*. Perhaps such an aura suffuses for many even Mrs. Langer's theory of the symbol, which Professor Kermode names as the form of symbolic theory with which the new poetics could establish a *modus vivendi* after he has consigned Blake, Mallarmé, and Rimbaud to nether darkness.

What still prevails, says the same writer in a chapter discussing "modern symbolist readings" of literary history in *The Romantic Image,* is "the symbolist conception of the work of art as aesthetic monads, as the product of a *mode of cognition* superior to, and different from that of the sciences." [24] Professor Kermode's use of "aesthetic monads" and "mode of cognition superior to . . . that of the sciences" as partners suggests some problems with terminology. Critical terms share the common fate of all language: they shift more or less in meaning. But one

might argue plausibly that historic associations and contexts of a term could and should serve as anchors which
nevertheless allowed some movement in current and
wind. For a poetry to be said to belong to the "symbolist"
heritage from Baudelaire and Mallarmé, it should be
"symboliste" (that is, "symbolist" or "symbolistic") in
two senses. It should seem to a reasonably sizeable family
of readers to be concerned with the "Holy Grail," that is,
qualities or structures that evoke religious feeling, perhaps
some sense of what Rudolph Otto called the "numinous."
Our walls will have windows and open-work; we are trying
to set up not a constrictive but a workable idea of a term
now hovering between confusion and meaninglessness.
Our emphasis is meant to be relatively more on what the
concentration of the reader apprehends than on what the
poet "intended" he should apprehend; for even Baudelaire,
who came upon the symbol in certain high moments he
characterized as "almost supernatural," knew that "le
symbole," to be recognized, called for a sensitive man of
good will. Again, religious feeling lives and changes within
broad limits, and we know no compelling reason to deny
use of the term "symbolist" to linguistic structures that
seem to afford a sense of the *presential,* which Philip
Wheelwright defines as "that quality which the primitive
myth-maker, the man of religious sensitivity, and the
developed poetic consciousness all have in common." [25]

The second criterion of a reasonably discriminating use
of the adjective "symboliste" ("symbolist" or "symbolistic"), is a linguistic structure thoroughly metaphorical,
with a tendency toward radical metaphor (or "diaphor"),
an indirectness of presentation with the symbol as component, the whole being "suggestive" and "musical." For
reasons already given, a poem or work of the "Goethean"
type could be considered "symbol" with a religious or
metaphysical connotation, but we should not be comfort-
able if we called it "symbolist." One might still hold that
all "poetry," meaning by this true literature in any genre, is
"symbol," without committing oneself to admiration of
the linguistic structures favored by the heirs of Baudelaire.

Such a nomenclature might be a useful tool if applied, let us say, in Germany to George, Hofmannsthal, and Rilke; in Spain to an Antonio Machado, Jorge Guillén, Cesar Vallejo, Garcia Lorca, Rafael Alberti; in Portugal to a Fernando Pessoa and Jorge de Lima; in Italy to Ungaretti and Montale.[26] It might help to establish an indispensable, if modest, degree of tidiness in our rubrics if it were applied not only to Hopkins, Eliot, and Yeats, to Ezra Pound, Hart Crane, and Wallace Stephens, to the later Frost, to the William Carlos Williams of *Paterson*, to Dylan Thomas, George Barker, Robert Lowell, Allen Tate but also to the various poets granted a chapter of their own under the caption, "The Ghostly Member" by Babette Deutsch in the immensely competent *Poetry in Our Time*.[27] What would be the result if our criteria, for instance, were applied to Edith Sitwell, Elinor Wylie, Kathleen Raine, Edwin Muir, Léonie Adams? Allegedly poets who often use the symbol as component in the expression of religious or metaphysical themes, to what extent are their linguistic structures also "symbolist"? Certainly a great tact would have to feel its way toward the spirit of forms, since we have already indicated that even the linguistic structures of Baudelaire, Mallarmé, Rimbaud, and Verlaine, the tetrarchs of Symbolisme, are to be distinguished from one another. Would our two criteria be useful in the novel—Joyce, Virginia Woolf? In plays . . . ?

What of Baudelaire, then, in whom we mark the turning point from symbolism to Symbolisme? We risk an analogy in conclusion. During the Crusades, though the goal for the zealous and the single-minded was the liberation of the Holy Sepulchre in Jerusalem, many knights were satisfied to set up fiefs for themselves along the way, sometimes in Asia Minor, sometimes even in Greece. The whitened stones of the *donjons* of French knights still stand on Acro-Corinth. With the religious impulse were mixed motives some of which, sooner or later, became predominantly or fully secular. Some historians nevertheless do not discount the reality or the potency of the religious impulse, and of the benefits it brought for individual souls and for Western civilization. Others work to resolve the religious impulse completely into conscious or unconscious secular motives. What cannot be denied is the increasing secularization of culture since the Crusades.

The course of thought about, and practice of, the literary symbol since Kant, Schiller, and Goethe suggests an analogy. The idea of the symbol in the German philosophers and poets was rooted in a cultural tradition receding into the Middle Ages and Neo-Platonism, expressing itself not only in Christianity but in those heretical and contentious fellowtravelers, the Kabbalists and esoteric philosophers. At work in the Middle Ages and the Renaissance, renewing their strength in the eighteenth century, the latter have developed on the off side, as it were, even into our day. The philosophical, the religious, and the esoteric tradition, effected a fruitful contact again during Romanticism. For some poets and for some critics and theorists, the modern poetic movement since the Romantics has sought to recapture an ancient power of language, a mode of symbolic and analogical seeing. For an Ivanov, a Fritz Strich, a Guy Michaud, the ideal was achieved in Dante, Goethe, and Claudel.

What of Baudelaire, both innovator and figure of transition? Certainly we must emphasize in his case the religious and esoteric matrix, though his relation to it, to be sure, was not that of a Dante or a Claudel. Therefore we are willing to accommodate ourselves to Guy Michaud's conclusion that Baudelaire gave us only a "foretaste" of "true symbolism," since he practiced the theory only "instinctively" and was satisfied with "le mystère poétique." We ourselves, less unilateral can be content with "le mystère poétique," though we believe that we have a right to insist on Baudelaire's real, if peculiar, grasp of its religious and metaphysical connotations.

For the theory of symbolism in the nineteenth century, as we have pointed out, even in the mode of its relation to Neo-Platonism developed in a philosophy of organism, of change and novelty. Yet the Romantic quest, as competent scholars have shown, was not for an escape out of time but for a means of validating time as the "moving image" of eternity, to confer upon time a positive religious and metaphysical status. Baudelaire's ideal of "intimacy" and "color" in his poetry, his insistence on a "modern" beauty, his kind of religious vision were Romantic. In some of his poetry he presented the absence of God, he even struck a Promethean note, sometimes in the tone of grievance, more often in a tone of grief whose resonance belied a flat despair. His special ardor for an experience of the infinite, *hic et nunc*, more earthbound than that of a Novalis, brought Paris and the modern world into his poetry and enlarged the area where those objects could be found which in moments "almost supernatural" reveal the depths of life and become its symbols.

Thus Baudelaire's real contribution to later developments in symbolism could be said to have taken the form of a peculiar offshoot of Romantic immanentism. Objections to this view are evident: Baudelaire's opposition to the idea of "nature" in a Wordsworthian sense. "Nature" for him must always be apprehended in the process of correction through "vision," and this was as true in religion as in art. Nevertheless Baudelaire did not permit "nature" to remain in the classical sense an independent, impersonal background. A second objection is related to the first: Baudelaire's sense of the evil in man making eventually, under Poe's influence, for political and social reaction. Nevertheless he could interpret some of the more dramatic sins—hashish, Lesbianism—as mistaken aspiration toward the infinite, nor did his sense of sin inhibit an ardent demand for an infinite of bliss *here and now*. The need of redemption before large claims can be made and the patient hope in a better world to come are not Baudelairean themes. It is the impatient demand for the divine to be more manifest here and now, in modern life, in modern beauty, to become flower even in hypocrisy and sin under conditions in which the divine seems absent— that is Baudelaire's link with immanentism.

On the aesthetic plane Baudelaire added to the old

symbolology a new symbolism drawn from the modern, the particular, and the changing. In accordance with the general pattern which we have been suggesting, Baudelaire's *symbolisme* has an oblique relation to the older *symbolique*, but it cannot be torn away. Nevertheless, just as emphasis on immanentism can be a bridge to a religious-minded naturalism, or to naturalism proper, so the oblique direction of Baudelaire's *symbolisme* could suggest ways to new theories and to new experiments with the symbol. After all, our problems with the symbol result from our attempt to reinterpret in terms of post-Kantian philosophies a conception of symbol grounded on a view of ultimate reality as static perfection. An exponent of a philosophy of change, even though clinging, as many Romantics did, to a mitigated form of eternalism, will tend to think in terms of "Imagination," an organic mode of apprehension, and not of the "imitation" of fixed structures. Imagination will unite the knower through symbol with a *natura* that is *naturans*. Baudelaire, we believe, became involved in this experiment without any great theoretical understanding of its terms or its implications, but with the decisiveness that marked his opinions. He insisted both on the "analogy" and on the "intimacy," on a storehouse of structures which a metaphor might fit with mathematical exactness and on "color," on discovery and creation. Whatever the theoretical difficulties of his position, aggravated by a poetry that sometimes presents a sense of the divine chiefly through despair or even revolt at its apparent absence in life, we must resist the temptation to over-simplify Baudelaire's "situation." What the symbol meant to Baudelaire is more than we can get into an "objective correlative" or even into a literary monad of an indirect structure. To return to our analogy drawn from the Crusades, Baudelaire did not take Jerusalem, but neither was he satisfied to settle in a fief outside of Holy Land.

NOTES

1 — From Plotinus to Dante

1. "The Concept of Romanticism in Literary History," *Comparative Literature*, I, II (1949), 1–23, 147–72.
2. René Wellek, *A History of Modern Criticism* (New Haven: Yale University Press, 1955), II, 339–40. My heavy debt to these masterly volumes in this section is gratefully acknowledged.
3. J. Isaacs, *The Background of Modern Poetry* (New York: Dutton, 1952), pp. 21–33 *passim*.
4. Wellek, II, 3, italics supplied.
5. Edgar De Bruyne, *L'Esthétique du Moyen Age* (Louvain: Editions de l'Institut Supérieur de Philosophie, 1947), pp. 87–88. Unless otherwise indicated, all translations are my own.
6. W. K. Wimsatt and Cleanth Brooks, *Literary Criticism* (New York: Alfred Knopf, 1957), p. 117. To this volume too my debt is considerable.
7. *Ibid.*, pp. 126–31 *passim*.
8. De Bruyne, pp. 90–92.
9. Wimsatt and Brooks, pp. 94–97.
10. *Convivio,* II.i.2–9; translated by Philip Wicksteed. Quoted in Wimsatt and Brooks.
11. De Bruyne, pp. 97–99, 200.
12. Charles S. Singleton, *Dante Studies* (Cambridge: Harvard University Press, 1954–58), I, 62.
13. *Dantis Aligherii epistolae: The Letters of Dante,* trans. Paget Toynbee, quoted in Singleton, p. 87.
14. Singleton, pp. 69–89, 31.
15. Francis Fergusson, *Dante's Drama of the Mind* (Princeton: Princeton University Press, 1953), p. 103.
16. Singleton, pp. 79–80.
17. *Kunst und Altertum*, V, 3 (1826), translated and quoted by Erich Heller in *The Disinherited Mind* (New York: Meridian Books, 1959), p. 161.

18. Dorothy Sayers comes close to the Goethean terminology. In the *Divine Comedy*, she avers, there is a "minimum of arbitrary, and a maximum of natural symbolism," where by "natural symbol" is meant a "particular instance of a universal." Yet she calls the work a "great allegory." *Further Papers on Dante* (New York: Harper, 1957) II, 53–58. Bernard Stambler in *Dante's Other World* (New York: New York University Press, 1957) compounds confusion of terms by only partially rejecting Singleton's "allegory of the theologians," accepting an essentially Goethean definition of the symbol, yet making of the symbol a "simple equation" (pp. 73–75).

19. C. S. Lewis, *The Medieval Allegory of Love* (Oxford: Clarendon Press, 1936), pp. 322, 61, 54, 268, 160, 154.

20. Etienne Gilson, *Dante the Philosopher*, trans. David Moor (New York: Sheed and Ward, 1949), p. 293 ff.

2 – Goethe and the Romantic Theorists

1. René Wellek and Austin Warren, *Theory of Literature* (New York: Harcourt, Brace and Co., 1949), p. 330, n. 11.

2. Quoted from Philip Wheelwright, *The Burning Fountain* (Bloomington: Indiana University Press, 1954), p. 89.

3. Karl Viëtor, *Goethe the Thinker* (Cambridge: Harvard University Press, 1950), pp. 175–76.

4. *Ibid.*, p. 69. *Conversations with Eckermann*, Sept. 18, 1823 and Feb. 26, 1824. Quoted in Viëtor, p. 163.

5. Viëtor, pp. 60–74, 179.

6. Antonio Aliotta, *L'Estetica di Kant e degli idealisti romantici* (Roma: Perrella, 1950), pp. 214–16.

7. Wellek, *History of Modern Criticism*, II, 156–57.

8. Quoted in Wellek, II, 41–42; see also p. 43.

9. Wellek, II, 42.

10. Wellek, II, 43, 44.

11. Wellek, II, 47–49.

12. For a discussion, see Gian N. G. Orsini, *Benedetto Croce* (Carbondale: Southern Illinois University Press, 1961), pp. 227–78 *passim*.

13. Fritz Strich, "Das Symbol in Der Dichtung" (1939), in *Der Dichter und Die Zeit* (Bern: A. Francke, 1947), p. 32.

14. See my "Charles Du Bos and Goethe," *Romantic Review* (Feb., 1959), pp. 41–54. I have paraphrased the French critic's "équilibre au sein de l'entrevision."

15. Philip Wheelwright, *Metaphor and Reality* (Bloomington: Indiana University Press, 1962), p. 68.

16. Quoted in Wellek, I, 207, 212.

17. Quoted in Wellek, I, 211.

18. *Oeuvres Complètes de Baudelaire*, Pléiade edition (Paris: Gallimard, 1961), p. 1257. Subsequent references to this edition of Baudelaire's works will be indicated only by *Oeuvres*.

19. Eliseo Vivas, *D. H. Lawrence: The Failure and the Triumph of Art*, appendix on "The Constitutive Symbol" (Evanston: Northwestern University Press, 1960), p. 273.

3 – The Esoteric Context

1. Margaret Gilman, *Baudelaire the Critic* (New York: Columbia University Press, 1943), pp. 140–42.

2. Paul Valéry, Variété II, *Oeuvres*, I, Pléiade edition (Paris: Gallimard, 1957), p. 608.

3. John Senior, *The Way Down and Out* (Ithaca: Cornell University Press, 1959), pp. 17, 27.

4. *Ibid.*, pp. 44, 133–50 *passim*.

5. Quoted in Albert Béguin, *L'Ame Romantique et le rêve* (Paris: Corti, 1937), 2nd ed., 1946, p. 310; italics supplied.

6. Baudelaire, *Oeuvres*, pp. 347–48.

7. Béguin, pp. 48–52.

8. For a recent publication of selected writings, see F. H. Maatner and H. Hatfield, *The Lichtenberg Reader* (Boston: Beacon Press, 1959).

9. *Novalis Schriften*, ed. I. Minor (Jena: Eugen Diedericks, 1923), number 194.

10. Maurice Besset, *Novalis et la pensée mystique* (Paris: Aubier, 1947), pp. 9–10, 202–10.

11. See my *Charles Du Bos and English Literature* (New York: King's Crown Press, 1949), pp. 100–104.

12. E. Spenlé, *Novalis* (Paris: Hachette, 1904), pp. 161–62.

13. Baudelaire, *Oeuvres*, p. 343.

14. Enid Starkie, *Baudelaire* (London: Faber and Faber,

1957), pp. 217–18, 17, 532, 225–26. Essentially similar views of the relation of Poe and Baudelaire will be found in André Ferran, *L'Esthétique de Baudelaire* (Paris: Hachette, 1933), part II, ch. 1.

15. Baudelaire, *Oeuvres*, p. 687. From "Théophile Gautier" (1859). Baudelaire is quoting an extract from his own "Notes Nouvelles sur Edgar Poe," his preface to the *Nouvelles Histoires Extraordinaires* (1857), where he adapted "The Poetic Principle."

4 – The Critic's Theories

1. Valéry, *Oeuvres*, II, 598–613. I quote from the translation by W. A. Bradley of "The Position of Baudelaire," in *Baudelaire*, edited by Henri Peyre (New Jersey: Prentice-Hall Inc., 1962), pp. 7–18.

2. See Baudelaire's review of L. de Senneville's (Louis Ménard) *Prométhée délivré*—*Oeuvres*, pp. 596–99.

3. Susanne Langer, *Philosophy in a New Key* (New York: The New American Library, 1951), p. 220.

4. Baudelaire, *Oeuvres*, pp. 1224, 1277.

5. Enid Starkie, *Baudelaire*, p. 326.

6. Baudelaire, *Oeuvres*, pp. 606, 709.

7. Northrop Frye in *Myth and Symbol*, ed. Bernice Slote (Lincoln: University of Nebraska Press, 1936), pp. 1–7.

8. Baudelaire, *Oeuvres*, pp. 1256, 974, 693, 883–84, 117, 1120, 704–5, 890.

9. *Ibid.*, pp. 1245, 348, 380.

10. Valéry, *Oeuvres*, I, 878.

11. Baudelaire, *Oeuvres*, 1036–66 *passim*.

12. *Ibid.*, pp. 687–88, 1040–44.

13. *Ibid.*, pp. 1099, 1042, 1296, 373, 771, 596, 1000, 1102, 712.

14. Gilman, p. 266.

5 – "Symbolique" and "Symbolisme"

1. Quoted in Lloyd Austin, *L'Univers poétique de Baudelaire* (Paris: Mercure de France, 1956), pp. 73, 77–78.

2. Jean Pommier, *La Mystique de Baudelaire* (Paris: Les Belles Lettres, 1932), pp. 154–58.

3. Austin, pp. 146–48, 158–61, 79.

4. Henri Peyre, *Shelley et la France* (Paris: Droz, 1935), pp. 148–70.

5. Austin, pp. 149–53.

6. *Ibid.*, 54, 47, 5. See Robert Vivier, *L'Originalité de Baudelaire* (Brussels: Palais des Académies, 1952); Jean Prévost, *Baudelaire: Essai sur l'inspiration et la création poétique* (Paris: Mercure de France, 1953). Jean Pommier, however, though in guarded fashion, stresses the importance for Baudelaire of his mysticism (*Mystique de B.*, pp. 100, 151, and *passim*); André Ferran does likewise, but more positively (*Esthétique de B.*, pp. 349, 361). Perhaps the posthumous publication of her volume on *Baudelaire the Critic* accounts for a certain elusiveness in Margaret Gilman's book. To take her at her most "reductive," like Lloyd Austin she makes much of Baudelaire's statement in his article on Marceline Desbordes-Valmore: "I have always taken pleasure in searching in external and visible nature for examples and metaphors which should help me characterize the enjoyments and impressions of a spiritual order." Gilman, p. 257 ff. Then he seeks for Mme Valmore's poetry a metaphor, settling upon the image of "un simple jardin anglais, romantique et romanesque." Baudelaire has made it plain that he is praising what is "in complete disaccord" with all his other passions and his doctrine, in the case of a poetess whose sincerity recompenses her with a "glory . . . as solid as that of perfect artists" (which she is not). It is important to observe that this article, appearing in the *Revue Fantaisiste* for July 1, 1861, had been preceded, on June 15, 1861, by the article on Victor Hugo with the famous pages, which we have already discussed, on Swedenborg, "les correspondances" and "l'universelle analogie." It seems far more likely that Baudelaire had reduced his definition of the symbol to the measure of his present subject than that the statement in the Valmore article should be interpreted as amounting to what Baudelaire "really" meant by the symbol.

7. Valéry, *Oeuvres*, II, 1404.

8. Austin, pp. 345, 133, 335.

9. *Ibid.*, p. 181.

10. *Ibid.*, p. 336, where Austin quotes with approval the definition of the Baudelairean symbol by F. W. Leakey: "une métaphore dont le premier terme est abstrait, le second concret."

6—The Poetic Elements

1. Baudelaire, *Oeuvres*, p. 724.

2. *Ibid.*, p. 186.

3. *Ibid.*, pp. 1205–37 *passim*.

4. Austin (p. 269) admits that the theological affirmation always implicit has "never been formulated so explicitly," but that it "had been contradicted rather than affirmed, by the experience of the poet, when he sought in nature divine correspondences." One might reply that in a world (even a poetic world) where Satan is taken seriously God must be taken even more seriously. To turn the world conclusively over to Satan is to make no sense of the task of transmuting "mud" into "gold," and it robs *les fleurs du mal* of their peculiar fragrance. In Baudelaire's world, in order for Satan to rule, God must reign.

5. Vivier, p. 176.

6. Prévost, pp. 309–37 *passim*.

7. Vivier, p. 281.

8. Prévost, p. 339.

9. Vivier, pp. 320–44 *passim*.

10. Austin, p. 191.

11. Baudelaire, *Oeuvres*, pp. 1248, 1261, 186.

12. Austin, pp. 201, 202 n., 237.

13. Wheelwright, *Metaphor and Reality*, p. 67.

14. Austin, p. 199.

15. Wheelwright, *Metaphor and Reality*, p. 73.

16. Langer, p. 204.

17. See also W. M. Frohock's discussion of this poem in Chapter 5 of *Rimbaud's Poetic Practice* (Cambridge: Harvard University Press, 1962).

18. Wheelwright, *Metaphor and Reality*, pp. 81–86.

19. Deborah Aish, *La Métaphore dans l'oeuvre de Mallarmé* (Paris: Droz, 1938), p. 8.

20. Peyre, ed., *Baudelaire*, pp. 100–102.

21. Baudelaire, *Oeuvres*, p. 1159. For a fuller treatment of Baudelaire's use of allegory, see Chapter 5 in Pommier's *La Mystique de Baudelaire*.

22. Gaston Bachelard, *La Poétique de l'espace* (Paris: Presses Universitaires, 1957), pp. 174 ff.

23. Peyre, *Baudelaire*, p. 140.

24. The poet in "Le Chat" will even present an experience of perfection that "bites," and he will use the image for the bitter-sweet of a certain ecstasy in "Le Flacon." Our study should ideally include examples of "cutting" and "biting" where these ideas are conveyed by other words and images, as in "Ciel brouillé" or "Le Vampire."

25. Wheelwright, p. 93.

26. Robert Penn Warren, *The Rime of the Ancient Mariner* (New York: Reynal and Hitchcock, 1946), pp. 70–75.

27. Quoted from D. A. Stauffer, *The Golden Nightingale* (New York: Macmillan, 1949), p. 35.

28. Wheelwright, p. 100 ff.

29. Charles Du Bos, "Méditation sur la vie de Baudelaire," *Approximations* (Paris: Crès, 1927), II. See translation by Hyatt Mayor in *Baudelaire*, edited by Henri Peyre.

7—Poetic Structures

1. Baudelaire, *Oeuvres*, p. 285. "Le Thyrse."

2. Judd Hubert, *L'Esthétique des Fleurs du mal* (Geneva: Cailler, n.d.).

3. Proceeding in a more or less chronological order and including the 1860 edition, we propose as samples: "A une Mendiante rousse," "Une nuit que j'étais auprès d'une affreuse juive," "Le Mort joyeux," "Confession," "Remords posthume," "Paysage," "Je te donne ces vers afin que si mon nom," "Tout entière," "Chanson d'après-midi," "Les Petites vieilles," "Semper Eadem," "Le Cadre," "Le Portrait" (the last two pieces are III and IV of "Un Fantôme"), "A une Passante." The series of "Femmes Damnées" also belongs to this category.

4. See in Maurice Beebe, ed., *Literary Symbolism* (San Francisco: Wadsworth, 1960), the protests against "symbolism" of Saul Bellow (p. 4 ff.) and of Mary McCarthy (p. 43 ff.). But they really accept symbolism of the first type.

5. Poems where allegorical personification pervades the entire structure are few, but there are many in which it is part of the whole. For a rather strained example of the type, see "La Haine" (1851), where hatred is a "drunkard in a corner of the tavern," thirsty for a liquor that multiplies like the hydra of Lerna, and who is denied the comfort of "falling asleep under the table." A famous poem personifies "L'Hor-

loge" as a sinister and impassive "god" raising a finger in warning, "Remember!" while "Maintenant," with its "insect voice," says "Je suis autrefois," and "I have pumped your life out with my obscene pump."

6. Baudelaire, *Oeuvres*, pp. 972–73.

7. "Une Gravure Fantastique," and "Le Masque," taken from a painting and an allegorical piece of sculpture, are two "Baudelaires."

8. In "Je te donne ces vers afin que si mon nom," the poet will use the term beautifully of Jeanne Duval who is more often associated with the diabolic: "Statue aux yeux de jais, grand ange au front d'airain." It is the "angel" in the dread impersonality of beauty.

9. I find it impossible to believe, from the evidence in the poem itself, that "Le Flacon" is the epilogue of the cycle as the editors of the Pléiade edition of Baudelaire's works assert (p. 1521).

10. Other poems of this general type are "L'Idéal" (1851), "La Fin de la journée" (1857), "La Sisina" (1859).

11. Further poems of this kind, where the poet achieves no more than a unity of impression, are "L'Irréparable" (1855), "La Mort des artistes" (1857), "Le Goût du néant" (1859).

12. Baudelaire, *Oeuvres*, p. 1253.

13. In "Parfum exotique" the poet's imagination travels again to a paradise of an exotic nature, this time through the "odeur de ton sein chaleureux." In "Le serpent qui danse," where the title describes his lady's walk, her hair launches the ship of his soul toward distant skies. But the poet never quite succeeds in bringing together the ship, the serpent's motion, the lady's ship-like motion, the sea water and the melting glacial waters of her kisses.

14. I am indebted to Henri Peyre in a number of ways for his discussion of the poem in *The Poem Itself*, edited by Stanley Burnshaw (New York: Holt, Rinehart and Winston, 1960), pp. 14–15. I have used his translation in the last two lines of the penultimate stanza.

15. Prévost, p. 343.

16. "The archetypal symbol *blood* is capable of an unusually tensive and paradoxical character." Wheelwright, p. 113.

17. Baudelaire, *Oeuvres*, p. 1666.

18. Among other poems of a similar type, "La musique

souvent me prend comme une mer," evokes a ship with a rocking or lulling effect of movement even during a tempest, or becalmed like despair. Poems of "plastic intention" are "Tristesse de la lune," with its Poesque infinite of sadness, and "La Géante," in which the poet combines a plastic imagination that created river gods of stone in Athens with a kind of surrealistic humor. See also "Ciel brouillé," "L'Ennemi," "Le Flacon," and "Le Rêve d'un curieux."

19. Baudelaire, *Oeuvres*, p. 598.

20. W. M. Urban, *Language and Reality* (New York: Macmillan, 1939), p. 408 ff.

21. Langer, p. 221.

8—Modern Theories

1. Guy Michaud, *Le Message poétique du Symbolisme*, 4 vols. (Paris: Nizet, 1947), I, 80.

2. E. Fiser, *Le Symbole littéraire* (Paris: Corti, n.d.), p. 38.

3. Georges Dumas, *Nouveau traité de Psychologie* (Paris: Alcan, 1934), IV, 13–14; quoted from Fiser, p. 52.

4. Stéphane Mallarmé, *Oeuvres Complètes*, Pléiade edition (Paris: Gallimard, 1945), pp. 869–70.

5. See on this point Suzanne Bernard, *Mallarmé et la musique* (Paris: Nizet, 1959), p. 56.

6. Georges Bonneau, *Le Symbolisme* (Paris: Boivin, 1930), p. 94; quoted in Fiser, p. 56.

7. Bonneau, pp. 74–75.

8. Fiser, p. 53.

9. In a note to his editor (1857) Baudelaire proposes to substitute for "mystiques" the phrase "to use the language of those books which are always dragging around on my table and which you look at wide-eyed." The books included Swedenborg's *Du Ciel et de ses merveilles*. (*Oeuvres*, p. 1605.)

10. Michaud, *Message poétique*, I, 124.

11. Burnshaw, ed., *The Poem Itself*, p. 39.

12. Michaud, *Message poétique*, I, 112–24.

13. Langer, pp. 221–22.

14. Strich, pp. 16–19.

15. Peyre, "French Symbolism" in *Columbia Dictionary*

of Modern European Literature (New York: Columbia University Press, 1947), pp. 291–94.

16. Michaud, *Message poétique*, II, 408 ff.

17. Michaud, *Message poétique*, III, 612–20.

18. G. Lehmann, *The Symbolist Aesthetic in France*, *1885–95* (Oxford: Basil Blackwell, 1959), pp. 14–15, 32, 67, 148, 175, 81.

19. Michaud, *Message poétique*, I, p. 74.

20. Lehmann, pp. 53, 276, 137, 270, 86.

21. *Ibid.*, pp. 302–7.

22. Austin, p. 18 n.

23. Renato Poggioli, *The Poets of Russia*, *1890–1930* (Cambridge: Harvard University Press, 1960), pp. 116–17, 140, 146.

24. Frank Kermode, *The Romantic Image* (New York: Macmillan, 1957), p. 153.

25. Wheelwright, p. 135.

26. Burnshaw, ed., *The Poem Itself*. The general reader is invited to read poems and commentaries relating to the foreign language poets named in this bilingual text.

27. Babette Deutsch, *Poetry in Our Time*, 2nd ed. revised and enlarged (New York: Doubleday, 1963), pp. 243–68, *passim.*

SELECTED BIBLIOGRAPHY

THIS LIST includes only items cited or especially helpful in the preparation of this book. The student is referred to Henri Peyre, *Connaissance de Baudelaire* (Paris: Corti, 1951), as the most valuable bibliographical guide to study of the poet. The poet's own work used in the study was *Baudelaire, Oeuvres Complètes*, texte établi et annoté par Y.-G. Le Dantec, édition révisée, complétée et présentée par Claude Pichois (Paris: Bibliothèque de la Pléiade, Gallimard, 1961).

Aish, Deborah A. K. *La Métaphore dans l'oeuvre de Stéphane Mallarmé.* Paris: Droz, 1938.

Aliotta, Antonio. *L'Estetica di Kant e degli idealisti romantici.* Roma: Perrella, 1950.

Austin, Lloyd James. *L'Univers poétique de Baudelaire: Symbolisme et Symbolique.* Paris: Mercure de France, 1956.

Bachelard, Gaston. *La Poétique de l'espace.* Paris: Presses Universitaires de France, 1957.

Beebe, Maurice, ed. *Literary Symbolism.* San Francisco: Wadsworth Publishing Co., 1960.

Béguin, Albert. *Le Romantisme et le rêve.* Paris: Corti, 1946.

Bernard, Suzanne. *Mallarmé et la musique.* Paris: Nizet, 1959.

Besset, Maurice. *Novalis et la pensée mystique.* Paris: Aubier, 1947.

Bonneau, Georges. *Le Symbolisme.* Paris: Boivin, 1930.

Burnshaw, Stanley, ed. *The Poem Itself.* New York: Holt, Rinehart, and Winston, 1960.

Cazamian, Louis. *Symbolisme et poésie: l'exemple anglais.* Neuchâtel: Editions de la Baconnière, 1947.

Chérix, R. *Commentaire des Fleurs du mal.* Genève: P. Cailler, 1949.

Chiari, Joseph. *Symbolisme from Poe to Mallarmé*. London: Rockliff, 1956.

Cornell, Kenneth. *The Symbolist Movement*. New Haven: Yale University Press, 1951.

Croce, Benedetto. *Poesia e Non Poesia* ["Baudelaire"]. Bari: Laterza, 1923.

De Bruyne, Edgar. *L'Esthétique du Moyen Age*. Louvain: Editions de l'Institut Supérieur de Philosophie, 1947.

Deutsch, Babette. *Poetry in Our Time*. Second edition revised and enlarged. New York: Doubleday, 1963.

Du Bos, Charles. *Approximations*, I and V. Paris: Corrêa, 1922, 1932.

– – –. "Meditation on the Life of Baudelaire," translated by A. Hyatt Mayor, in Henri Peyre, ed., *Baudelaire*.

Fergusson, Francis. *Dante's Dream of the Mind: A Modern Reading of the Purgatorio*. Princeton: Princeton University Press, 1953.

Ferran, André. *L'Esthétique de Baudelaire*. Paris: Hachette, 1933.

Fiser, Eméric. *Le Symbole littéraire*. Paris: Corti, n.d.

Foss, Martin. *Symbol and Metaphor in Human Experience*. Princeton: Princeton University Press, 1949.

Frohock, Wilbur M. *Rimbaud's Poetic Practice: Image and Theme in the Major Poems*. Cambridge: Harvard University Press, 1962.

Gilman, Margaret. *Baudelaire the Critic*. New York: Columbia University Press, 1943.

Gilson, Etienne. *Dante the Philosopher*, trans. David Moor. New York: Sheed and Ward, 1949.

Hubert, Judd. *L'Esthétique des Fleurs du Mal: Essai sur l'ambiguité poétique*. Geneva: Caillier, n.d.

Isaacs, J. *The Background of Modern Poetry*. New York: Dutton, 1952.

Kermode, Frank. *The Romantic Image*. New York: Macmillan, 1957.

Langer, Susanne. *Philosophy in a New Key*. New York: American Library [1942], 1951.

Lehmann, G. *The Symbolist Aesthetic in France, 1885–95*. Oxford: Basil Blackwell, 1950.

Lewis, Cecil S. *The Medieval Allegory of Love*. Oxford: Clarendon Press, 1936.

Mansell-Jones, Paul. *The Background of Modern French Poetry*. Cambridge: Cambridge University Press, 1951.

Michaud, Guy. *Message Poétique du Symbolisme,* 4 vols. Paris: Nizet, 1947.

― ― ―. *Mallarmé, l'homme et l'oeuvre.* Paris: Hatier, Boivin, 1953.

Orsini, Gian N. G. *Benedetto Croce, Philosopher of Art and Literary Critic.* Carbondale: Southern Illinois University Press, 1961.

Peyre, Henri. *Shelley et la France.* Paris: Droz, 1935.

― ― ―, ed. *Baudelaire,* a collection of critical essays. New Jersey: Prentice-Hall, 1962.

― ― ―. "French Symbolism" in *Columbia Dictionary of Modern European Literature.* New York: Columbia University Press, 1947.

Poggioli, Renato. *The Poets of Russia, 1890–1930.* Cambridge: Harvard University Press, 1960.

Pommier, Jean. *La Mystique de Baudelaire.* Paris: Les Belles Lettres, 1932.

Prévost, Jean. *Baudelaire, Essai sur l'inspiration et la Création Poétique.* Paris: Mercure de France, 1953.

Raymond, Marcel. *De Baudelaire aux Surréalistes.* Paris: Corti, 1947.

Sayers, Dorothy L. *Introductory Papers on Dante,* 2 vols. New York: Harper, 1954.

Senior, John. *The Way Down and Out: The Occult in Symbolist Literature.* Ithaca: Cornell University Press, 1959.

Singleton, Charles S. *Dante Studies,* 2 vols. Cambridge: Harvard University Press, 1954–58.

Slote, Bernice, ed. *Myth and Symbol: Critical Approaches and Applications.* Lincoln: University of Nebraska Press, 1963.

Spenlé, E. *Novalis: Essai sur l'Idéalisme Romantique en Allemagne.* Paris: Hachette, 1904.

Stambler, Bernard. *Dante's Other World: The Purgatorio as Guide to the Divine Comedy.* New York: New York University Press, 1957.

Starkie, Enid. *Baudelaire.* London: Faber and Faber, 1957.

― ― ―. *Arthur Rimbaud.* Norfolk, Connecticut: New Directions, 1961.

― ― ―. *From Gautier to Eliot: The Influence of French on English Literature, 1851–1939.* London: Hutchinson, 1960.

Strich, Fritz. *Der Dichter und die Zeit.* Bern: A. Francke, 1947.

Tindall, James Y. *The Literary Symbol*. New York: Columbia University Press, 1955.

Urban, William M. *Language and Reality*. New York: Macmillan, 1939.

Valéry, Paul. *Oeuvres*, 2 vols. Edition établie et annotée par Jean Hytier. Paris: Editions de la Pléiade, Gallimard, 1957.

Viëtor, Karl. *Goethe the Thinker*, trans. Bayard Q. Morgan. Cambridge: Harvard University Press, 1950.

Vivas, Eliseo. *D. H. Lawrence: The Failure and the Triumph of Art*. Evanston: Northwestern University Press, 1960.

Vivier, Robert. *L'Originalité de Baudelaire*. Edition révisée. Brussels: Palais des Académies [1921–24], 1952.

Warren, Robert Penn. *The Rime of the Ancient Mariner*. New York: Reynal and Hitchcock, 1946.

Wellek, René. *A History of Modern Criticism, 1750–1950*, 2 vols. New Haven: Yale University Press, 1955.

Wheelwright, Philip. *The Burning Fountain*. Bloomington: Indiana University Press, 1954.

———. *Metaphor and Reality*. Bloomington: Indiana University Press, 1962.

Wimsatt, William, and Brooks, Cleanth. *Literary Criticism, a Short History*. New York: Alfred A. Knopf, 1957.

INDEX